Unstoppable

ALSO BY CHIQUIS RIVERA

Forgiveness

Perdón (Spanish)

Chiquis Keto

Chiquis Keto (Spanish)

Unstoppable

HOW I FOUND MY STRENGTH
THROUGH LOVE AND LOSS

CHIQUIS RIVERA

with CECILIA MOLINARI

ATRIA PAPERBACK

New York   London   Toronto   Sydney   New Delhi

An Imprint of Simon & Schuster, Inc.
1230 Avenue of the Americas
New York, NY 10020

Some names have been changed and some dialogue
has been re-created.

First Atria Paperback edition February 2023

ATRIA PAPERBACK and colophon are trademarks of Simon & Schuster, Inc.

For information about special discounts for bulk purchases, please contact
Simon & Schuster Special Sales at 1-866-506-1949 or
business@simonandschuster.com.

The Simon & Schuster Speakers Bureau can bring authors to your live event.
For more information or to book an event, contact the Simon & Schuster Speakers
Bureau at 1-866-248-3049 or visit our website at www.simonspeakers.com.

Manufactured in the United States of America

1   3   5   7   9   10   8   6   4   2

The Library of Congress has cataloged the hardcover edition as follows:

Names: Rivera, Chiquis, author. | Molinari, Cecilia, author.
Title: Unstoppable : how I found my strength through love and loss /
Chiquis Janney Rivera, with Cecilia Molinari.
Description: First Atria books hardcover edition. | New York : Atria Books, 2022.
Identifiers: LCCN 2021043858 (print) | LCCN 2021043859 (ebook) |
ISBN 9781982180683 (hardcover) | ISBN 9781982180690 (ebook)
Subjects: LCSH: Rivera, Chiquis. | Singers—United States—Biography. |
Mothers—Death. | Conduct of life. | LCGFT: Autobiographies.
Classification: LCC ML420.R64 A3 2022 (print) | LCC ML420.R64 (ebook) |
DDC 782.42164092 [B]—dc23
LC record available at https://lccn.loc.gov/2021043858
LC ebook record available at https://lccn.loc.gov/2021043859

ISBN 978-1-9821-8068-3
ISBN 978-1-9821-8948-8 (pbk)
ISBN 978-1-9821-8069-0 (ebook)

I dedicate this book to YOU.
I hope it inspires and empowers you.
Through pain, loss, and love,
may you find the best version of yourself.

CONTENTS

Contents

INTRODUCTION

*I*n December 2012, my world came to a standstill with the sudden loss of my momma. I was left gasping for air, wondering if life was still worth living without her. But there was no real time to grieve, no space to make sense of this sudden and excruciating void she'd left behind because my brothers and sisters needed me. So I sprang into action to help piece back some sense of family for the five of us. I knew that's what my momma would've wanted. I had to help heal their bleeding hearts—mine would have to wait. That's when I wrote my first book, *Forgiveness.* In those pages, I felt the need to share my story, to clear the air, to tell my truth. It also gave me the chance to forgive others, forgive myself, and pick up the broken pieces of my life. But what happened after that?

Having to continue life without the force of nature that was Jenni Rivera at times felt paralyzing. Stepping into her shoes and taking on a mother figure role for my youngest brother and sister, Johnny and Jenicka, was a challenge on its own. But giving up was not an option. In these pages, I share with you the lessons that taught me how to stand on my own two feet like never before. This is my journey from nerve-rattled singer to Grammy-winning performer, from first-time business owner to full-blown Boss Bee entrepreneur; it's how I navigated the turmoil of my relationships, how I figured out the balance between satisfying my family's needs while no longer putting my own dreams on hold, and how I became a wife and then watched it all crumble before my eyes.

Yeah, I've been through hell and back a few times, but I'm still standing. I survived. I figured it out. I learned that nothing and no one will ever stop me from following my heart and my dreams, and becoming the best version of myself possible. *Unstoppable* is a new chance to speak the truth about the last five years of my life, but it's also my chance to inspire you. No matter what you face, no matter what people say, no matter how defeated you may feel, I'm living proof that we have the power to get back up, dust ourselves off, and become unstoppable.

1

SURVIVING LOSS AND DEVASTATION

An eerie feeling crept over me as the long and fiery days of summer softened into the nostalgic autumnal glow of 2020. I usually love this time of year, when the weather begins to turn and the crisp, cool nights beg for me to do a deep dive into my closet and pull out the sweaters and cozy layers that have been patiently waiting for their seasonal turn. But this time, it was different. My heart was fractured. Simple day-to-day activities demanded every last ounce of strength I carried in my exhausted mind and body. As I switched off the lights in my home and slowly walked upstairs to my bedroom, I just couldn't shake this feeling, a déjà vu of sorts, that I was reliving the fall of 2012 all over again. After brushing my teeth, washing my face, and mindlessly motioning through the rest of my nightly routine, I climbed into my king-size bed, curled up under the soft white covers with my fluffy pillow, and then slowly turned to the empty spot beside me. My stomach tied up in a thousand knots and the agonizing pressure on my chest was unbearable. I . . . felt . . . so . . . alone.

I had already survived the worst possible unimaginable loss. The pillar in my life, the one person I had relied on, trusted, adored, and forgiven beyond the grave, was long gone. And now, the person I believed was my soul mate, my ride or die, the one who vowed to love and cherish me, was gone too. Surely I'd get through this type of crushing devastation again. My mind was telling me that I'd been through worse, that I could and would handle this too, but somehow I was back to square one emotionally. WTF? How did I get here?

After my mom passed away in a plane accident on December 9, 2012, it was as if someone had said "Kill the lights" in my life. I patted my bleeding heart dry and blubbered through that first year, trying to figure out how to fill the gaping hole she left in our family.

"Do you guys ever wonder what Momma is doing?" I asked my brothers and sisters during our first sibling getaway about a year after she passed.

In honor of a promise we'd made to take a yearly family vacation, I rented an RV and invited my brothers and sisters on a road trip to the Grand Canyon. In the past year, I had dealt with anger, frustration, and excruciating pain, and then I forgave . . . I vowed not to hold any resentment toward those who hurt or left me, I gracefully accepted all that had gone down, as I detailed in my first book, *Forgiveness*, and reconciled with the idea that, although I didn't quite understand why the glue that kept us together was gone, I knew it was up to me, as the eldest sibling, the one who had already been taking care of my brothers and sisters throughout their lives, to step into my mom's shoes and push us forward.

"I do all the time," said Jacqie, my younger sister, who was twenty-four at the time and living in her own house with her husband, Michael, whom she'd married about a year earlier, and her daughter, Jaylah.

"I dream about her a lot," said Johnny.

"What do you dream about her?" I asked.

"Just her laughing," said Johnny in a hushed tone.

Johnny was twelve years old back then, my youngest brother, but really, he'll forever be my little kid. When he was born, Momma, who was determined not to put her career on hold, handed me her baby and said, "Mija, I really need you. Now more than ever." And just like that, Johnny became my son. I remember like it was yesterday, standing in the backstage area with this little baby boy in my arms, feeding and cuddling him, while my mom rocked the house onstage. She toured nonstop during the following years, focused on making something of her career and giving us all a better life, and I stayed home with my four siblings, taking care of them as best I could, while being barely seventeen years old myself.

"I wish I could be like you guys," interjected my bighearted brother Mikey, then twenty-two years old, who had become a father only a year earlier to beautiful little Luna.

"What do you mean?" I asked, as we sat around a firepit on the last night of our Grand Canyon vacation, staring up at the endless sky swarming with flickering stars.

"I'm not at peace at all about it," said Mikey, referring to our still-recent loss.

"Me neither," murmured my little sister Jenicka.

For the first time in our lives, my siblings and I had to start learning how to live without the force that was Jenni Rivera, yet the mere idea of moving on without her felt absolutely paralyzing.

"I don't think I'll ever understand it," I said.

"I still don't understand why my dad's gone, and it's been four years," said Jenicka movingly.

My heart dropped when I heard Jenicka express herself so openly. That night, I saw my two youngest siblings in a different light. Johnny was eleven and Jenicka was fifteen when our mom passed away. They'd lost their dad only a few years earlier, so on that unimaginable day they'd also become orphans. Ever since then, I was determined to make sure they knew I would never abandon them. I switched into full-on protective momma bear mode.

My mom's trust apparently determined that the kids' guardian had to live in the house with the children. Tía Rosie had been appointed their legal guardian—a pill that was hard to swallow for me, given that I had raised those kids since they came into this world—but I was still their emotional guardian. So when the kids asked me to move back to the house, I was very hesitant because I had finally begun to get used to being on my own, and I knew the situation was less than ideal. But they needed me. That's why, despite the awkward custody arrangement, where I had to ask my aunt for permission for something as menial as picking them up at school, I said yes to Johnny and Jenicka, determined to make it work for them.

These kids were so strong—they were my heroes, and honestly, the key ingredients to my survival. While I was fighting to keep them alive, they were keeping me alive, inspiring me to stay strong, hold it together, and pull through no matter what.

By September 2, 2014, about a year after this sibling road trip, once tía Rosie and I had come to an agreement, I was made their official legal guardian and she and her family moved out. "Congratulations," Johnny said in a serious tone on the day we received the all-important documents, "you just gave birth to a couple of teenagers." They were no longer just my siblings, they were now officially my kids, and everything I did from then on wouldn't be just for me, it would be for them too. I vowed to never turn my back on them.

Although we easily fell into our old routines, stepping in to raise a preteen and teen was not easy. Where I was once spending quiet evenings decompressing in my tiny garage apartment in Van Nuys, I now worried about getting the kids to school on time, making sure they made it to their doctor appointments, and going to their parent-teacher conferences—you name it, I was doing it. I'd take Johnny on my Target runs, then we'd hit up his favorite GameStop shop. We went to the movies or watched them at home and ordered pizza. I'd also bring him along with me to my boyfriend Angel's place. He was basically glued to my hip during those first couple of years, and so was Jenicka.

I made sure she had driving lessons so she could get a permit and eventually her driver's license. That was a game-changer for me because Jenicka was then able to help by going to the grocery store and dropping Johnny off or picking him up from any scheduled appointments. Even though the two of them would fight a lot—as most siblings do—Jenicka has always been an incredibly mature and wise young lady, and her support was absolutely invaluable. She gave me a little extra space to breathe.

Jenicka was going to a public high school at the time, but since there was a strong Latino population there, everyone and their mother knew about our mom's passing, and it was really affecting her sensitive soul.

"Pretty please," she finally said to me one day at home, "can I go to Johnny's school?"

Johnny had recently started at Fusion Academy in Woodland Hills, a private school dedicated to one-to-one teaching, meaning one teacher for every student. Although he was still reeling from losing our mom, the personalized attention did wonders for him. They were used to seeing and dealing with celebrity children—Paris Jackson, Michael Jackson's daughter, also attended that school—so I thought it would be a good fit for Jenicka too. She was so relieved to finally be able to focus on school instead of the outside chatter that had been bogging her down that she even graduated a year ahead of her class.

This move meant not only that both my kids were doing better at school, it also meant I had to drive them to just one school in the morning, cutting my time on the road significantly—I relished any spare minutes I could get.

Although I had been their mother figure in the past, this was different because I was quietly devastated and still trying to process my own grief. When I moved back to my momma's house to take care of the kids, Mikey was sleeping in my room, so I took Jacqie's old room, which meant that every time I walked to and from my new bedroom—every freakin' day—I had to pass by my mom's room, which we had left untouched since she died. The flap of the sheet on the left side of her bed was folded over from when she'd last climbed out. The cute striped pajamas she had worn the night before were by the sink in the bathroom with her undies, and there was a dress she'd taken off in her closet and left on the floor. Everything else was clean and tidy. But those few items remained as they were for a few years. Sometimes I was fine with it; other times I had to close the door to avoid the constant reminder of her absence. And there were moments when I would step inside, sit on her bed, and simply let the tears gush out, gathering whatever strength I could from her waning presence.

It was difficult and awkward, but, ultimately, I knew I was doing the right thing by being there for my siblings. I knew how much Momma loved these children, how much she loved all of her children, so moving back home with them was also my way of honoring her legacy, and it was allowing me to slowly heal. I chose to stick it out and put on a strong face for my kids. Jacqie was married and had a daughter, Mikey had a daughter too, so it was just me, Jenicka, and Johnny now, and I needed them to be all right.

But I didn't do it all alone. First, I rehired Mercedes, the same babysitter we had when my mom was alive. Johnny really loved her and felt comfortable around her, so, although Momma had let her go, I made an executive decision to bring her back, knowing the reason they'd parted ways was more of a misunderstanding than anything else. She was a godsend, helping with the cooking and the kids during the day, which offered me a few precious hours to figure out what I was going to do with my life, something I barely had time to think about during those first few mom-less years.

Then, when Rosie and her family moved out of the house, my boyfriend Angel really stepped up for us. We had been together for a few years, and although at times it had been a rocky ride emotionally, which led us to break up and get back together more than once, when my world came undone, he was there, steadfast by my side, providing me with love and support, pushing me to succeed and offering priceless advice.

First, he started spending more nights with us to make sure we were safe.

"You guys are all alone," he said, worried. "It's just you and them." He actually wanted us to move out of the house and go live with him, but I didn't feel any of us had the bandwidth to deal with yet another big upheaval in our lives.

"Let's just take it little by little," I replied. We were all craving some sense of normalcy and stability, and he got that; he was okay with it.

A lot of people never quite understood my choice to stay with him—including some of my family—given the feud he'd had with my mom before she died. But I knew that, although mishandled, it had all been to protect me and come to my defense. He was a solid guy, not the gangster many made him out to be.

Angel never moved any of his stuff to the house or left anything there other than a toothbrush because he really didn't want to live in my mom's house—it just didn't feel right to him. He was determined not to let anyone think that he was taking advantage of the situation in any way. This meant that sometimes he'd head off to work early just to get ready for the day in his office, yet he always came back, night after night, to make sure we weren't alone.

"Here, take it," he'd often say, handing me a wad of cash. "I use electricity and water when I'm here with you. Please, pay for whatever you need; go buy groceries." He was an innate provider and, although the current arrangements weren't what he'd wished for, he rolled with it, giving us the space and time to heal, while also lending me the love and care I desperately needed.

As if that wasn't enough, he also stepped in and gave me a hand with Johnny. Angel would help me comfort Johnny when he crept into our room in the middle of the night scared or sad. He made Johnny feel safe and slowly became a true father figure in his life. Angel wouldn't scold him, but when Johnny was acting up or doing something that was stressing me out, Angel would step in and say, "Come here, Johnny, let's go for a ride," and he'd guide him to his car and give me the breather I needed to get my head back in the game.

"Hey, your sister's going through a lot," he'd say to Johnny in the car. "So, if you need to talk to someone, you can talk to me." Angel would take him to the office or they'd simply go for a spin while listening to music, and Johnny felt at ease and at home with him.

Those were difficult years because Johnny was smack in the middle of puberty and exploring his sexuality, and I had only recently discovered that he liked boys at the time. Even though Angel didn't quite relate to this because it was something so new and different to him, he didn't judge Johnny and never made him feel bad. On the contrary, Angel was there for him, willing to listen, understand, and talk to him, and that meant the world to a little boy who'd lost both his parents and was now trying to figure himself out. I think this also factored into why Johnny was so close to Angel and looked up to him so much, and still does to this day.

Although our relationship was tumultuous—likely because we were both going through so much and had a lot of growing up to do in different ways—Angel always took care of me and made sure I felt safe. Every relationship is a master teacher in our lives, and I learned so much from him and will be forever grateful for his presence during those years of inexplicable heartache as we adjusted to our mom's permanent absence.

I truly believe that nothing God sends our way is something we can't handle. That's why I always say, Dios nunca se equivoca (God is never wrong). Everything comes our way for a reason. It may sound cliché, but I live by that saying.

I don't wish this type of pain on anyone—losing a parent, losing a partner, losing friends, whether it be through death or the end of a relationship, can drive anyone to a dark place. I know, I've lost them all. But I think that people are meant to be in our lives for a certain number of seasons to teach us the lessons we need so we can enter the following years of our lives with some evolution under our belt. Easier said than done, right? Especially when it comes to the death of a parent. When you're in the thick of it, you feel like that sense of devastation will never truly go away. But I always tell myself and those around me going through a rough time: This too shall pass. Maybe not right now, maybe not as quick as we'd like, but it will eventually, especially if you're intentional about getting through it. It's never going to be easy, it's just going to get easier. You eventually learn to live with that void.

These are the questions I began to ask myself when I was going through that painful turning point in my life: What am I supposed to learn from this? How am I supposed to grow? How can I be a better friend? How can I be a better daughter? How can I represent my mother's legacy? What can I learn from her, mimic, do differently? How can I improve my life through this pain? When you start searching for the answers to these profound questions, you are opening the door to growing and evolving into the person you're meant to be. You'll see my answers flourish in these pages and become an essential learning: Each and every loss adds up to an emotional, physical, and mental gain. And one day, you'll wake up from that dreary black-and-white movie and see the colors shine again.

I've always had to grow up faster than people my age, but those first years without my momma taught me how to be a full-blown woman. She had been my advocator, my cheerleader, my biggest critic, and my protector, but now I had to stand up and protect myself and my siblings. I realized I couldn't depend on anyone but myself, and I learned to be strong in every way imaginable. Pain provides lessons. It helps us grow and become more aware of our surroundings. It's a gateway to change and evolution.

So, now what?

That's what I kept thinking while navigating those first few years with the kids. *Shit, now what do I do?* I thought when I found out that Johnny had been exchanging explicit photos with a guy and misusing his Instagram account, where he had hundreds of thousands of followers.

"First of all, why are you sending pictures with your face in them?" I asked Johnny. "I can't stop you from sending pictures of your penis, but don't put your face in them because you're the son of a famous woman and part of a well-known family."

He stared back at me with a blank face. He knew he was in trouble, and as his mom, I had to teach him a lesson so he could fully understand the gravity of the situation. I mean, come on, the only reason those photos didn't get out was because he was underage and publishing them would be considered child pornography. That really saved our asses, but I was furious. I realized he was too young to handle his own social media account, so I shut it down, deleting absolutely everything, and he was fuming, but I didn't care.

"Look, you're a little boy," I said to him firmly, "and you don't need this, plus it's causing you problems."

Then, to make sure he didn't keep doing any stupid shit, I moved him to the office area located directly across from my room. I removed the door and placed his mattress in the hallway so I could keep a close eye on him at night.

OMG, what am I going to do? Who do I run to now? How am I going to take care of all of this, of them? I thought as this situation unraveled along with countless other freak-outs that came with raising two teens.

And then it happened. I heard my mom's voice loud and clear: "Figure it out," a phrase she often used. When I was growing up, there was no babying in my house. Momma always threw me into the deep end of anything in life, and then said, "Swim." Figuring it out was the rule we lived by. That's when it hit me, *I know who I am. I know who raised me. And I will get through this.*

You may not see the way out just yet, but if you stay focused on the light, you will make it to the other side without even realizing it.

2

GIVING UP IS NOT AN OPTION

*W*hen you don't grow up with much, it makes you value everything that comes your way so much more. As a child, I saw my mom fight for us, fight to survive, fight to become a singer, a performer. That grit was my example—it's all I've ever known—that's how she raised me, throwing me into the sea of life, where I either swam or I drowned. And you better believe I swam. I swam through the ups and downs, the loss, the devastation, figuring it out, because giving up was not an option, at least not in our house. Momma always said, "When you fall, you have to get back up, dust yourself off, and keep going." There was no room for victims, no time to feel sorry for ourselves.

I don't stop to wallow in the fear of endings because I know they make way for new beginnings. And I know how to fend for myself. I'm not afraid of failure. If my career ever ends, I am ready to grab a cart and sell oranges on the side of the freeway. And I will take pride in my stand and strive to sell the juiciest oranges in the city. I'll make them shine because I'm determined to do all I can to be successful at whatever I set my mind to. I will make it work, no matter what. Deep inside, I know I will be okay. My momma never quit, and neither will I.

Another driving force in my don't-give-up mentality is my siblings. I'm the eldest of the five of us, and I was taught since the very beginning that I must set the example for them. I constantly strive to make my mother proud, to make my siblings proud, to make myself proud, and to do what's best for all of us, even when that means facing our fears head-on and making the tough calls.

"Jenicka," I called out to my youngest sister from the tufted cream-colored sofa next to the grand piano in the formal living room of what had been our home since 2009.

"Yes, sister," she replied, in that soft and peaceful tone that makes everything feel better.

"Come here, and call your brothers for me, please," I asked my sweet and oh-so-mature baby sister, who was now a full-blown eighteen-year-old.

"Are we in trouble?" asked Johnny as he walked over to the couch, where we'd had so many talks in the past as a family.

Johnny was fifteen going on thirty, but he will forever be my little kid.

"You and your meetings, Chiquis! You take this Boss Bee thing way too seriously," said Mikey, as he walked down the stairs to join us, who in the spring of 2016 was twenty-four years old.

"I am a boss!" I snapped back. I love Mikey. He's a supersmart, all-around great guy with a huge heart, but he always has something to say about everything.

"I wanted to call this meeting because it's important," I said, once they'd all sat down. "I was talking to tía Rosie. I don't know . . . there's no easy way to say this, but we have decided that it's time to sell the house."

Their eyes shot down, and in an instant their expressions went from relaxed and cheerful to straight-up glum. My heart was beating fast. I knew this would be a tough talk, but I also believed Momma wouldn't have wanted us to remain stuck within those walls, immersed in her memories and constantly living in the past for years to come.

"Why, though?" asked Johnny, breaking the beat of silence among us.

"Because I feel bad having to pay for this house and taking that from what's in the trust. That money can be used for other things—for your school, for your college—and realistically, I can't afford this house."

Up until then, money from Mikey, Jenicka, and Johnny's trust funds was used to pay for the mortgage, but I didn't want to do that anymore. That money was meant for their future, their educations, their survival, not to pay for a $15,000-dollar-a-month mortgage. Listen, my mom was Jenni Rivera, the top-selling female artist in Regional Mexican music, aka a banda superstar, who Billboard called the "top Latin artist of 2013," but I was just getting my feet wet when it came to my singing career. I still had a long road ahead of me before music would become a profitable business in my life. So, as much as I would've loved to pay for that house and keep it going, I wasn't making nearly enough to step in and make it happen—it just wasn't within my means.

"Mikey wants to move out," I continued as they stared back at me sullenly, "which means it would just be us three—"

"Jenicka is getting a little grown now too. Are you dealing with that well?" interrupted Mikey.

"Yeah, but she's not planning to move out anytime soon," I replied. "She has to go to college." Then I turned to Jenicka. "There's no reason for you to move out. Why are you looking at me like that?"

"Because, what if there's a chance that I do?" she said, shyly.

"All I want you to do is go to school, I'll take care of you—"

"Wait," said Mikey, raising his hand. "What about what she wants to do?"

"What do you mean?" I said, a little annoyed.

"Have you heard yourself? You said, 'All I want you to do . . .'" pointed out Mikey.

"But what I want for myself is the best for her," I replied with a half smile. I knew what he was getting at, but I just wasn't ready to accept it.

"You sound just like mom," said Johnny.

Mikey continued, "Johnny's going to want to go to college too and—"

"No, I can't be on my own," interrupted Johnny. I can't imagine staying at the college dorm by myself."

"Are you going to live with your sister when you're thirty, though?" asked Mikey.

"Yeah," replied Johnny somewhat defiantly.

Picturing change was hard for all of us at the time. I knew it was time to move on, but, honestly, it scared me shitless.

"They're both going to stay with me until they're like twenty-nine," I said, knowing this was wishful thinking.

I finally understood why Momma always said, "It's us against the world." Making sure my siblings and I stayed close and stuck together during those first three-plus years after she died had been super important for our healing process. But for me, there was an added layer of why I didn't want to part from them: I felt that they were all I had left of her. I had come to terms with selling the house, I had gotten used to Jacqie living in her own home with her growing family, and I knew Mikey would fly the nest soon to make a home for himself and his four-year-old daughter, but I was far from ready to let my babies go. Johnny and Jenicka had been my lighthouse, shining the rays of hope that carried me through that tempest in our lives.

I shook off these thoughts and attempted to steer the conversation back to the main point: moving out of Momma's house.

"Nothing is going to change," I said, "it's just going to be a different house."

"We're really not going to have this house anymore, are we," said Johnny, with sad eyes, realizing this was actually happening. "It's hard for me to envision it belonging to anyone else."

"I know," I said in a softer tone. "I know this is hard."

That house was more than just a building. It represented Momma's tireless work and sacrifice, the countless tours, the never-ending TV and radio shows and promotional interviews, all of which made her miss important moments in our lives, like birthdays. She did all that to take care of us and give us a life she had only dreamed of while growing up in the gang-ridden streets of Long Beach, California, then struggling to survive as a teenage mom. Hell, I went from calling a garage my home as a kid and sleeping with my mom on a mattress on the floor, to having my own room and a two-story custom-made closet in a sprawling 10,000-square-foot mansion resting on four acres in Encino. She didn't just buy this house, she turned it into our home, our little oasis where we could take shelter from the outside racket. In the short time we spent there, we filled each room with memories: family meals, arguments, laughter, and tears. You name it, we did it. That's why it took me three years to finally decide it was time for us to move on. And that's why this conversation and the idea of closing this chapter in our lives was so excruciatingly difficult to swallow for all of us.

"Don't look at me like that, Jenicka. I'm not crying," I said as I dabbed the inner corners of my eyes with my fingertips. "Oh my god, why am I crying? I was expecting you to cry, Johnny. I don't know why I'm crying. I think about you, Johnny, a lot, because I know how hard all of this has been on you."

Johnny was about nine when we moved into this new home—many of his most heartfelt memories with our mom had taken place within those walls during the last three years before she passed. It hurt me to think of how painful this transition would be for him.

"We're just going to find something for us, and you, Mikey. You're more than welcome to come."

"We'll see," said Mikey.

"Me too," added Jenicka. "We'll see."

"Jenicka, no," I replied, shutting that idea down. "Alright, so the meeting is over."

"This sucks, dude," said Johnny as he slowly got up from the sofa.

"I know, I'm sorry," I said, "but you're going to thank me later—I hope."

In the following days, I spoke to the real estate agents and set up times for them to start showing the house. That's when Johnny realized this wasn't just talk, this wasn't just a plan, this was for real. And he wasn't happy about it. When the first round of prospective buyers came to the house, he tagged along the showings adding his own commentary to the tours. He told a couple who was doing a walk-through with their dog in the lady's arms, "We had three dogs, two of them ran away and one of them went missing, and then we heard coyote screeches." "Oh my gosh," said the woman, clutching her dog a little tighter. When this same couple was viewing the master suite, he blurted out, "We had a poltergeist upstairs a few years back." They looked at him, slightly taken aback. He was being rude and a little obnoxious, hoping to scare them away so he could cling to the house a little longer.

When Jenicka came to one of the rooms I was frantically cleaning before the prospective buyers walked in to check it out and told me what was going on, I called Johnny over.

"Are you doing this on purpose?" I asked him.

"Maybe a little," he said with a nervous giggle.

"Johnny, this isn't funny."

Regardless of his efforts, within a month, we had a solid offer, and the house was in escrow.

Meanwhile, Jenicka was still determined to pursue the idea of living alone. She didn't quite know how to talk to me about it because she knew it wouldn't be easy, but one afternoon, she finally gathered the courage to walk into the ground-floor office—a place where I had had so many talks with our mom, including the time I wanted to bring my boyfriend Angel to Jacqie's wedding and she said no—where I was holding a meeting with my manager and assistant.

"Hi sister, can we talk?" she said, as they left the room, and she pulled out a chair and sat down across from me, the enormous wooden desk between us giving the moment an extra air of formality.

I flashed back to all the times I had sat there with my momma: planning her wardrobe, coordinating her schedules, figuring out what to do with the kids, sharing big laughs as well as having some tough confrontations, like the time I overheard her telling Jacqie that she shouldn't invite my boyfriend to her wedding and I burst in demanding that Angel be there by my side. It was the last big argument we had in that room before she kicked me out of the house in March 2012.

"So, what do you want to talk about, Jenicka?" I asked, already suspecting where this conversation was heading.

She took a deep breath and said, "I'm going to move out. I'm not going to go with you and—"

"Okay, wait. You're asking me to move out or you're saying you're going to move out?" I said, interrupting her.

She locked her hands and replied with a soft, yet determined tone, "I'm saying I'm going to move out."

"This is a decision that you've already made," I replied, trying to hide the pain I felt in the pit of my stomach.

"Yes, I thought—"

"Wait," I interrupted her. "So, because you're eighteen, you feel that you need to move out."

"Yes," she replied.

"Why?"

"I want to go explore and be able to take care of myself," she said quietly.

"But you don't have to take care of yourself. I can help you take care of yourself," I said to my baby sister, hoping to change her mind.

"I know, but I want to take care of myself," she said in that sweet voice of hers.

Taking care of herself . . . I felt she had no idea what she was stepping into.

"I don't know exactly where I'm going. I thought about San Diego—"

"What?" Hold the phone. She wasn't just considering moving out of the house, she was thinking about moving to another city? Aw, hell no.

"Sister, listen," she said calmly, as she read the mini freak-out on my face, "I don't want you to have to take care of me."

"I don't feel that you're thinking this through all the way, Jenicka. You have to think about it."

"I have thought about it," she replied, "and I think I can handle it."

22

"There's no changing your mind at all?" I said, scrunching my face and giving away the hurt I felt inside.

"You're going to make me cry," she said with a nervous smile.

"I know you're a good girl. You're responsible . . . but if you're living on your own, you could get into a lot of trouble."

"Yeah, but I'm smart, sister. I'm not going to go get pregnant."

"Jacqie came home with a piercing on her tongue, all kinds of tattoos, and a kid in her uterus. I don't think Mom would like this idea. You know how Mom was," I said, still trying to get her to see this wasn't necessary just yet.

I still had the memory of Jacqie leaving the house a couple of hours shy of her eighteenth birthday fresh in my mind, even though it had happened nine years earlier, in the fall of 2007. I was dating Karla at the time, whom I talk about in *Forgiveness*, which made Jacqie really jealous and overprotective, emotions that were likely boosted further because she had to keep it under wraps for me— my mom wasn't aware of my relationship at the time, although she could sense something was up. After being so close for years, this caused a lot of tension between Jacqie and me, and it exploded into a huge fight that night in November, a blowup that drove Jacqie to pack her things up and leave the house. She was going through a major rebellious streak and yearned for her independence, and now that she was practically eighteen, there was no stopping her.

As she stormed toward the door with her bags, I was so upset at how bratty and extreme she was being that I grabbed her hair and pulled her back inside.

"Where are you going?" I yelled. "Don't you disrespect me like that!"

But she wriggled away and continued stomping over to her car, stashing her stuff in the back. Then, as she fixed her ponytail, she turned to me and said, "People like me make it in life. People like you are remembered." She honestly thought she was going to get out there and do her thing. We laugh about the drama of that phrase now, but it stung back then.

Nevertheless, soon after she left, we made up, and I continued to see her in secret because Momma wasn't having it. No one disrespects her like that and comes out unscathed. So I'd send Jacqie money and keep an eye on her as much as I could. It was hard because, as a mother figure, I knew how she'd handled leaving home was wrong, but I also wanted to be a good sister and have her back.

What Jacqie didn't realize when she left home was that her new life would involve rooming with a friend, working at Denny's, and returning home a year later, all tatted up, pierced, and pregnant.

"How do I tell Mom?" she asked me shortly after reconciling with our mom.

"Just tell her. She's so happy you're back home, I'm sure she won't be upset."

Jacqie had a special place in our mom's heart because she was rebellious, and Momma could see herself in her. She'd always say, "Jacqie's like me."

So, that day I pushed her into our mom's bedroom and followed her in.

"What's going on?" Momma asked, waking up from a power nap.

"Go ahead," I said to Jacqie, "tell Mom what you have to tell her."

Mom sat up in her bed.

Jacqie started crying.

"Mom, I'm pregnant," she finally blurted out.

"Oh my goodness, okay," said Momma, and then she took Jacqie in her arms and hugged her.

"It's okay, don't worry about it," said Momma in a soft and comforting voice filled with love and patience.

"We're going to be fine," I said.

"I'm kind of ready to be a grandma," said Momma.

My mom knew what it was like to be a teenage mom, and I knew what it was like to be the daughter of a teenage mom, so we were very supportive throughout the whole process. At the end of the day, we were just happy Jacqie was back home with us.

But it wasn't easy, and like any parent, I wanted to prevent Jenicka from traveling down the same difficult paths some of the women in our family had to experience.

Back in the office, I stared at Jenicka in disbelief and sat back in my chair, quietly trying to process this conversation. I wanted to support her decision, but it felt like she had drop-kicked my heart. At the time, I felt like I had given up my life for Jenicka—well, I did, I put things on hold just to raise her and Johnny—and with so much change on the horizon, I wasn't ready to let her go. I didn't want our trio to break up. She and Johnny were my rocks.

"I want you to be my sister now, not my mother," Jenicka said honestly. She thought I had become a little overbearing in my mom role. "I want to be able to do my own thing and figure out what I'm going to do with my life without Mom," she added in that mature tone that makes me think she's wise beyond her years.

That made my heart stop. I understood. It was one of the reasons we were selling the house to begin with—we all needed to figure out our lives and move on.

"This breaks my heart into a billion pieces," I said to her as I took a deep breath to control my emotions. But I respected her decision.

"I'm going to be around," she said, trying to comfort me.

"Just know that it hurts me very much, and that whenever you want to come back home to live with me, the door will always be open."

Jenicka stood up, walked around the massive desk and, as I peeled away from my chair to face this new reality, we fell into each other's arms.

"It's okay," she said, after hugging me long and hard. "It'll be fine, I promise."

Jenicka was a good girl, mature, and smart. She'd been open and honest and done everything right by approaching me with her plan. Even though I was broken by this decision, I got it. She wanted to follow her path, and I wasn't going to stand in her way. So I swept my hurt aside and decided to trust that she would be okay.

Once we accepted the offer for the house, we only had two weeks to move out. I honestly thought it would all take a little longer, but the buyers, Nick and Vanessa Lachey, offered to give us above the asking price on the condition that they could move in as soon as possible. The deal was struck and the clock was ticking. That's when it hit me, *Oh shit, we need to get out of here.*

Reality was starting to sink in. We had two weeks to not only pack up all of our things, but to also finally confront something we had been avoiding for the previous two-plus years: the storage containers in the garage, the ones that had all of our mom's things.

Jacqie came over one afternoon, and the five of us hesitantly walked over to the garage. We stood there quietly as the door slid up and revealed stack after stack of clear plastic containers.

We took a collective deep breath, and I said, "Alright, guys, let's get to it."

"What are we going to do with all of this?" asked Mikey, somewhat overwhelmed.

"Well, we have to look through it, we have to pick and choose what we're going to store, what's going to be in the Grammy Museum, and what you guys are going to take," I said as I approached one of the bins and pulled off the lid.

Although our hearts felt tight and we were filled with dread, we did our best to keep it lighthearted as we began to unpack the containers filled with memories. Suddenly, I pulled out a bright fuchsia wide-brimmed hat and yelled, "Oh my god, see? I get it from Mom. She still has tags on her stuff too!"

"Sixty-eight dollars," said Jacqie, reading the price out loud and shaking her head.

"Thank you, Momma," I said, looking up to heaven. "I was feeling really bad about myself."

"Would she even wear this?" said Jacqie, grabbing the hat from me and playfully putting it on her head. "Oh my god, this is my new Sunday church hat. Praise the Lord!"

"You know what," I said, "why don't we give some of Mom's hats to Grandma?"

"Grandma does like hats," said Jacqie, removing the hat and placing it back in the bin.

We started moving some containers to one corner, while opening others, trying to quickly sort through her stuff, because as cheerful as we were trying to be, it was incredibly difficult. I mean, her bedroom had remained the way she had left it up until a few weeks earlier when we cleaned up a bit for the house showings, and even then, we left her last change of clothes intact. But we powered through a little while longer.

"Oh, this is pretty," I said, pulling out one of Momma's glam black-sequined dresses and holding it up to my body to get an idea of how it might look on me.

"I think she wore that on a red carpet," said Jenicka.

27

Each piece brought back a memory. It hurt to see Momma's stuff, remember the moments, and then come to terms with the reality that she was no longer there with us.

I grabbed a red halter dress from another bin, and Jenicka said, "She wore that dress to tía Rosie's wedding and then I wore it to a gala. I want that one."

The air was growing heavier, together with our hearts.

I gave the red dress to Jenicka and pulled out a simple red romper with a front zipper and held it against my body to see if it would fit, thinking I could maybe even wear it one day. That's when I looked over at Jenicka and noticed her expression change.

"Are you going to cry?" I asked.

"I don't know," she said softly, looking down.

"It's okay," said Jacqie. "She never cries. She needs to let it out."

Meanwhile, Johnny and Mikey had been on the quiet side, making only small comments here and there. I guess they were trying to cope with this moment as best as they could.

I had been doing everything in my power to keep it together, but as soon as I saw the tears clouding Jenicka's eyes, and while still holding that red romper in my hands, I broke. That piece of clothing was part of Momma's loungewear. She'd wear it to go to the movies with us, to go grocery shopping, and to just hang around the house. The mariachi dresses she wore onstage make me miss her, but not as much as her everyday clothes and sneakers. That was my momma, Dolores Janney Rivera—her essence in all its beauty.

"I can't do this," I said, dropping the romper into the box and walking to the back of the garage, as tears welled up in my eyes. "I don't want to do this," I sobbed.

Mikey silently walked over and gave me a hug, and I rested my head on his shoulder.

"It's so fucking unfair. I hate it, I hate it, I hate it," I murmured. "I'm sorry. I'm supposed to be strong for you guys, but it's so fucking hard."

As I continued to let the tears roll down my face, Jenicka started to cry, then Johnny followed with his own waterworks. Jacqie came over to me and we shared a long, emotional hug.

"Where is she? Where is she?" I said softly. "I want to smell her and it pisses me off that I can't."

"Nothing smells like her anymore," said Jenicka.

"It's been a long time," said Jacqie, trying to hold down the fort as we crumbled around her.

"I just want to know where she's at. What she's doing?" I said as I attempted to compose myself a little.

"She's chilling," said Jacqie.

"She's sleeping," said Jenicka.

"Resting for all the years she wasn't able to rest," I added. "So, what do we do with this?" I said, patting the black suitcase, the elephant in the room. That piece of luggage carried everything that had been salvaged from the plane wreck.

"It needs to go. It has really bad energy," said Jenicka.

"A lot of it I don't want to see ever in my life again. I just want to bury it," I said. "But there's that one dress, the pink-and-yellow one she wore that night."

"[The suitcase] is perfectly fine," said Jacqie, "which is so unfair. I hate that suitcase. Everything in it is unscratched. It makes me wonder why she couldn't come out unscratched or alive."

We didn't have the emotional strength or courage to open the suitcase that afternoon, so we pushed it to the side and decided to call it a day and get the rest of our family involved. We needed their help. We couldn't get through it all alone. As we started gathering ourselves to leave the garage, Mikey said, "Stop. Stop with the whole sadness, the crying." He put his arm around my shoulders.

"I know, I know. I'm sorry. I was the one who started the fountain of tears."

"It's okay," said Jacqie reassuringly. "It has to happen."

I was doing my best to believe in destiny, in things happening for a reason, but in the garage that day stood five kids who had all lost their parents. Why did we have to lose our mom so soon? It's hard to comprehend, to make sense of it all. What *was* clear, though, was that with the sale of the house, we all felt that she was slowly slipping away from us. But we realized it was up to us to reclaim her in our hearts—she would always live on with us.

The days that followed were bittersweet. I was looking forward to this new chapter and what the future held for all of us, but I dreaded having to close the door on this one.

The five of us decided to have one last family barbecue in the backyard with my uncles Juan and Pete, my aunt Rosie, my grandma and grandpa, as well as everyone's spouses and children. It was a beautiful send-off to the house that had held us together for this long. We had a mariachi band play some music at twilight as we took in the beautiful city views for one last time.

"As much as I'm going to miss this house," I said that evening to my family, "I'm pretty much ready. It hurts me, but I think it's the best decision we could've made. And we're going to make new memories."

Johnny and my tío Juan, who were sitting next to each other at the other end of the backyard table, began to cry. Mikey walked over to Johnny and hugged him, and then he was also overcome with emotion.

"What makes us sad are the memories, but honestly, the house doesn't feel the same without her," said Jacqie, as she stood next to

Juan, who remained seated at the table with tears still in his eyes. "It's not a home."

"It's just the memories we live by," added Jenicka, who was sitting by my side. "Right now, I can't help thinking of that day she was here, sitting on Esteban's lap and just smiling. At any party, she would be laughing and super happy to just be home." Tears flooded her eyes as she recalled memories of our family gatherings with my momma in this backyard.

"When I was little, I never thought we'd be in this situation that we're in," said Johnny, between sobs. "I'm still trying to face it. It's breaking me."

"You're just letting go of a physical house," said Mikey to Johnny. "She's always with you."

Although more than three years had passed, we were all still sharing the pain of her loss and that had kept us close.

"You guys are overwhelmingly impressing me," said Juan. "It's unbelievable how strong you are as kids."

Later that evening, we each wrote a note to Momma, taped it to a balloon, and released them into heaven, hoping our messages of love and appreciation would reach her somewhere up there.

That home was our safe place, and it was hard to accept that we wouldn't be able to come back to it. On that last day, as we all stood in the empty living room and took one last look around, I said, "Let's go. We have to be strong children. Children of the corn," which was something our mom used to say to us when we misbehaved because she thought we were acting like the evil kids from that movie. It was a running joke from then on.

"That's us," said Jenicka as we left the house through the grand front door for the last time.

As hard as this was for all of us, letting go of the house didn't mean letting go of her. We carried her laughter, her love, her lessons, everything within us, and no matter where we went, we'd make sure her presence and legacy lived on. We'd finally managed to pick ourselves up from the wreckage of her loss. Now it was time to dust ourselves off and move forward.

May your faith in the future be much bigger than the false illusions of the past.

3

BIRTH OF THE BOSS BEE:
PERSIST, PERSEVERE, PREVAIL

When my mom asked me to move out of our home in March 2012, she also fired me from my role as her assistant and revoked my access to her credit cards. She thought I needed a wake-up call, and she was right. I had grown comfortable in my situation. When I began working for her, after high school, she started me off at $1,600 a month. But with time, as my responsibilities continued to grow—from personal shopper, to assistant, to taking care of the kids and the house, paying the bills, and making sure everything was running smoothly—I decided to renegotiate my salary. "Okay," she said, "for everything you do, what if I give you one thousand dollars a week?" I gladly accepted. That meant I would be making $4,000 a month. My car was paid off and I didn't pay rent, or utilities, or my phone bill because they were taken care of through the business, so that salary was basically money in my pocket. And I began to spend it more mindlessly. Once, I bought my mom a $2,600 pair of limited edition Jimmy Choo shoes and threw in an extra pair for myself—I still have them in my closet. The same would go for clothes. I'd buy her outfits and use the business credit card to charge some cute clothes for me too, clothes I didn't need because I lived in workout gear and barely ever went out.

Momma was aware of what was going on because I was using her credit cards, but she let it slide at the beginning because she knew I worked hard for her day in and day out. But I took advantage of this situation. The truth is I had lost touch with the value of money. I get it now that I have to take care of my mortgage, my bills, my groceries, and my everyday expenses with my own hard-earned cash. I still treat myself, but I learned my lesson the Jenni way—the hard way.

In that month of March, I went from going on spending sprees and living the life in a 10,000-square-foot mansion, with my own room and ginormous closet and constant access to my brothers and sisters, to having the rug blatantly pulled out from under me. Suddenly, I was out of the house and out of a job. The first thing I thought was, *Fuck, I should've gone to school!* I had lived for my mom and my kids; they were my life, my job, my purpose. Without them and without a degree to lean on, what was I supposed to do now?

My grandparents were really big on making sure their children got a solid education, but that was never really pushed on me when I was growing up. As a kid, I was introverted and, although my mom didn't know it at the time, I was quietly dealing with my father's abuse, so my mind was clearly in turmoil, which was reflected in my schoolwork. For a while, I was behind in my reading skills and even needed special tutoring. Then, by the time I hit my teens, I began taking on more chores at home. While my mom was out working, as the eldest, I was in charge of the house and the kids. That meant cleaning our home, making sure my siblings did their homework and were fed, and so on. By the time I was done with all of that, the last thing I wanted to do was sit down and do my own homework, so I would half-ass it, doing just enough to get by. That meant maintaining a C average, with some A's and B's in the mix, because although education wasn't first in my list of priorities, I knew that coming home with a D or an F was met with an ass whooping.

The funny thing is that when I expressed any interest in a career, my mom, the straight-A valedictorian and all-out nerd, would say that I didn't need to go to college. She'd always say, "I was the ugly duckling at school and had no other choice than to put my face in my books to get ahead." Then she'd add, "God didn't give you the brains, mija, but he gave you the beauty, so you've got to capitalize on that."

That stung. It messed with my self-esteem and actually pushed me to make it my mission to be smart, to read, to constantly feed my brain. When I misspelled a word and my mom called me out on it, saying I was "stupid," I started reading the dictionary to learn a new word on the daily, and I still do this today, only now it's through an app, because I never want to be considered stupid again. I'm not stupid. I hate that word.

Despite this backlash, I still had college aspirations. For a while I had thought about becoming a psychologist. I wanted to help other people navigate trauma the way my therapists had helped me after my dad molested me. But when I shared this with Momma, she said, "But that's a lot of school, mija." And although I expressed a true interest, she made me feel as though I wouldn't be able to handle it. Nevertheless, I continued bringing up the conversation. But she insisted, "You don't need to go to school to learn how to make money."

Finally, after graduating high school and turning eighteen, I came up with a plan. I told her I was thinking of joining the Air

Force. I figured it would give me time to think about what I wanted to major in and it would also pay for college, which was a win-win in my eyes. But the timing was off. My mom was going through a divorce, she needed my help with the kids, her singing career was starting to take off, and she needed me by her side. "I can't do it without you," she said. "I'll give you a job. I'll pay you cash." And that's how I began my fourteen-to-twenty-hour workdays as my mom's personal secretary, counselor, wardrobe stylist, shopper, accountant, cheerleader, and babysitter. I had officially enrolled in the University of Jenni Rivera, and to be honest, I liked it. I felt needed by Momma and by my siblings. I felt useful, and it satisfied the one constant I've always known I wanted: to help people. I dedicated my twenties to helping my mom and my family.

I wasn't thinking about the future back then, I was living in the now. That's why I was so lost in the spring of 2012, when my mom gave me the boot and pushed me out of the nest at twenty-six. I had grown so codependent on her that I didn't know how to use my wings to fly on my own. I thought I was too old to go to school to pursue a career in my late twenties, and I assumed I had missed that boat. So I turned to what I knew best: how to run a business. And I slowly discovered that I actually did have an education up my sleeve; it just wasn't from a traditional four-year college. It was Jenni Rivera's school of hard-knock life.

I learned so much through working side by side with my mom. I opened all of her corporations, closed contracts, and really helped build her empire. But after working tirelessly for years, sharing all of my ideas, taking part in the big and small decisions and tasks, when I finally was out on my own, I realized that none of it was really mine. And it hit me like a lightning bolt. I had created so much. I started her perfume line, the jeans, the tequila, the makeup, the skincare—and yet I had nothing to show for it.

However, what was mine was the priceless knowledge I had acquired throughout those years. And when my mom kicked me to the curb, she gave me the chance to put it all to the test, and I couldn't be more grateful for this now. In a way, it was the last and most important lesson my mom taught me: Don't depend on anyone, not even your mother. She stripped everything from me when she kicked me out. And that's when I realized I had to figure out my life and start doing things for myself. In that moment, I vowed to never depend on anyone again.

Even though, at first, I felt like I was drowning, my mom had already given me the tools to survive, and it was time for me to put them to use. So came the birth of my first business: Blow Me Dry. Dry bars were superhot at the time, and I would go to them all the time. So I figured that would be the perfect business venture for me: a service that I loved (yes, I got my hair and makeup done in my salon all the time!) and a business I could call my own.

I wanted to show my mom what I could do. I wanted her to be proud of me. So I grabbed the money I had saved up from my *Chiquis & Raq-C* reality show, reached out to a realtor, and signed a five-year lease for a space on Ventura Boulevard in Encino. Then I hired an architect and planned out the salon.

My goal was to beautify my salon space while also making it profitable through regular services, including wash and blow-dry, makeup, and add-ons like hair masks and deep conditioners. I wanted women to walk into the chic aqua-and-white space and get beautified on the outside by doing their hair and makeup, but I also wanted them to leave with something in their mind that inspired confidence from within. That's why I placed carefully chosen quotes all around my salon, thoughts that helped me get through some tough times, like the Serenity Prayer, or something as simple as "Confidence is sexy." In the restroom, I had one that said, "Commit an act of kindness every day."

This was my first business venture without my mom, and I wanted to keep it as separate from her as possible. That's what drove me to open it in Encino near our home instead of in a Latino neighborhood. When I told her about my decision, she was not happy; she just didn't get it.

"What the fuck, mija. Why not? Use your mother's name. This is why I work my ass off every single day. I've done this to set a foundation for all of you. So I don't understand why you won't do it in Long Beach or somewhere like that, where people know me and they would go to your salon. I'll promote it."

"Momma, no. That's exactly what I don't want to do. I want to show you that I can do this by myself. Go someplace where no one knows me, provide good services, and be successful on my own." I didn't want my success to ride on my mom's coattails.

"I just don't fucking get it." She was very upset. "What's wrong with you?"

Even though she didn't get it, I was determined to do this my way. Yes, I had chosen a more Anglo-driven community, and sure, it could've been more successful if I opened it somewhere like Long Beach and cashed in on being Jenni Rivera's daughter, but that's exactly what I wanted to escape. I didn't want to give the media or my mom any chance to throw it back in my face later and say, "Oh, it's successful because of me," or "Because her fans go there." No. This had to be all me and all mine. I needed to prove to her and to myself that I could do it on my own.

When opening day came along in the summer of 2012, I was a bundle of nerves. All the main Spanish-language TV stations had sent reporters to cover the launch party, and I had invited my mom, but I honestly wasn't even sure if she'd show up. As the evening began to unfold, I stepped up to face the media on my own in a little red carpet area in front of the salon, my hair pulled back in a chic bun to highlight my dangling gold earrings and clean-cut white jacket over a short mustard-colored formfitting dress. I felt nervous yet also ecstatic because I had made all of this happen. I started chatting with the media and then glanced to my left, and my heart skipped a beat. There was my mom, walking over in a classic blue button-down shirt and sunglasses, and I practically jumped for joy, interrupting the interview to call her over. We gave each other a big hug and, while the reporter interviewed her, my eyes filled with tears as I realized that no matter what, Momma always had my back. Her support and approval filled me with inexplicable joy and strength.

"We're businesswomen," she said to the reporter, "and we're here to support each other and try to be successful in all of our ventures."

Later, as I walked Momma around the salon—I hadn't let her see it until that night!—I soaked in her words of wisdom, words I still live by today.

"You need to embrace the fact that it is difficult," she said to me that night about running my own business. "Things aren't just put in your hands. Things are difficult. You have to fight and struggle and cry about it. And then you need to get up and shake it off and keep going, mamacita. What you did today, opening this place up and standing firm in front of everybody, saying, 'I did this,' cause you did it on your own . . . I'm very proud of you."

I'll never forget the hug she gave me right after that, and the look of joy and pride in her eyes. It's a moment that will stay with me forever.

I was excited about this journey because I felt it would help me grow and allow me to really spread my wings and see what I was capable of. It meant the world to me.

Yet the timing was off for me once again. Not because I didn't calculate it right, but because God had other plans. A few months after it opened, I lost my relationship with my mom because of our fallout over her far-fetched suspicion that I had slept with her husband (which I had not), and a couple of months later, she was gone for good. By then, my head was no longer in my business. I was doing what I could to stay above water and not drown in the grief and devastation of that loss. Then I moved into my mom's house to take care of my younger siblings, and they became my life all over again. I was devoted to them, so I was unable to give the salon the attention it required. I was on mom duty, and that was my life raft, what was allowing me to survive emotionally, but I didn't have the bandwidth to also keep up with my salon.

At the start of the business, I had managed to break even most months, but in the course of those four-plus years, I had to hire a manager because I couldn't be there every day as I had originally planned, and that meant putting more money into the business just to help keep the ship afloat.

Too many responsibilities were piling up, and something had to give. I was losing so much money, but I was hell-bent on not failing, so I held on for longer than I should have, refusing to close it until I couldn't keep it going anymore. I finally understood the meaning of the saying, "Si tiene tienda que la atienda, si no que la venda." If you're not there at your shop, giving it your all, especially during those first few years, it's really hard for it to take off. It was draining me dry, and the time had come to cut the bleeding.

Life had taken an unexpected turn, and I had to come to terms with that and realize that this business no longer fit my path. As much as it pained me to let go of my wonderful staff—people who felt like family to me—and accept this failure and financial hit, when I finally shut down Blow Me Dry, it released me. I felt like I could breathe again. It also taught me my first big lesson as an independent businesswoman: In order to succeed, you have to know how to fail. Not to be confused with giving up. Failure is a lesson in and of itself. It means something didn't work. But it doesn't mean we must give up.

Those following weeks hurt deeply. Blow Me Dry was my first business baby. I had had plans to turn it into a brand and to sell merchandise. The sky was the limit, and now it was gone. I cried so much during the following weeks, especially when I drove by and saw the sign still hanging there above the now-empty space, but I was also grateful for the opportunity it gave me. With that salon, I took my first steps into launching and managing my own business. It showed me what I could do, and that filled me with confidence and strength. It also taught me that in business and in life, you have to know when to let go.

By closing this door, I suddenly opened a new one, where I had the time and space to pursue other avenues of revenue and new opportunities. This allowed me to home in on the other things I had already started cooking up and make them even more successful. I was finally becoming a true Boss Bee (Built On Self-Success, Babe Embracing Evolution).

The term Boss Bee comes from my old friend Gerald's go-to phrase "Boss Bitch." He used to say that all the time to encourage us when we were winning at life. I later gave it my own twist and turned it into Boss Bee. My goal was to inspire and empower women with this name. I started using the bee emoji, and from there, my fans ran with it. I've never liked calling people who like what I do and follow me my fans, so they became my Boss Bees. I wanted to give this community a mission, a purpose. That's why I started Boss Bee Nation: "Changing the world one heart at a time." I wanted my Boss Bees to be all about positivity, spreading good, empowering one another. It's not a fan club or an official nonprofit organization, it's simply a mission. I haven't gone through that long and arduous process of creating an official foundation, like I did with my mom's Love Foundation. I've just been funding it myself through investing in and selling Boss Bee merchandise to do good. I deposit the profits in a separate account and use it for scholarships to help further a Boss Bee's education, to adopt a family for Christmas and fill their house with gifts, to help a single mother, and more. And if a story touches my heart, I'll donate $1,000 to $2,000 to that cause in the name of Boss Bee Nation to encourage all of us to do and spread good in the world. When my Boss Bees invest in a hat or a shirt, they're helping me help other people, and I love that.

I really came into my own as the OG of Boss Bees once my mom was gone. There was no inheritance waiting for me, so I had to "figure it out" and learn to fend for myself, take care of my kids, and step into my own power as a businesswoman. And I embraced this evolution like no other.

Once *I Love Jenni* aired its last episode, networks began to approach my siblings and me to do a new family reality show. By that point in 2016, I had three reality shows and seven years of experience under my belt in this media, and I was very grateful for this medium because it honestly helped me get out of my shell. It all began in 2009 when the idea of *Chiquis & Raq-C* was being floated around. I honestly fought hard against it. Up until then, I had been behind-the-scenes helping my mom launch and grow her career and businesses, and I was happy in that role, but my mom thought I could do more. "Please, mija, you could help people, you could be an inspiration." Help people? Be an inspiration? Those words sealed the deal. I pushed my fears aside and was all in.

Raq-C was a radio host, so she was already used to being in

the public eye, and she was great at it, but I still had to go through many growing pains. First off, I had no idea how to behave in front of the camera. I kept thinking, *What am I doing here?!* I didn't have a voice yet, and I was still very shy and introverted. But Raq-C pushed me to do more, to get out of my comfort zone. "Girl, you gotta talk," she'd tell me off camera. And she was right. I didn't know how to own my presence in the spotlight yet. I also didn't know what I should and shouldn't talk about. I didn't want to make any mistakes. So I set out to watch and learn.

Even though Raq-C and I had a falling-out, I will always remain grateful to her. Just watching her unapologetic and outspoken ways were an inspiration. But she was also generous with the spotlight. Oftentimes, she'd say, "Here, Chiquis, you go and do the interview for us."

"Okay, but what do I say?" I'd ask her. The thought of having to face the media on my own turned me into a nervous wreck. But she'd patiently coach me through some talking points and really taught me the ropes.

The show was released in 2010 on Bravo. People loved watching these two Latinas in LA living their lives. It was the first time our Latino community saw themselves reflected in the reality show boom. *Chiquis & Raq-C* became so successful that it opened the doors to our first family reality show. Although I really loved doing this first reality show, I was hesitant to do another one. I had seen the issues this type of show can cause in families. Jessica Simpson and Nick Lachey got divorced after their show; the Osbornes started having issues. "Momma, I don't know about this," I said, but she was determined to do it, so we moved ahead. Raq-C and I had the first Latina reality show in 2010, and *I Love Jenni* aired the first Latino family reality show in 2011, which ran for a total of three seasons. I also did my own show in 2012 called *Chiquis 'n Control,* which started off following my life after my mom asked me to leave home and became an opportunity to show who I really am as an individual to an audience that had been marred by endless gossip about my family.

As the years went by with *I Love Jenni* and *Chiquis 'n Control,* I stopped overthinking my every move on the shows and was finally not only able to let loose on camera but also begin to gain my own fan base, which eventually became my beloved Boss Bee Nation, which I mentioned earlier. I found my voice, I began to feel comfortable speaking my truth, and that led me to become the unapologetic, outspoken, and unstoppable chingona I am today.

When we were approached to do *The Riveras*, before saying yes or no, I needed to check in with my siblings. So I called a family meeting, and the five of us sat down to explore this new opportunity. I said to them, "Hey, this would be a good way to make some money, save some money, and start our own businesses." But I was also a little worried. It's really hard to draw the line with reality shows, to know what should be kept private and what should be shared publicly. "We need to make sure that this doesn't affect our relationships. We have to stick together, that's what matters most." This was essential to me, and I also knew it was important to our mom because she would always say to us, "I want you guys to be different from my siblings and me." My siblings were all I had left, and I wasn't going to let anything come between us.

Once we agreed to not let this get in the way of our relationships, we also agreed that the new show would be a logical source of income. It was something we all knew how to do, and, financially, we needed the money, so we said yes.

The Riveras started filming in February 2016 and was released in October 2016. It allowed us to show everyone that despite all we'd been through, we were doing okay. And it gave us the chance to spend more time together. But things started going south during the last two seasons. Jacqie was annoyed because she had a long drive to our house in Encino for filming, plus she had other responsibilities, including raising her three kids—the show was starting to weigh on her. Meanwhile, Jenicka and Mikey didn't like doing the show, so it was really hard to get them to participate in scenes. I was an executive producer and trying to hold down the fort at home while coordinating schedules and dates with all of them, which was causing me to get frustrated with my brothers and sisters. It was starting to take a toll on us, but we signed on for a third season, thinking we could make it work. And that's when it all went to shit.

Some of the producers began to make things up to cause more drama among us, and in the process we were losing our authenticity, which didn't fly with my work philosophy one bit. I always aim to represent what is really happening in my life, and that's what I wanted for *The Riveras*, but our stories didn't seem to contain the level of drama the network required. When we first started filming the show, the producers protected our image, but eventually they caved under the network's pressure.

Then, as executive producer, I began to butt heads with production too. I noticed how they were going behind our backs to start trouble between my siblings and me, and that's when they crossed the line in my book. It was tough because I had been working with this company since the start of my reality career. The network would've gladly kept the cameras rolling for more seasons because our ratings were good, but after talking to my siblings and realizing it was having a negative effect on our relationships and stressing us out, we called it off.

I wasn't willing to lose my family over a show and its ratings, no matter how good the money was—and it sure did serve as great financial security for a long time. But I couldn't sell my soul to the devil. The love for money will never be more important than my family. The beauty of this decision is that by closing this door, it opened a new one for all of us. That's when we all started hustling and doing our own thing. Mikey found a job and started making his own money. Jacqie began to focus more on her music and invested in her T-shirt line, in addition to also helping with our mom's businesses, the boutique, and the Love Foundation. Jenicka began to explore possible career paths as a plus-size model. She also got into makeup instructional videos and started focusing on developing her social media. And Johnny had money in his account that he would be able to access a few months later, when he turned eighteen. Putting an end to this reality show gave us all the time and energy to look for other avenues of income that also made us happy. It was a welcome break from years of exposing our lives to the public through a medium governed by rules where drama is the goal and you have to keep your real self in check. I'm very grateful for my reality career, it truly helped me, but now it was time for each of us to focus on ourselves. To me, that meant continuing to develop another relatively new endeavor that I had launched in 2016, a side hustle and a dream that I was now ready to take to the next level.

Each and every step described here, from assisting my mom, to opening my salon, to the years of reality TV, to dealing with grief and raising teens, helped put me on a path to finding myself and manifesting a new and "flawless" dream.

I've been taking care of my skin since I was sixteen. The interest was first sparked by the magazines I loved to flip through, like *Seventeen*. I gobbled up all their tips and tricks for clear and beautiful skin. That's also when I really started caring about what I looked like in general. And then there was this boy—(isn't it always about a boy??)—Junior, my first boyfriend. I wanted to look pretty for him. I started noticing how he'd check out the girls on TV. One day, we were sitting on my living room couch and he blurted out, "Oh, she's so beautiful. She has beautiful skin." That might have been one of the first times I felt that kind of jealousy boil my blood. "Whaaat?" He tried to backtrack, "It's not like I could ever have her. I'm just saying she has beautiful skin." My insecurities kicked in big-time, and I thought, *Wait, I want to have beautiful skin too!* And so began my skincare journey, though I never imagined where it would lead me.

I met Judi Castro about five years after that incident. By my early twenties I had graduated from at-home care to aesthetic treatments, like facials and Botox, with Judi, a professional aesthetician. Yes, I started getting Botox at a very young age for preventative reasons. I loved her treatments and how wonderful my skin looked and felt after I visited her spa, so I kept going back and quickly became a loyal customer.

Several years later, in 2014, while lying on a spa bed watching Judi's daughter hard at work on my face, I said, "Hey, I really want my own skincare line, and I know your mom has hers, but I'd love to talk to her about it." Boss Bees gotta ask for what they want! She said she'd talk to her mom and then we'd set up a meeting to discuss it further. I knew Judi well, she'd been in the industry for years, I loved her work, and her expertise would be invaluable.

Meanwhile, as much as I wanted to make this happen, I was also still debating if partnering up with someone was the right way to go. I had helped my mom develop her own beauty business—it was actually my idea, as Momma was more into makeup. I sat down with my mother's business partner, who like Judi had her own aesthetics spa, where my mom would go to get her facial treatments. And that's how it all began for them too.

I was so excited and fully invested in this new venture, handling all the day-to-day tasks that went into developing and launching my mom's skincare line. I went to the manufacturer's office with my mother's business partner to check out the progress, try the products, and make sure the quality was up to par with my mom's standards. The line was amazing. I was really proud of what we had accomplished. However, as we progressed, we realized something was off. I started digging into the purchase orders and they didn't add up. After finding several discrepancies, I drove to the bank and asked to see our account information. There was no money in there. We were at zero. We'd been swindled, scammed, it was all gone!

This woman had been making up the purchase orders. She'd print them out herself, claim she'd already paid her half, and ask us to pay the rest. We're talking purchase orders of $40,000 to $50,000. And we trusted her, so we'd send her our half, none the wiser. After all, it was a 50/50 partnership, or so we thought. It turns out that we had actually banked the entire venture ourselves, while she was receiving 50 percent of the cut.

Maybe my mother's business partner took advantage of the fact that I was only twenty-two and as naïve and gullible as they come. I'll never know because once we caught on to what she was up to, she disappeared and took half of everything. To make matters worse, we came to discover that the logo—which I have tattooed on my body—wasn't even registered under my mom's name; it was registered under hers! We face-planted with that one but you better believe I will never make that mistake again. Now I trademark everything myself and make sure there's a contract (which I triple check before signing). The hard lessons are the ones that stay with us forever.

So you can understand why my excitement was slightly tinged by the fear of partnering with someone again. But I quickly noticed this was a completely different story; it was my journey, and I couldn't have asked for a better business partner. Judi is absolutely amazing. When I sat down with her, I acknowledged that she already had a line, although it was more clinical than what I envisioned. I wanted to create affordable products packed with quality ingredients. She loved the idea. We met up again, came up with a business plan, dotted our i's, crossed our t's, and began our journey as 50/50 partners for what would soon become Be Flawless.

It took us two years to develop our six-step skincare system. I was over the moon with it, but it was really hard to introduce it to our community. Now everyone's all about skincare, but five years ago it wasn't really on everyone's radar. We knew the goal was to attract customers, so Judi and I decided to pivot slightly to grab their attention. That's how the cosmetics line was born. I figured, if I'm known for my juicy lips, why not come out with a line of lipsticks and lip glosses that would bring the public to our brand and help push the skincare. We launched Be Flawless Diamond Skincare and Cosmetics in March 2016. The makeup did so well that we expanded the line to what it is now, including everything from eye shadow to face coverage.

I have to glam up for work, putting on layers of makeup, and I love feeling like a diva, but I also relish peeling it all off at the end of the day and letting my face breathe and rest. That's why, when I take my social media breaks or I'm in between projects at home, I love being bare-faced, no makeup, no nothing. I take great pride in my skin. I want my face to shine and radiate my inner beauty, and in order for that to happen, I need to take care of it. That's why skincare continues to be my passion. Plus, if you want your makeup to look good, girl, you've got to take care of what's underneath it.

For the last couple of years, Judi and I worked hard to reformulate and revamp our skincare line, which we relaunched in March

2021 as Be Flawless Skin. I wanted to upgrade the logo, streamline the name with our cosmetics line, and continue procuring quality active ingredients at an affordable price. I also wanted to focus on calming skin issues like rosacea (something I have) and hyperpigmentation, which is a huge problem in the Latino community, because we all deserve healthy, gorgeous skin. I'm hell-bent on never promoting or selling something if I don't use it and believe in it first. That goes for other brands and my own too. I need to love it in order to push it.

It's funny, some naysayers (even some family members) think that Be Flawless just pays me to promote the line, and that I owe money to Judi and her husband, Luis, but that couldn't be further from the truth. Our 50/50 partnership means doing everything equally, from investment to making and agreeing on the biggest and tiniest of decisions. We are kicking ass when it comes to co-parenting this baby of ours. There's a beautiful mutual respect we have for each other that I value so much. We sit down, share ideas, inspire each other, and get it done. We've been working together for so long that our relationship has grown beyond just a business partnership; we treat each other like family. Judi is like a mom, a sister, and a friend all wrapped into one. I will be forever grateful to her and Luis for believing in me and standing by my side no matter what hills and valleys I had to traverse along the years.

Blow Me Dry was like my business boot camp, so I knew I had it in me. My momma had unwittingly trained me for this, and I had gotten a taste for it through her businesses and my first venture with the salon, but with Be Flawless I truly came into my own as a businesswoman. I realized I am an entrepreneur at heart. Developing and launching new endeavors ignites my passion.

There are people who can work under someone and others who can't. I don't mind taking direction, but I'm a leader through and through. I like to be my own boss and make my own schedule, because that's what I've been doing my entire life, as the eldest sibling, as my mom's right hand helping to build her career, and that's what makes me thrive and shine. However, don't be fooled, taking the reins and building your own empire requires focus and tireless work. You've got to stick to a schedule and remain disciplined in order to reach those goals.

What helps me are checklists. I have been making checklists since I can remember. Nowadays, I title them "Things to Accomplish," because I live for that feeling of accomplishment I get when I check off an item from my list. The more I check off, the better I feel. I'm so attached to these checklists that if I lose one or accidentally delete it from my Notes app, I freak out—just ask my team!

Aside from my beloved lists, creating and sticking to a schedule is absolutely essential for success too. Sure, you could sleep until eleven in the morning if you wanted to, but will that help or hurt you in the end? I personally need to wake up early and start attacking my priorities and getting stuff done. I begin my day by praying, meditating, filling myself with gratitude, repeating some key affirmations, working out, and taking care of my dog, and that's all before the actual business portion begins.

That essential morning me-time sets me up to slay the rest of the day. And my vision board helps me set and manifest my goals. The words of affirmation that I write down on my board also hold me accountable, such as: *I want to be consistent. I want to have more willpower. I want to be on time. I want to be courageous.* Many times, I jot these phrases down on Post-it Notes and leave them around the house to feed myself positive messages throughout the day. It helps me counteract the slumps, the hardships, the unforeseen negativity, and any other bad energy I may encounter. There's so much toxicity and contamination in the world that it's super important to feed yourself words of affirmation, of life. I've been doing this for years. So much so, that while I'm brushing my teeth in the morning, I write some of my affirmations on the bathroom mirror: *I am beautiful. I am confident. I got this.* Once I say these phrases out loud, I take a deep breath and exhale, sending that energy into the universe. I truly believe in the power of words.

Whether it's exercising on the regular and eating what's good for my body, or teaming up with like-minded collaborators to create a kick-ass business, my schedule, routines, and spiritually aligned affirmations allow me to feel as though I'm consistently making strides toward my dreams. In those first years after my mom passed, I had gotten a handle on my businesses, I knew what I was doing, and I was loving it. And so, the time had finally come to turn my focus to what truly makes my heart soar: music.

Get up, get out, and do something!
Because if you don't, someone else will.

4

MY TURN: TIME TO TAKE THE STAGE

Music has always been a part of me, even before my mom decided to venture down that path. I spent the first few years of my life at the Paramount swap meet with my family, learning about beepers and first-generation cell phones with Regional Mexican music blasting in the background. That was my early childhood soundtrack; it ran through my veins. I loved corridos so much that the first song I learned when I was four years old was "La puerta negra" by Los Tigres del Norte. My grandpa would sit me on his lap and I'd sing to him. Sometimes he'd grab one of those handheld video cameras from back in the day, the ones with the tiny cassettes, and record me, and I loved every minute of it.

When my grandpa used to rent out El Farallón, a space he'd use to hold competitions as he searched for new talent, I was held captive by the performances each year. I paid attention to the contestants' song choices, watched them move, and listened to their voices, until one day, when I was ten, I said, "I want to try it." I chose to sing "La Chacalosa," one of my mom's corridos, and I placed second. I was thrilled. (Abuelo, I still owe you a corridos album!) That was the first time I sang in front of Momma. She looked on, but didn't say anything.

Singing was something I had always been drawn to, but as I grew up next to my mom and quietly observed how much she suffered and struggled to make a name for herself in that industry, I began to feel a little hesitant about giving it a shot myself. That didn't stop me from dreaming of doing something in the entertainment world. I even thought about becoming a weather girl because I loved watching Jillian's sunny forecast on Los Angeles's channel 11. She looked so beautiful and rocked awesome outfits together with her signature upbeat attitude.

Then, when I was twenty-four, I sang in front of my mom for a second time. We had just wrapped a day of work and had taken the team out to get some food at La Sirenita Mariscos in Van Nuys, a Mexican grill and seafood restaurant, which had a little stage area in the back for mariachi bands and karaoke. Jacqie went up and sang a tune, and I followed her with "No llega el olvido," one of my mom's songs that I loved, and one of the few that I knew enough to sing at the time. We were all just unwinding and having a good time, but when I stood in front of everyone to sing, I was a bundle of nerves. I didn't know what my mom was going to think, what she was going to say. Momma observed me attentively, and all I heard her say as I moved through the song was "that's my daughter."

She knew I had been wanting to take up singing for a while. At first, I set it aside and put all my efforts into helping her build her career, thinking that my moment would eventually arrive—it was a dream I hadn't been able to let go of over the years. But whenever we talked about it, she expressed deep concerns.

"Think about it, mija. It's a very hard career for a woman. The long nights; I don't know if you can handle it. I don't know if that's what I want for you. You see how hard it's been for me, how I've had to prove myself, and how mean people can be," she said to me often.

I understood where she was coming from. Hell, I experienced it all firsthand. I saw her struggle through many setbacks and slowly rise to the top. It took her three albums to start to really get noticed and be considered a success. Her first Grammy nomination came from her fifth album. Her ninth album, *Mi vida loca*, was the first one to reach number one on Billboard's Regional Mexican Albums chart. This was in a span of seven years, and I'm not even counting all the years prior to that when she was struggling to just get heard. But nothing could dissuade me. When you have a passion tugging at your heart, you have to go after it.

"Momma, I have thought about it, and I want to give it a shot."

"Okay, if that's what you want, then fine. Just wait until I can manage your career."

So I stood on the sidelines and continued to wait. But God had other plans.

As I slowly emerged from the fog of heartbreak and internalized emotions due to her sudden death, I realized the time had come for me to finally use my voice. I sat down and cowrote my first song, "Paloma Blanca," in response to "Paloma Negra," the song my mom dedicated and sang to me onstage during her last performance in Mexico.

But, as many of you know by now, when my song was released in 2014, it got the cold shoulder. The haters came out swinging:

"She's just riding her mom's fame."

"Since when has she wanted to sing?"

"She sure didn't inherit her mom's talent."

I dodged their comments left and right. I'd be lying if I said the public's reaction didn't sting. Each passing phrase burned a hole in my heart. I was still so vulnerable, so raw from losing my momma. Yet, I must admit, some of the professional critics were right. That song was not ready to be released. I sang it with raw emotion, tears streaming down my face as I did each take alone in the singing booth. That cathartic moment was also my very first time in a studio. I now know I should've paced myself, given myself the space to perfect it, had other people there to guide me, taken the time to master it the right way, because I was too green.

But before I could reach any of these conclusions, Angel released it as a surprise. He had the best of intentions, hoping to give me something to smile about, something to look forward to, but it kind of blew up in my face instead.

Climbing out of that darkness was like scaling up Mount Everest. At times, I was about ready to give up, thinking my mom had been right all along, that this industry wasn't for me. But then that inner drive that pushes me to be unstoppable, to work harder, to do better, to commit to proving that I was capable of this and so much more just took over. I didn't react or fight back like my mom usually did with her haters. I did it my way. I ignored them, I didn't let their comments consume me or tear me to shreds. I thought, *I can do this. And this is something I want to do*. And I let my thoughts be my inspiration. No words, no matter how devastatingly harsh, were going to get in my way.

Then I focused on my mom, on how many closed doors and critics I saw her endure before she became a legend. And I sat down and wrote a second song, "Esa no soy yo," with my vocal coach and close friend, Julio Reyes, which I released a few months later. And that's the one I used to officially step into the music scene in 2014, with my debut on an international stage as a singer at Premios Juventud.

My Turn: Time to Take the Stage

Every time I'm about to take the stage, I feel my momma. When doubt invades my mind, when I start to feel those pre-performance jitters, and when I'm praying I don't forget the lyrics to a song, I can almost feel her giving me that last push that says, "Don't bitch out. You got this." And off I go soaring through the songs with that head-to-toe rush I have fallen in love with, feeding off the sea of people singing along with me. That first performance was no different. She was there with me, in spirit, and she remained in my mind as I belted out my song into her diamond-studded mic, which my family agreed I could use for my debut.

People think I've only been in the music industry for seven years—they forget that it's been part of me my entire life. My training began early, at home and on the job with my mom, where I started from the bottom, doing everything from scheduling and selling dates to drawing up contracts and dealing with her management team. Then, once she was gone, and I was paralyzed by grief, Angel stepped in to help me fill the gaps. It's much easier to do stuff for other people, but when the tables are turned, and you have to do it for yourself, sometimes you don't even know where to begin. When I decided to pursue my singing career, he was there to shake me up and remind me that I already knew how to get this done. I had the business side down, and he taught me more about the industry, giving me a push and lending support when I needed it most. He urged me to open my own record label, my own publisher, and to make sure I owned the masters of any of my present and future songs. Putting into practice everything I learned through my mom and Angel gave me an edge over other new artists at the start of their careers. I knew what to do to avoid getting screwed over, and Angel helped me keep the industry sharks at bay.

Armed with this knowledge, I went back to the studio to finish recording my first album, *Ahora*. I was still trying to find myself musically, searching for my sound, where I felt more comfortable, what genre spoke to me. As the producer of this album, I had free rein to do whatever I wanted, and I felt like I was taking steps in the right direction. In the end, I like to call it my experimental album because I included everything from banda and norteño tunes to even a pop song in English. I really wanted to see this through, so I gave it my all in time, energy, and money. I rerecorded "Paloma Blanca" because I wanted to get it right for the album. "La malquerida" was another highlight because that's the song Gloria Trevi gave me. She'd written it for a novela, but when it wasn't used for that project, she sat me down one day and said, "I like this song for you." And she gave it to me, just like that. From then on, she became my singing career's madrina, and she's been supporting me ever since.

"Paper Bullets" is another song from my freshman album that means a lot to me because I wrote it thinking of my mom. It later evolved and was mostly directed to the people who've talked shit about me, except for this verse, which came straight from my heart to my momma:

The rumors and lies were like a hurricane
I'm still cleaning up all the mess it made
All I wanted was to make you proud
But I'm left to wear this broken crown.

Ahora was my firstborn in music. I was so proud of what I had accomplished, but it turned out to be a very expensive project. There's a song on there, "CPR," that cost $5,000 to make. When the recording, production, mixing, and mastering wrapped, I had spent almost $60,000 on the entire album. What was I thinking? It was way too much, I know that now, but I felt I had to give it everything and then some to erase the mishaps that came with the release of my first single and prove that I was worthy of being taken seriously. Living in the shadow of my mom was out of the question. I wanted to express myself freely so that people could see me as Chiquis through and through.

Yet nothing ever seemed to be enough for a crowd that was hungry to crap on my parade. The backlash I received after my debut release in the summer of 2015 really took me by surprise. Even though my mom's diehard fans loved her, some of them didn't like me—that's still true today—and both they and the media immediately started to draw comparisons between me and my mom. It was the same old, same old: I didn't sing like her, I didn't act like her, I wasn't at her level. What they didn't realize was that they were comparing a newbie, who was just beginning her career and barely tapping into her potential and was still unsure of what sound or genre she wanted to pursue, with someone who had already become a legend. How quickly they all forgot how my mom got her start, all the years of hard work it took for her to not just make it, but to perfect her craft. It didn't happen overnight. She worked tirelessly to improve her singing and to own her title as the "queen of banda." Of course I wasn't where I wanted to be vocally yet, but we all have to start somewhere.

My momma had broken the glass ceiling when it came to women in Regional Mexican music and no one had been able to surpass that until the release of *Ahora*, which sold 7,000 copies in its first week and was certified gold by the Recording Industry Association of America. I became the first female artist to reach Billboard's Regional Mexican and Top Latin Album charts since my mom opened at number one with her posthumous *1 Vida – 3*

Historias in December 2014. That was a huge accomplishment for me.

So you can imagine how difficult it was to ride this high and try to make sense of why so many people wanted to see me fail regardless. They didn't give me a fighting chance. The frustration and exasperation that welled up inside me made me want to say, "Fuck this. I'm out. I'm done. I give up." But I reconsidered. I had decided to give singing a chance because I wanted to do something that made me happy. And the passion and joy I had felt while in the studio making music was deeper and stronger than any backlash thrown my way. I needed to explore this further, and no one was going to stop me.

I never set out to replace my mom. From the very start, my musical journey has been all about finding and expressing myself as Chiquis. Being Jenni Rivera's daughter careerwise has helped and hurt me. The level of pressure and responsibility thrown on my shoulders is at times unbearable, but I get over the negative comments by channeling her. I remember how it all began. My mom wasn't a great singer from the start. I witnessed her tireless effort to become better and her growth throughout her journey. These thoughts gave me strength. I knew I couldn't let the critics deter me from a dream I had carried in my heart since I was four years old. I had to *figure it out*. I had to work hard like she did. I had to improve. I had to grow. So I started taking singing and vocalization lessons. I'd wake up before dawn to go to my video shoots after spending all night in the studio recording take after take of each song until I felt it was right. Whatever it took. The music bug had bitten me, and I was hooked. I knew I had it in me. I just needed more time to find my path.

Now, as I look back, I take pride in seeing how far I've come. I've stopped beating myself up about that first single. It was a learning curve, it gave me the push I needed to grow as a singer. I'm also at peace with the comparisons to my mom because I realize that, no matter what I do, they are inevitable.

In the end, the good always outweighs the bad. After I released my first album, people started approaching me and wanted to work with me. They began to believe in me as a singer in my own right. Then came my first concerts, which included a pop and a banda section. I loved the variety, but every time I started singing my banda songs, I just lit up. It gave me a thrill no other genre did, and the electricity and connection I felt with the audience and how they reacted to those tunes was out of this world. That's when I knew banda was my calling. There was no turning back, no giving up, because that's what truly made me happy. So I took the plunge and began to gestate my second music baby, *Entre botellas*, my first all-banda album, which dropped in 2018.

What has kept me going since the start, no matter how rough it has gotten, is the passion I feel for music, the dream I carried for so long, the desire to make it all come true. I don't like living with that nagging woulda, coulda, shoulda feeling. No matter what people think or say, if I feel something is right in my heart, I will not shrink back. I will pursue it. I held on to the high I felt after each performance, the joy I could sense from the audience, the satisfaction that came with expressing myself through music, and I pushed forward. I wanted to work on my singing, my performances. To this day, I always aim to outdo myself so that my next concert, song, or album is better than the last. I'm my own competition in every aspect of my life. I refuse to compare myself to anyone, even when people insist on comparing me to my mom. I embrace her as my guide and inspiration while sticking to my own pace, my own style. When the cards were stacked against me, I wasn't ready to quit on my dream and what I had visualized for my future. My fearlessness kicked in and I kept going. I was determined to see this through.

I wasn't born ready . . .
I had to surpass all the obstacles in my path
to KNOW I was ready.

5

HEARTBREAK AND CHOCOLATE

When the Encino house was in escrow, a few weeks before we closed and had to pack up and move out, I realized I still had to figure out where Johnny and I would live next. Angel and I had been talking about moving in together for a while, but when tragedy struck our family, he totally understood my wanting to be close to my siblings and our need for a sense of stability. He'd been incredibly supportive and patient, and now that he finally saw a clear opening, he decided to take the leap and ask me one more time. It was one of those late nights when he'd come over to the house after work and I was done with my mom duties for the day—those precious hours where most of our important conversations took place.

"Well, I think it's time. Why don't you and Johnny move in with me. I've been waiting for the right time to ask you."

"I feel like we should be married before we move in together, though," I said. He knew I was hesitant given our track record of breakups.

"Okay, let's just try living together. We are engaged," he replied.

"Sure, as long as Johnny's okay with it. If he's good with the plan, we'll do it."

As I tried to catch some z's that night, my mind was racing. *Was this the right thing to do? Were we ready? Should I insist on getting married first? Would this be the best move for Johnny?* That's when I knew that I had to run this idea by my abuelita Rosa before talking to my kid. I needed her love and her words of wisdom, and I wanted her approval.

The next day, I drove over to her house in Lakewood and stepped into my safe haven, her kitchen. She was busy at work making chocolate paletas and I fell in line to help. While we hung out and poured the chocolate into molds, I cautiously said, "Sooo, Abuelita . . . Angel asked me to move in with him."

She just squawked, "¡¿Que qué?!"

Oh no, here we go. But I continued to plead my case, explaining that once he knew we were selling my mom's house he'd invited me and the kids to move in with him.

"Nothing scares me anymore," she said, referring to how no one gets married before moving in with each other these days.

"It scares me," I confessed.

"Enjoy. Que sea lo que Dios quiera, ask God to bless this decision," she replied, taking it all much better than I had imagined. She suggested that I should give it a shot, make sure we get along, and then get married.

Her words gave me comfort. I always headed to my grandma's house when I needed love, advice, or just some of her delicious home cooking. Her love means everything to me, and her stamp of approval was just what I needed to hear that day.

Now I was ready to talk to Johnny. He was only fifteen at the time, so anywhere I went, he had to go with me. Aside from being his legal guardian, he's always been my kid, and it was important for me to give him the respect to ask for his opinion before final-izing this decision. So I took him out for ice cream to sweeten him up a bit. Johnny grabbed his cup of bubble gum ice cream and sat at one of the tables, digging in while I picked up my mint chocolate chip and cookies and cream sundae from the counter and walked over to join him.

"How would you feel if we moved in with Angel?" I asked, ten-tatively.

"Are you ready to take that step?" he asked, and when he heard me hesitate, he pushed further: "What happens if you break up again? Have you thought about that?"

Angel and I had broken up quite a few times in the four and a half years that we'd been together, and Johnny was pushing to see if I was sure it would work this time around. He needed stability—hell, I needed stability too, and I honestly thought moving in with Angel, someone he looked up to, someone who had proven to be a provider, who'd been there for us, would bring us just that.

"I have thought about that, but I want to be as positive as I pos-sibly can."

"You know I love him," he added, "but do you feel like we'll be good there?"

"Sometimes. I'm not going to lie, there's always a plan B in the back of my mind," I replied openly and honestly, because that's the type of communication I've set out to have with my kid-siblings from day one. I saw my momma suffer through the end of her mar-riages, so I learned from a young age that a backup plan is always needed because, no matter how fairy tale–like things may seem, you never know how they might end. "If you don't want us to move in together, then I'll find a house for us," I said. I needed to make sure Johnny was on board and comfortable; if not, I wouldn't go through with this.

"I'm fine," he said.

"Oh, okay. That was a lot easier than I thought. I was really nervous. I was trying to sugar you up with ice cream and make sure that we were good."

"I love you, sister," he said.

"I love you," I replied.

I was relieved to have my grandma's and Johnny's okay, but I think I was subconsciously hoping to see my doubts reflected in their answers.

My relationship with Angel had been packed with beautiful highs and excruciating lows. When we first started dating, I knew going in that he had five kids but wasn't married and didn't have a girlfriend. I wasn't afraid of kids, but I did want to know a little more about them. That's when I found out his youngest was only five months old.

"Oh my god, it's a baby!" I exclaimed.

"Actually, no, she's five months pregnant."

"What the heck!?! And you're not with the mom?"

"No, we broke up, but we hooked up after that in Vegas and had sex and that's when she got pregnant. We're not going to be together, but we decided to keep the baby."

My mind and behavior were still that of a girl back then. I looked up to him, and I felt slightly intimidated by his maturity—he was sixteen years older than me—and I didn't really know any better.

He'd always say I was a mama's girl, and my urge to prove him wrong helped me evolve into a woman who could handle herself in life.

Angel stood by my side when I went through hell with my mom, he was there for me when she passed away, and he gave me the push I needed to swim through the ocean of grief toward my passion for music. Plus, in a sense, he filled the void my parents had left: his energy and role as protector and provider reminded me of my mom, and he was also an older father-figure type of guy. I loved him, but I think, given all that I was going through, what I was really attracted to was that protection and security and sense of peace he made me feel. His energy felt familiar and comforting, and I latched on to that and didn't want to let it go. I didn't want to see what wasn't working, until my first big wake-up call on February 11, 2015.

That day, we were at his office listening to new music by Ariel Camacho, one of the artists he represented. Gerardo Ortiz, another artist, was also there. As we went from tune to tune, I noticed he'd left his phone on the table. He was talking to the guys, so I casually picked it up and punched in his passcode (which he'd given to me). I'd never looked through his phone before, and I don't know what urged me to do so that day, but as I scrolled down his messages, I suddenly stopped at a name I recognized. It was a model who would hang out at his office a lot and take pictures with his merch, a girl I was actually really cool with. I tapped to see the message thread, and my heart hit the floor. There were pictures of her ass and texts from him that said, "Yummy."

What the fuck!

My pulse started throbbing. I stood up, walked over to him, and grabbed him by the neck in front of his clients. "You fucking asshole!" I yelled as my grip tightened in my fury. He just stared back at me in a drunken stupor. Then I released my hold on him, turned to my two assistants, who had been in the room all along, and said, "Let's go." I took his phone with me.

He followed me home, and we had a massive fight and broke up that night. I was absolutely devastated and felt so humiliated. It was very hard for me to trust a man after suffering the abuse by my father, which started when I was eight when my parents separated and continued until I was twelve. So feeling that sense of betrayal with Angel hit me like an extra hard gut punch. That was it, this time there was no going back . . . or so I thought.

Two weeks later, tragedy struck. Ariel Camacho, the artist who had been showcasing his new music at Angel's label the day we broke up, died on February 25, 2015, in a car accident. I was so sad and shocked by the news that, after days of not talking, I reached out to Angel. One chat led to another, which ultimately gave way to his heartfelt apology. He had fired all the models, cleaned up the shop, and promised things would continue to change for the better. And I chose to believe him.

We got back together. Yet something had cracked within me that day, something I was able to patch up but not fully heal, and I was never quite the same with him again. We had been engaged since December 2013, but that ring felt heavy on my finger now. So as soon as we made amends, I gave it back to him. I told him it was tainted, dirty, that he'd hurt me, and that I didn't want it anymore. He accepted it without fighting back, saying he understood, and promised to make it up to me. So yes, I chose to stay with him, but I was skeptical.

Trust has never come easy for me. I saw too much while growing up. In addition to the abusive relationship I suffered with my dad, I also witnessed my momma's troubled relationships fall apart. I experienced her pain, her tears, her heartbreak firsthand. And that made me feel as though I always had to be on my toes, two steps ahead of any guy I dated, because I didn't want to give anyone the power to hurt me. Nevertheless, Angel and I continued to move forward.

That year, 2015, was a big one for me: I launched my music career, I was in the middle of conceiving my skincare and cosmetics line, and I was turning thirty. I love throwing parties for my family, my friends, and even my pets, so you know I wanted to go all out for my thirtieth birthday. I was hoping to rent a beautiful hall, decorate it to my liking, and invite all of my loved ones. When I shared this idea with Angel, he said, "Don't worry, I'll build it for you." It was such a wonderful gesture, especially after all the conflict we'd experienced just a few months earlier, so I said yes.

He basically built me a nightclub in two weeks. I think, for the most part, it was for me, but that spot was likely also a safe place for him. He knew my family would be there, and his relationship with them had been rocky from the start, given the public confrontation he'd had with my mom back in 2012 when she and I were no longer on speaking terms, so I think he probably felt more powerful and at ease in his own space. Whatever the reason, he came through.

The night of the party, I put on a beautiful white flowy dress with a flattering V-neck that made me feel like a queen. Angel picked me up, and when we were in the car on our way to the party, he started stirring up trouble with me. The issue: my cleavage. As the controlling and macho guy that he was, he didn't like it when I exposed my breasts. Jealousy had started to seep into our relationship ever since that day in February. Maybe he thought that since he'd betrayed me, it was only a matter of time before I did it to him? That wasn't the case at all, but he couldn't see clearly anymore. Anything and everything became a trigger, including my birthday party dress. It was the first important birthday without my momma, and I just wanted to feel beautiful and sexy on my special day. In retrospect, I realize that this was the beginning of the end of us.

When we arrived, he was in a bad mood, which set the tone for the rest of the night, but I still tried to brush the pangs of sadness aside and go with the flow. As I walked into the venue, I was surprised by the decor he'd chosen: it was almost like a wedding. There were king and queen chairs, where the two of us were supposed to sit, and I was wearing white. It was a little weird, but again, I said nothing.

My family was there for me, but their guard was way up given the bad blood between my mom and Angel before she passed, so there was a lot of tension in the air. At one point, as the night unfolded, Angel, who had had one too many drinks, said some harsh words and forcibly pulled me toward him. My tío Juan saw the whole scene and flipped out. He was about ready to pounce on him, and things continued to escalate until Angel started a cake fight to air out the tension that was on the verge of exploding. It was one of the worst birthdays ever, but we survived.

This was all happening at the start of my music career. I had just launched my first album a few weeks earlier, and I was laser-focused on giving it all I had to make it a success. So after my birthday fiasco, I went on tour to promote *Ahora*. That's when things took a turn for the worse in our relationship. Angel couldn't let go of the fear that I would eventually cheat on him because of what he had done. It was really his guilty conscience messing with his mind. He kept projecting on me something that he had done, without taking a step back and realizing where it was coming from. When trust is broken, it's really hard to recover, even more so when the aftermath is packed with jealousy and accusations.

Yet I continued to try to fix us.

I invited him to join me as I promoted my music across the United States and Mexico, but he was afraid of flying, which meant even more time apart. That's when his insecurities kicked in even harder. I had to call him each night when I got back to my room to prove that I wasn't out partying without him. It was so confusing, because he was really supportive of my career and he knew how long I'd been wanting to do this, but his jealousy began to take over and it pushed him to hold me back.

As the months rolled by and I booked more gigs, he started insisting I stay home and consider working at his office, which would give him a front-row seat to where I was and what I was doing at all times. It was like he suddenly wanted a housewife. He was older than me, his business was already up and running successfully, and he was definitely an old-school macho guy—who knows, maybe that was exactly what he had wanted all along. But I had other plans, and he knew it.

It's not that I didn't know how to be a wife—that was the role I had taken on for years with my mom—but the time had finally come to do something for myself. And I wasn't about to throw it all away for a man. I was so excited about developing my career as an artist and my life as a businesswoman. My first book and album were released in 2015, then in March 2016, I launched Be Flawless—I was on a roll, thriving and loving the fact that I was working and making my own money.

Support from him was one thing, but I was determined not to give him the power to take it all away from me the way my mom did back in 2012. After she kicked me out of the house, I vowed to never depend on anyone again, and I aimed to keep that promise to myself. You live, you learn. As excruciating as that year had been for me, my mom taught me the value of being an independent woman, and no one was going to steer me away from that now.

Perhaps, when I began to sense this shift in the relationship and his need for a housewife that so clearly clashed with my goals as a businesswoman and singer, I should've ended it, but I didn't. During one of our countless arguments on this subject, I finally said, "Just give me three years. I want to do this, and I want to give it my all."

"No, I want a wife and a family; plus, I can't travel with you. Why do you want to keep pursuing this?" Maybe he figured one album was all I needed to get the singing bug out of my system.

"Because I'm not where I want to be," I said to him. "I really want to get further. I want a Grammy."

He just stared back at me in silence.

"Look, you're already well-established, and I can easily just sit here and leech off you, but that's not what I want to do. I'm with you because I love you and I want to be with you, not because I need to be with you."

I felt like he understood my point, so I bypassed the accumulating red flags I should've paid attention to—his controlling nature, his jealousy, his need for a housewife, and his cheating heart—and decided to take the plunge, ignoring what my gut was desperately trying to tell me. The signs were there, I had seen this go down between my mom and dad—he'd also wanted a housewife and she'd also had bigger plans. Yet I silenced my doubts and hesitations and, with grandma's approval and Johnny's support, I said yes to moving in with him. It turned out that Mikey would also be living with us temporarily until he found a place of his own, which made me happy, because having my brothers with me was almost like having a piece of my momma—they made me feel safe.

Angel and I went house hunting in Woodland Hills and Encino, and when I told him I really liked Toluca Lake, we searched for a place in that neighborhood and found the perfect house. It was a huge 7,000-square-foot home with six bedrooms, which was perfect because it would comfortably fit us, Johnny, Mikey, Angel's kids when they stayed over, and my future glam room. Since it was in the heart of Los Angeles, it was also easy for Angel to get to work, to his mom's house, and to visit his children. To make matters even better, the owners were fine with a one-year lease—that gave us one year to put this living together thing to the test before we made any other major decisions.

I was excited to start this new chapter with my boyfriend, but

I was also jittery with nerves. I'd never lived with a guy before—I had to adjust to the idea that it would no longer be "my" house, it was "our" house now. And although I was a little afraid of commitment, I went for it. In June 2016, we moved into our new house. I chose a closet in our room, started unpacking my clothes, and set out to make a home for us. But it wasn't the type of home I had imagined. We had a weird relationship. He'd leave the house at nine in the morning and come back at ten at night, and sometimes he had to work weekends—or so he said. This meant that during the day it was almost as if I was single. It wasn't the companionship I had dreamed of, but I was dead set on making it work. After all, being in a relationship is all about compromising, but sometimes I wondered, *Am I compromising too much?*

I was pretty sure he was going to propose to me again on my birthday that year. I overheard him talking about a diamond, and I shared this with my friends. It made me nervous but happy too. After five years, I had gotten used to him, to our relationship, to our ups and downs. I didn't want to have to start all over with someone else. I thought that would be it.

Then came a new wave of drama.

He started acting weird with me, picking more fights than usual, trying to exercise more of his machista control over my life and career, but he wasn't getting anywhere. I was raised by a strong, liberal, independent woman, and I wasn't about to blindly follow his lead. If I have questions, I will ask them. If there's an issue, I will bring it up. And if I have a dream, I will follow it.

A few weeks before my birthday, once we had already moved into the Toluca Lake house and I had begun to set it up, decorate it, furnish it, hoping to make it feel like a home, I had to travel to Miami to record a two-song Selena tribute for that year's Premios Juventud. I was over the moon with excitement. To be called to participate in a tribute to someone I looked up to and admired so much while growing up was an amazing blessing, and I was determined to work hard to give my best performance yet. Meanwhile, J Balvin happened to be in Miami at the same time. Cue the drama.

In February 2016, a photo of J Balvin and me had gone viral and stirred up rumors that we had a thing going on—let me set the record straight right now: not true. The photographer captured a candid moment, where J Balvin and I were crossing paths at an awards show. He has his hand on his heart and was simply saying hi to me as I turned and greeted him with a smile. We were about two feet apart. That was it. The media blew it out of proportion and started speculating that we might be dating. They didn't really know much about my relationship with Angel because I kept it under wraps to protect our privacy. They had a field day, and Angel, with his jealous streak at full blast, began to wonder if the rumors were true. So when he heard that J Balvin was in Miami that June while I was there, he totally lost it.

At one point, even his aunt texted me: "You need to get ahold of Angel." I thought it was because she knew we were arguing non-stop during those weeks. But no, she told me he was convinced that I had cheated on him with J Balvin. Oh my god, what did I need to do for him to trust me? This was insane. I never cheated on him, my mind wasn't even there. I was always faithful to him, yet no amount of texts or phone calls could persuade him otherwise.

The night of the Selena tribute video shoot, as I pulled on my black mariachi jumpsuit and slid my arms into the matching bolero with gold details, I let out a deep sigh. I was about to take the stage and sing Selena's classics, "Si una vez" and "Bidi Bidi Bom Bom," but instead of feeling overwhelmed with excitement, I was overcome by sadness. Even though I knew it was just Angel's own insecurities coming into play, his lack of trust was wearing me down. The jealous streak had turned into a permanent fixture in our relationship, and I couldn't handle it anymore. I was so tired of being accused of shit I didn't do. I was reaching my breaking point and, deep down, I knew it, but in that moment the show had to go on. I adjusted my black wig, puckered up for an extra coat of red lipstick, and like so many other times before, I pushed aside the heaviness and focused on taking the stage and, for one brief moment, embodying one of my idols.

After that show, I made a pit stop in Las Vegas for another event, and then I finally returned to our new home in Toluca Lake.

"I just can't do this anymore. I'm tired of it," I said to Angel that night in our bedroom.

He was convinced that I had gone to dinner with J Balvin. He was believing everything the media was publishing, and none of it was real. It was absolutely insane.

"This is no way for either of us to live," I continued. "I can't take that you think I'm doing things I'm not. I'm working and all you do is stress me out."

We didn't end things that night, but it was only a matter of time before the shit hit the fan for good.

As if all of this wasn't enough, my dad, who was in prison serving a thirty-year sentence for sexually abusing my tía Rosie and me, had suddenly resurfaced after ten years of silence. A cousin from that side of the family texted Jacqie: "Just wanted to give you a message from your dad. He loves you. He wants to know how you're doing. And he's very happy that you had your third baby." She also let her know that he wanted to see her. It had been twenty years since Jacqie had seen our dad. She wasn't sure what to expect but began to contemplate the idea of going to visit him. Before making a decision, she decided to approach Rosie and me separately to make sure we were okay with it.

"We promised once that if we ever got the chance to go see Dad, we'd do it together," she said to me one day, just after we'd inaugurated a women's shelter in our mom's name. "But he's been trying to contact me for a very long time, and I've been ignoring him because in the letters he mentions me and Mikey. And I asked about you and he hasn't but—"

"I wonder if that would hurt his case if I go," I interrupted, trying to give this extremely painful conversation a pragmatic twist.

"There's just a lot of emotions that I'm feeling," explained Jacqie. "I don't want to see him unless he does say sorry. I need him to say sorry because I need him to recognize that his choices did mess everything up."

"I just want you to know, if you want to go see him and he wants to have a relationship with you, I'm going to be okay with it," I said with tears in my eyes. "I don't think you should live with that what-if, especially if he's looking for you."

"I just need that closure," she replied. "Whether it's going to be that we're going to keep a relationship or whether it's just the closure of 'I got to meet you' and I'm fine with or without him. And if he does say sorry, then I do want that relationship. But if he doesn't, I don't."

I'm not going to lie, that was really tough for me. Just talking about him stirred up so many memories. I can recall things that no little girl should ever know. My dad molested me for four years, and when it finally came out, he called me a liar. He never admitted to it or apologized for doing that to me. All he did was say that my mom had put this in my head, that she was the monster of the story. I wish that were true. I wish I didn't remember what he did to me, but I do.

"Is it really okay?" she asked.

"Yeah, I'm fine with it, sister, of course," I said.

I tried to separate my experience and my feelings from what my sister needed. I didn't want her to live with any type of regret. If she felt she needed to see this through, then I would support her decision, even though I had my doubts. I didn't want my dad to get the wrong idea. Jacqie's visit didn't mean that all was forgotten. Nothing could really change or move forward without a sincere apology and admittance to what he had done.

Once she had my go-ahead, as well as Rosie's, she filled out the forms and drove to the prison with her husband. It was the day before my birthday. We often wondered if our dad remembered our birthdays. On her way back home after seeing him, she called me and told me that he did remember, every year. I went silent. Tears were rushing down my cheeks. So many clashing emotions. As I cried, Jacqie said he did express that he was sorry, but it was a blanket apology, focusing on his absence from our lives and not on what he had done to Rosie and me. My sister felt that it was a first step in the right direction. I wasn't as convinced, but I let her follow her own path.

And so came my thirty-first birthday on June 26, 2016.

The past few weeks had been so intense. With my relationship on the rocks and my dad coming back into the picture, my heart was so heavy. I was also still lugging around the grief and pain of the past four years. But I got out of bed, dressed up, and headed to church for the christening of my nephew, Jordan.

I was actually supposed to get together with Angel that day in Malibu. I assumed he was going to propose, but I couldn't bring myself to meet him. I couldn't be there; I couldn't go through with it. I had been asking God to give me signs: *What do I do? What's my next step in my relationship with Angel?* I was so torn, heartbroken, and confused that, as the pastor spoke, my eyes welled up with tears. My family could see I was hurting, so they took my arm and led me up front to the pastor. As he began to pray for me, he put his hand on my forehead, and I started to cry unconsolably. Then I felt something inside me say, "Let go," and I fell back into the arms of the congregation, and then to the floor. As I looked up toward the church's ceiling, I began to bawl even harder. My grandma quickly kneeled beside me and took me in her arms. When I slowly stood up, I felt lighter, more at peace, but I also had a rush of new emotions.

All I really wanted right then and there was my mom. I wasn't sure if I was making the right decision, and I knew that if she'd been there, she would've known what to say. Hell, I probably wouldn't have even been in that situation because she would've likely grabbed me awhile back and pulled me out of that relationship when it started to really go downhill a year earlier. She'd already forewarned me back in 2012, when I first started dating Angel: "I don't understand, you can be with any guy you want. I molded you into this hardworking young lady who knows what she wants—I don't get why you choose to stay with this man who has two baby mamas in tow, plus five kids."

"You know what, Momma, you have five kids too," I snapped back.

"Well, if that's what you want, I give you three months. You'll be over it."

I can see her point now. She noticed things I couldn't see at the time. If she had lived, I honestly don't think she would've allowed me to get so far into this relationship. As soon as she saw me upset over one of our many breakups, I'm sure she would've said, "You deserve better anyway. Don't worry, I'll find you a boyfriend." She was obsessed with hooking me up with a doctor or boxer. "Don't ever be with a guy who's in the same industry as you," she said to me more than once, "because you're going to regret it." I wish I would've paid more attention to this pearl of wisdom. I could've used it down the line too.

I still miss her advice and how I knew that, no matter what, at the end of the day, she'd protect me and save me from anything. But now it was up to me.

I had been fighting for my relationship for so long, and had so many second thoughts because I loved Angel. I also felt that if I gave up on the relationship and walked away, it meant I was failing. Yet I was exhausted from trying so hard, from carrying the weight of our issues on my shoulders. Angel was a provider by nature, he supported me in many ways, and I learned and grew so much with him, but he didn't know how to take care of my heart. I wanted to be valued for the woman I was, I didn't want someone questioning my every move—that wasn't fair. It was time to make the wise decision and take care of myself.

During the next few days, we talked, we fought, and I came to terms with the fact that we were no longer on the same path. He was set on having a wife and more kids and my heart was set on my career. Then came the final blow.

It was July 1, the night before what would've been my momma's forty-seventh birthday. Jenicka had come over to our house with her dog to visit Johnny and me, and as we settled in and started to chat, Angel said in passing, "Oh, aquí está todo tu circo."

What?!? How dare he call my kids a circus!

This was supposed to be my home as much as it was his, and my family should always be welcome no matter where I live. The comment threw me over the edge. I had reached my limit. Enough was enough. I looked at the kids and said, "We're leaving." I booked a hotel room; packed Jenicka, her dog, and Johnny into my car; and took off. I couldn't take it any longer.

The next morning, Johnny got ready and went to the venue where we were holding *La Noche de la Gran Señora*, a concert celebrating our mom's birthday, because he was scheduled to sing that evening and was over the moon with excitement. My family had been planning this event for months. We'd decided to make this one more intimate than the last two. It was an emotional day for all of us, so we always put our hearts into it.

After I peeled myself from the hotel bed and slowly got dressed, I drove back to the house to pick up my outfit for that evening. I parked in the driveway and walked up to the front door, only to realize Angel had locked me out. I rang the doorbell repeatedly, then called him on the phone several times. Nothing. He knew I had that event, he knew it was important to me, and he knew I needed to get my outfit, which was inside along with all of our stuff. I walked back to my car a crying mess, not knowing what to do. Devastated, I called my makeup artist, and she said, "We can get you ready at my house." As I drove over, she rushed to a department store and got me an outfit and shoes and saved my ass.

After she was done working her magic, I got back in my car and drove to the event, my mind racing a mile a minute. How could he lock me out knowing I had Mikey and Johnny to look after? I had trusted him with my siblings, who were my everything. I had dragged them into this hot, unstable mess and now we suddenly had nowhere to go. I felt I had let them down, but I promised to make it up to them.

When I arrived at the venue, I took several deep breaths and did my best to brush it all aside. Though my heart was in pieces, I forced a happy face for the media and for my family. I wanted to enjoy the night. I wanted to be there for Johnny and his debut on stage. And I wanted to celebrate my momma.

Once the event was over, Johnny and I hopped into my car and drove back to the hotel. We spent the next two weeks sleeping in that box with a double bed on Highland, while I went on the hunt for a place to rent. I finally landed on a house in Van Nuys. It was way beyond my budget, and I had to furnish it from scratch, but it was the only decent one available, so I took it.

There I was, yet again, with nothing to my name, with all my stuff held hostage by Angel. But this time I was armed with experience, and I knew that I would get us through this. I would make this work no matter what.

Right around the time Johnny and I were about to move to our new house, after a weekend of arguing over text with Angel, I finally arranged to stop by and pick up our stuff. One of his assistants opened the door, and I walked in and went straight to packing. Angel had said I should take everything, furniture included, because he didn't want any of it. So I chose some pieces for my new rental and gave away the rest. I honestly didn't want any of it either. That place had never felt like home.

I spent the rest of that month on the comfy recliner couches I had purchased, watching movies, eating chocolate, and nursing my feelings. I cried so much I thought the salt from my tears would crack my skin. There was a huge void in my heart. I'd fall asleep at night with my fingers intertwined because Angel and I used to hold hands when we went to sleep. I knew he wasn't good for me, but I missed him.

Sometimes we're forced to make painful decisions. They help us grow and become more aware of our surroundings and of the things that need to change within us.

6

A GUIDING LIGHT

I discovered God when I was ten years old. My abuelita would take me to church, and I loved it. I'm talking church on Wednesday, Friday, and Sunday—I was all in. My momma was a Christian, as is my family, and that's how they raised me, and from ten to twelve years old, the Bible became my guiding compass. But then I hit a snag.

As I entered that preteen stage, when you start to perk up your ears and actually pay attention to what's going on around you, I discovered that there were a thread of affairs happening among the churchgoers. *Thou shalt not commit adultery* quickly went out the window. Then it was revealed that one of the pastors at our church, our shepherd and guide, wasn't all that honest either. His integrity came into question when news spread that he was inappropriately touching the women in our congregation. This was around the same time I finally found the courage to speak up about the abuse I had suffered at the hands of my father. The disappointment was deep, two-fold. I really loved my pastor and that environment, but how could I continue believing in a congregation that didn't even respect the basic laws of Christianity? What felt like a safe place was now one I didn't feel like visiting anymore. So I began to step back and distance myself from that church, but not from God.

As the years passed, I continued to pray to God; my relationship with him never let up. With him in my heart, I carried on in my quest to find a religious space that spoke to me. But it wasn't easy. I never felt quite at home in the structured environment of a church. The sermons were laced with too much fear. They literally aimed to put the fear of God in the congregation and the churchgoers, then took it upon themselves to spread this fear.

I clearly remember this one time at my uncle Pete's church, when, as I walked down the aisle to take my seat, some lady blurted out, "I'm sorry, but you shouldn't be wearing those tights to church." Momma had gone ahead of me, unaware of this comment, and I had Johnny by my side, who was about seven years old at the time. I chose to mind my own business, but she pressed on, "Because they're see-through, and that's too tempting for the men." I was so stunned that I didn't know what to say. Wait, so I had to avoid wearing tight pants or leggings so that I didn't entice men, meanwhile— at least at my first church—everyone was screwing everyone else? WTF?

How can what I wear make men sin? That shouldn't be on me. It shouldn't be on anyone. No, if I wear a body-hugging outfit I'm not asking for it, and I'm not out to tempt men to stray from their moral compass. I'm just embracing my body and celebrating me. I'm not going to change who I am to make men more comfortable. They should be so stuck on God that they're too busy to look at my ass. I've come to realize this now, but back then I didn't know how to react, so once I caught up with my mom, I told her what the woman said. She stormed right over to her and set her straight. And that moment has stayed with me.

I don't want to be afraid of God. I don't think my relationship with him should be based on fear. It should be founded on respect. The respect for a higher power. And it should be a choice. I choose to be a good person and do what's right, not because I'm afraid that if I don't I'll go straight to hell, but because it's the right thing to do. I don't want to be threatened with a journey to the fires below in order to keep me in line. I don't like that. I witnessed it firsthand and came to the conclusion that I personally don't believe in that type of religion.

The sum of all of these experiences led me down my own spiritual path. Along the way I discovered Buddhism, meditation, the power of lighting candles and burning sage—the first time I did this, Momma asked, "Are you into brujería now?" As I explored these different beliefs, I remember that she was puzzled. "What is going on with you?" she'd say. "Did you smoke a joint?" But she didn't make me stop. She allowed me to continue my quest and made me feel comfortable enough to share with her whatever I was learning at the time. Like when I invited her to sit in the corner of my room I had named "Serenity," which was basically a spiritual nook that I created for mindful practices, and she quietly watched as I closed my eyes and showed her how I went about connecting with my inner self.

"How often will you be doing this praying thing?" she asked.

"I have to do it every morning." I aimed to do it daily because it put me in the best frame of mind.

"And are you going to be okay now? Because I've noticed you're a different Chiquis, and I'm like, *What is wrong with my baby?*" she said to me with tears flooding her big brown eyes. "When I wake up, the first thing I think about is you guys. If you were in my shoes, you would know what it is to be mom to all of you and just how bad I worry."

"Don't worry. I don't mean to make you worry, I'm sorry," I said, also getting emotional.

"I do worry, baby. I'm not saying you *make* me worry, it's just part of the whole journey. You were born, and all of you guys are here, and you're mine. It's part of the journey of being a mother," she said, as the tears escaped her eyes. "I can't help but worry sometimes, I mean, what's going through your mind, where are you confused, what can I help you in, what can you trust me with, what do you not want to tell Mommy . . . I mean, you'd have to be a mom one day to understand where I'm coming from. Being your mother is my favorite career. I need you to know that I'm so proud of you."

Her genuine expression of concern and care honestly made me feel so loved in that moment; it was like she was seeing me not as her partner in crime, but as her kid, and it filled my soul with warmth.

Even though my mom never understood it, she accepted that I was different and even held me accountable: "I'm gonna see if you do your little prayer thing every morning." She respected my spiritual journey even though it wasn't going down the traditional church route, and I will be forever grateful to her for allowing me to be me.

When I was a teenager, my mom revealed that my name, Janney, which is also her middle name, means "precious gift from God." I want to continuously honor my name by paying it forward. So, I continued to attend different churches. My heart remained open, and when a pastor preached something that rang true to me, I received it with joy—like the time I let go and fell back at my nephew's christening. But now, my focus was on my relationship with God, not the church.

My God is not tied to one religion, he *is* the higher power. This realization has allowed me to take the passages from the Bible that I love, as well as Buddha's teachings, wherever I go, and this makes me feel complete.

Meanwhile, my grandma still doesn't quite understand my beliefs. She hates that I have a huge Buddha fountain outside my house. She thinks it's a demon. I've tried to explain to her that it's just a symbol of peace and Zen, but she's not having it. Even yoga makes her cringe; she thinks it will send me to another dimension, where I'll run into the devil. "Grandma, no," I say, but I've stopped trying to reason with her on this point. She's set in her ways, and I get it. I respect her beliefs and know I will never change them, nor do I wish to. Each of us has the freedom to choose our faith.

Nowadays, I don't consider myself a Christian, but I do have a pastor, actually two pastors. I call them Mom and Dad because I consider them my spiritual parents. I met them through my sister Jacqie in 2018, at my goddaughter Jaylah's birthday party. Jacqie is very Christian, and she had connected with them through their shared religious network. I got to talking to them that day and liked what they had to say; I also enjoyed their energy. Every time I ran into them after that, we'd end up having amazing and inspiring conversations, and eventually they became my mentors.

I feel like I can be completely honest and open with them; I don't have to hide any part of me. I can cuss in front of them and they won't flinch. There's no judgment, and they never make me feel bad about who I am. They don't tell me not to drink—we even share a glass of wine once in a while; they don't make me feel the way I dance is too provocative; they don't tell me not to enjoy sex. God isn't going to love me less because I got drunk on tequila one night, and they don't make me feel that way either. It is so refreshing. I can be me.

Pastor Mom and Dad check in on me, and I know I can reach out to them whenever I need some guidance. Yes, they have a Christian church, but my pastor doesn't yell at his churchgoers or force religion down their throats. It's a conversation, and I appreciate that.

They let me and other people congregating there simply be—it's a refuge. I can go to that church with holes in my pants and no one will say anything to me. I can also not go to church and no one will make me feel guilty for that either. It's very nontraditional, which is why I feel safe with them. That doesn't mean they won't point out when I'm wrong. And I appreciate that because I want them to call me out; I want to learn from my mistakes and correct my errors. That's the only way we can evolve and grow.

Nevertheless, I still allow teachings from different religions to feed my spirituality. Through this process, I have learned to be open, to be patient, and to forgive. I forgive others and I forgive myself because God forgives us all. Furthermore, each and every one of the lessons I have come across on my spiritual journey have led me to create my own religion: Love.

With love as my compass, I want to bring hope to the world. I want to be a positive force on this planet and in the lives of those who surround me. God doesn't give us anything we can't handle. No matter how much drama, loss, or heartache I may be experiencing, I always try to anchor myself in one thought: *My blessings are so much bigger than my problems, because God is good.*

Love is the moving force of the universe.
Love is what I practice every day.
Love is my guiding light.
I want to be love.

7

KINDRED SPIRITS

When my relationship with Angel ended, I set out on a quest to find balance. Tensions were running high with my siblings as we faced yet another move in less than a month. The Van Nuys house I rented for Johnny and me to live in was a 2,500-square-foot, two-story property with four bedrooms and three bathrooms, beyond my initial budget, but I was desperate to find a place for us to land on our feet. It was located on a quiet street with a welcoming front yard, garage, and spacious backyard. My room had a master bath and two walk-in closets. I was planning on making another room a closet and glam room. That left Johnny's bedroom and an extra one for guests. On such short notice, I was pretty satisfied with this outcome.

Move-in day came and all my siblings pitched in, carrying boxes from the moving trucks into the house, except for Mikey. He was still at Angel's house with his daughter, Luna. He thought he would be moving to his new place with Jenicka (yes, they'd decided to be roommates), so he didn't pack his stuff into my trucks. But the clock was ticking and with no new apartment in sight, I needed him to get out of there asap. The last thing I wanted to do in that moment, surrounded by scattered furniture and sealed boxes that needed to be situated and unpacked, was to return to that place to pick up after my brother and haul his belongings and his ass over to our new rental, but I also didn't want Angel to get home and find Mikey still there, especially after he called my family a circus. Why didn't my Mikey have his shit together? I was pissed. Now, I not only had more to do, I ran the risk of running into Angel.

Standing between the open kitchen and the living room, I stared out a window and took a long, deep breath to calm myself down. The stress was eating at my nerves.

"You're already doing enough having to worry about this move and this house," Jenicka said, as she stood by my side glancing over at me with concern, "and having to also worry about us is not fair."

"He needs to step up and be responsible," said Jacqie, sitting on the couch in what was my new living room.

"I'm physically and emotionally tired and I have to unpack; it's just a lot," I said, grasping the back of the sofa, overwhelmed and slightly defeated.

But I had no choice. I needed to get this all over with so I could move on to the next chapter in my life. I walked to my car and drove to Toluca Lake to get Mikey, and when I arrived, of course I ran into Angel, which was exactly what I had been hoping to avoid because I was still feeling so raw and vulnerable.

I walked into the house and he gave me the cold shoulder, which is what he usually did when we were fighting. He never made the first move to reconcile because he was too proud. It was actually something we'd discussed many times. "You need to change that," I'd say to him, "because your pride is going to kill you." But you can't teach an old dog new tricks. Seeing him was gut-wrenching. I was still trying to digest it all. When I closed that front door for one last time and followed Mikey to my car, it hit me, *Oh shit, this is for real*. After so many years, it was over.

As we drove back to what was now my home, I was seething, doing my best to control the need to just scream and let out all the bottled-up emotions. When we arrived, I walked inside and got back to work, channeling everything into unpacking as much as possible. Later that evening, as Jacqie, her husband, Mike, and their newborn, Jordan; Jenicka; Mikey; and I sat on the two sofas in the living room, chilling after what had felt like an endless day, the conversation turned to Mikey. It started out calm enough.

Jenicka expressed that she was frustrated because she was the one who had taken on the house-hunting responsibilities while Mikey just sat back and was like, "Whatever will be, will be." She wanted him to be more hands-on. I was still upset about having to move him from my ex's house in the middle of my own big move. And Jacqie shared that she felt Mikey needed to own up to his responsibilities. We were going around in circles, walking on egg-shells, trying to carefully choose the right words to express to Mikey that we needed him to step up his game, knowing all too well that talking to him about stuff like this usually led to a full-blown war.

"You're going to turn twenty-five. Dude, you have a daughter," I said, chiming into a conversation I wish could've happened on any other day.

"It's frustrating because I don't want to be a burden on Jacqie and Mike, dude. They need their space, and I get it," said Jenicka. She was living in Jacqie and Mike's garage at the time.

"Are you frustrated with me too?" said Mikey to Jacqie as things began to escalate.

"Have you called about apartments?" she replied. "The other day you were saying you needed to find an apartment now, but what have you done?"

"What do you mean, what have I done?" asked Mikey defensively. "If you're all going to get so frustrated, I can do it by myself," he said, now clearly agitated.

"You don't have to get so upset," I said, trying to calm him down because I knew this was heading nowhere good.

"Well, it's not my fault," replied Mikey.

"We're not saying it's your fault," I said.

"That's kind of what it sounds like, and no one has any reason to be frustrated because I don't know what I did today."

Oh no you didn't. That was just the last straw for me.

"Mikey, it is not my responsibility. You are a twenty-four-year-old man. It's not my responsibility to be moving your shit out."

"You didn't have to move any of my shit!" he exclaimed.

"You know what, whatever," I said, giving up, knowing we were getting nowhere. "One day you're going to appreciate everything—"

"I do appreciate you!" he said, his voice a few notches louder.

"Listen, I'm not yelling at you," I replied calmly, trying to de-escalate the situation as he continued rumbling on. "Do not yell at me."

"I'm not yelling!"

"Yes you are. It's so hard to talk to you because everything offends you. Let's be motherfuckin' real," I said, clapping my hands to release my own tension and wake everyone the fuck up. "Have you been motherfuckin' responsible? You're very irresponsible, Mikey. I have a lot going on, but you know what, let me tell you how many apartments I called for both of you guys. But we can't say anything to you because you always get mad."

"I'm not upset about this," he answered, holding his forehead in visible frustration.

"You always get pissed," I continued, totally heated at this point. "You guys, be honest," I said to my sisters, when I realized that suddenly I was the only one having this argument with my brother. They just stared back at me blankly. Why was I having this fight alone? Why didn't they step up too? They'd been complaining all day about him. I was reaching my limit with all of my siblings at this point. I was the one who needed support that day. I couldn't continue carrying all of them on my shoulders when I was drowning in my own shitstorm.

"Whatever, fucking who cares. We're done. Are we done?" I asked my sisters, who remained dead silent.

"Yeah man," said Mikey, standing up from the sofa and punching a bag on the floor as he stormed over to the stairs.

"Don't be throwing shit in my house, motherfucker!" I yelled at him.

"Stop, guys, stop," said Jacqie, getting up from the sofa and finally chiming in again.

"Get the fuck out of here," I said to Mikey. "You're such a fucking idiot."

"No, Chiquis, don't," said Jacqie.

I was done, with all of them. I thought we were going to sit down and have a family discussion about what was frustrating all of us when I suddenly found myself fighting their battle alone.

"Both of you guys had all of this shit to say, and you didn't say anything!" I yelled to my sisters.

"You were saying it for us!" yelled Jenicka.

"Because I always have to do it!" I yelled back, reaching peak frustration now.

The screaming match continued until Jenicka burst into tears.

"It's cool. I'll handle my own shit," said Mikey, and he walked up the stairs to his room.

Looking back, I get it. Emotions were running high for all of us. We had just left our mom's house for good. We were all trying to find our way without her guidance, and it was an all-around fucked-up situation, but we had to figure out a way to navigate it. Mikey still had to work on not blowing up anytime we tried to tell him something that was bothering us. He'd become incredibly defensive and sometimes disrespectful, and that just fired me up, which was a recipe for disaster. Thankfully he's much better now, but that fight was a real slap-in-the-face wake-up call for me.

I had been bending over backward for everyone but myself since I was a teenager. And there I was again, nursing a broken heart, running around trying to find a new home at the drop of a dime, working tirelessly to fend for myself and my siblings, and still chasing after them as the overprotective eldest sister, and it was too much. My momma was no longer with us, and my siblings were grown-ass adults. It was time for them to figure it out for themselves. As painful as it was when my mom left me with nothing, I'm actually stronger because of it, and I thank her for that. Now it was time for my siblings to learn that same lesson. Something had shifted within me. I had to draw a line, take a step back, and let all of them find their own damn wings rather than carrying them on my back while I hopelessly tried to fly for all of us. I was the one hurting now; I was the one who needed support.

A few days after that big blowup with Mikey, I was outside Jacqie's garage helping her, Jenicka, and Johnny sort through clothes for a yard sale we were having that weekend, when Johnny brought up the fact that I was working nonstop that summer and, just like Momma, I was never around. This was it, my shot to honestly express what was going through my mind.

"I feel like for a long time, I was all about you guys. And it's not that I don't want to be. I guess I just want to feel appreciated by all of you," I said.

I knew the kids missed me, especially Johnny, because I'd been working in Mexico and hadn't been around much, but it was tough to hear Johnny complain about not having time with me when I was busting my ovarios trying to make a life for us. I already had to live with the guilt of not being around, so much so that I made sure someone was always there to cover his needs, which, at the end of the day, wasn't allowing him to grow up either.

"Omi helps her a lot, Johnny," chimed in Jenicka. "You take her and a lot of people like her for granted." It's true. My assistant, Omi, always goes above and beyond for me.

"I knooow," said Johnny.

"So maybe be tough love and have Johnny do everything by himself, so that he can learn to appreciate it—that's the only way you learn," said Jacqie to me. "Are you going to help Chiquis do what she needs to do?" she asked Johnny.

"You barely take out the trash," added Jenicka.

At his age, I was taking care of Jacqie and Mikey, making sure they did their homework and were fed, ironing their school clothes, and cleaning the house. And you best believe there was no room for complaining with Momma. I didn't expect Johnny to do it all, but I needed to stop taking care of everything for him so he could learn to look after himself.

"I'm honestly at a point in my life where I'm done giving too much when it's not appreciated. This needs to be fair, that's it. So if you want Omi to go home," I said, turning to Johnny, "then I need you to help me around the house. That means that if you need to grab a vacuum, do it, because she goes above and beyond and helps me with those things. I'm not going to pay someone to come and clean the house and cook for you. I'm sorry, you need to make yourself an egg."

"Sister, I don't know how to cook!" he whined.

"You have to learn. I learned when I was ten years old."

"Who's going to teach me?" he asked, visibly upset now.

"Youuu!" I replied, absolutely exasperated. "You think Momma taught me how to make an egg? She didn't. You know what Momma would tell me all the time? 'Figure it out.' I'll never forget that. When I asked her, 'How do I deposit a check?' her answer was, 'I don't know. Figure it out,' and she'd wave me off—a gesture I have etched in my mind forever. And guess what? I figured it out. I'm sorry, I'm not trying to be tough. I have no other choice, Johnny."

Johnny was still ten years away from accessing his share of our mom's inheritance. Anything could happen in those ten years. With tears streaking my face, I continued.

"With you, papi, I know that I've babied you a lot, and it makes me mad at Angel because he was supposed to help me with you. I don't know what to do."

I was always on him about taking out the trash, cleaning his room, and cooking for himself, but when he didn't do it, I took care of it myself.

"You have to understand, brother," added Jacqie, "you think it sucks to be the little one, but it sucks to be the older one too."

"No one taught me any of this!" yelled Johnny between sobs.

"Johnny, I try to teach you," I said.

"I know, sister, but Mom left and she didn't teach me any of this."

"I understand that. I'm going to teach you. I'm going to do my best to teach you," I said.

"You have to want to learn," added Jacqie wisely.

"I do, sister! This is just how I grew up."

In that moment, all I really wanted to do was run over to him, hug and protect him, and tell him everything was going to be all right, but that was exactly what I couldn't do anymore. That's not life. I always plan to be there for him, but what if one day I'm not? It was time for him to learn how to figure it out.

I was starting to question all of my actions. Even though my brothers and sisters sometimes upset me and hurt my feelings, I always went above and beyond when they needed me, especially financially. But then I thought, *Am I spoiling them too much? Am I doing them more harm than good?* They knew they could always fall back on me, but it was a lot for me to handle, especially at a time when I needed to fall back on someone myself.

I suddenly understood where my momma's tough love came from. She did it to help us get on with our lives, but now I was experiencing how heartbreaking doing right by your kids can be. The tears, the rebelliousness, the pain. I could hear her voice loud and clear, "You'd have to be a mom one day to understand where I'm coming from." Now I got it, Momma.

Jenicka was eighteen and exploring her independence, and now it was time for Johnny to step up and pull his weight at home too. I didn't have it in me to be as tough as our mom, but I still laid it all out for him, telling him that I was willing to guide him so that he could learn to take care of himself while I was on the road. I had to start to prepare Johnny for the realities of life. And that included a hardworking sister-mom who couldn't be around 24-7. I had to continue living, expanding my career, and seeking that hard-to-come-by balance. I'm still a work in progress in that area; it's not easy, but I'm getting there.

Neither Johnny nor I were ever really too crazy about the Van Nuys house. I was working so much it took me forever to unpack all of the boxes, so it didn't feel like a home for a long time. Everything was happening so fast I barely had a chance to digest that this wasn't my mom's house, it wasn't my boyfriend's house, it was my own space, and that was an important moment.

As we slowly eased into our new routine, I spent the rest of the summer mostly in Mexico as a judge on a TV competition show.

Mikey and I reconciled soon after our fight. And, although my heart still hurt from my breakup, with every passing day I was starting to feel a little bit better and stronger. There was a sense of relief as I rediscovered my old self. I felt lighter.

My ex was now trying to get back together with me. It was tough because I still loved him. We'd been together for so long. He'd been in the trenches with me. But I wasn't in love with him anymore. And I was determined not to go back. So I poured my heart into my work and into the creation of my second album. Now that I had no one trying to keep me at home or feed me guilt trips for traveling to expand my singing career, I was free to do whatever I wanted, and I wanted more. I was ready to take the next step and pursue a distribution deal to back my second project.

As I planned these next moves, a new guy unexpectedly appeared on the horizon. The first time I remember meeting him was on July 2, 2016. Yes, the day after I broke up with Angel, the night of my momma's birthday tribute. I was sitting with my whole family in a small VIP section, flush right to the club's stage, feeling uneasy in a jumpsuit outfit my makeup artist had so kindly pulled together amid my desperation when I found myself locked out of my own home. I didn't feel as cute and confident as usual and my heart was in pieces. Once again, I smiled to mask the pain, hoping to get through this event as quickly as possible. But my life was about to take a radical and unexpected turn, and I knew it.

"You know that singer wants to fuck you, right?" whispered Johnny in my ear, jolting me back to reality. I'll never forget that.

"What?!" I exclaimed.

And he repeated it super matter-of-factly, "Yeah, he wants to fuck you."

"Stop, no he doesn't. Stop it," I said, laughing off my little brother's observation.

"Yes he does," he insisted.

Curious, I quickly turned back to the stage, leaning forward to catch a glimpse of the performance, and that's when I noticed he was totally checking me out. I just smiled, and when he smiled back, I thought, *Oh shit, maybe he does.*

Lorenzo Mendez was the vocalist for La Original Banda El Limón, a band I had listened to for years, a band my momma loved. I had actually heard of him in passing through Omi, who said he was a really cute guy I had to check out and follow on Snapchat. "He's the boy version of you!" she had exclaimed. "You're both so funny."

Okay, he's pretty cute, I thought, as I leaned back in my seat. No one had looked at me like that for a while because I had been in a relationship for close to five years, so it did make me feel a few fluttery butterflies in my stomach. But I was so heartbroken I wasn't ready to let my mind go there.

When the band wrapped their set and started climbing down the stairs, I glanced up and our eyes met. Then, with his signature wide and charming smile, he approached me and casually said, "Hey, can we take a picture?"

"Yeah, okay," I answered. I stood up and leaned over the staircase railing. He put his arm around me, and we posed, cheek to cheek, and smiled for the camera. Then I said bye and sat back down, reveling in how good he smelled.

That's how I first crossed paths with Lorenzo. He posted the photo on Instagram later that night and we started following each other there and on Snapchat, but I didn't hear from him again until August—about a month after our meet-cute.

It all began with him commenting on my posts and sending me DMs. He'd say things like "You look pretty, babe," which actually made me cringe a little. *I'm not your babe,* I thought. I've always found it weird when anyone calls me "babe." So much so that I even brought it up with him. But then, as we continued to chat, one day he said, "Hey, I don't know if you pray, but if you do, try praying at night, on your knees, by the side of your bed. You're going to feel the difference." That really caught my attention. *Wow, he's spiritually connected.*

Then we exchanged numbers, and within a few days, we were on the phone having our first conversation—it lasted four hours. While Angel was more on the reserved side, this guy was a burst of fresh air. We went from discussing our favorite rappers to realizing we both loved the same food and couldn't hear a good song without getting down on the dance floor. He made me crack up laughing. Then we shared how tired we felt after finishing a performance. I loved that he understood the music industry from my same perspective, as a banda singer no less.

Up until then, I never thought I would date someone in my industry—my mom had warned me about this and my abuelita always said "Don't ever be with a musician"—but I felt Lorenzo was different. He could've been anywhere else boning girls, but he was on the phone with me instead. As if all that wasn't enough, he then opened up a little about his first marriage and confessed he wasn't sure he wanted to get married again or have more kids.

"Oh my god, I don't know if I want to get married or have kids either," I replied, amazed at all we had in common. Omi was right, he really was the male version of me!

"Yeah, I'm good with my daughter. I just want to be with someone, and sometimes marriage ruins things."

Coming from my relationship with Angel and his need for a housewife, I thought, *This guy is perfect for me.*

As the chats and phone calls continued, even though I usually preferred older guys, I couldn't help myself, I immediately started to form a bond with him.

Two weeks after our first conversation in August, he flew to Los Angeles from Texas and took me out on our first date to a Thai restaurant (one of our favorites). He walked in wearing a checkered shirt and a hat on backward and had this swag about him that I instantly felt drawn to. I had on a flannel shirt and some tight green pants, and he took one look at me and said, "Damn, you're cute." We hugged, and I noticed he smelled really good again—he loved his cologne. When the waitress came to take our drink order, we both chose water.

"Oh, you don't drink soda?" I asked.

"No, I try not to," he replied.

"Oh my god, neither do I."

He opened my straw and put it in my drink. Those details really made an impression on me. When we chatted about our music again, and I expressed how I had just gotten out of a relationship with someone who didn't want me to sing anymore, he came back with a "Hell yeah, you should keep going," encouraging me to continue to pursue my dream. As the evening flew by, we cracked up like little kids the entire time.

To say we totally hit it off is an understatement. It was like I had known him for years—maybe we'd crossed paths in a past life. Was he my kindred spirit? That night, after dinner, we headed over to my friend Ellen's apartment complex, and that's where we shared our first kiss, and it just felt right.

How could someone sweep me off my feet so soon after my breakup? I know I should've given myself a little more time to heal, but I couldn't help myself. Lorenzo was there for me, making me laugh, listening to me as a friend, helping me heal my broken heart and move on. He was also the exact opposite of Angel—he was younger, he liked to travel, he loved dancing—and I was drawn to these qualities like a bee to honey.

Meanwhile, it was almost as if Angel could sense I was talking to someone new. He started to try harder to connect with me, to win me back, almost like he'd suddenly realized he didn't want to lose me after all. He'd text me, "I want to see you. I miss you." He'd send me flowers. As a man of few words, he'd call me and play meaningful songs to me. And that put me in an awkward crossroads. I was just starting to get to know Lorenzo and felt so comfortable with him, but I didn't want to hurt Angel and, although I was no longer in love with him, I still had love for him. He'd been by my side through some of the worst moments of my life. That's why I initially didn't tell him I had started seeing someone. Why put him through that pain when I didn't even know where it was going?

Then, on September 16, 2016, just a few weeks after Lorenzo and I started seeing each other, we decided to go on a Las Vegas getaway, and one night, Lorenzo pulled out a ring pop and asked me to be his girlfriend. *How cute,* I thought, and I immediately said yes to this sweet move. But I wasn't ready to make it official in the media yet. I was still dealing with my breakup and balancing the start of my singing career and my evolving relationship with my siblings. I just needed a little more time. Making public appearances with a boyfriend was new to me. I was used to keeping my relationships private. That's how Angel and I handled our four-plus years together, and it worked well for us on that end. I was hoping to continue with that vibe, but Lorenzo was different. It seemed like everywhere we went together—Vegas, a restaurant, out for a drive—the paparazzi followed, and he seemed to enjoy the attention. I actually brought it up with him a few times.

"It's funny, I used to go out everywhere with my friends and I never got caught by the paparazzi."

"Maybe it's because they don't care to see you with friends, but they do care about seeing you with a guy," he replied, matter-of-factly.

"Yeah, maybe, but we got into some pretty crazy things and they never caught us," I insisted.

He'd just brush it aside and change the subject. I would've preferred to keep it private a little while longer, but it was almost as if Lorenzo had wanted to make sure Angel knew we were now together. It felt like his ego was at play, marking his territory, telling Angel, "This is my woman now." I just decided to go with the flow because I didn't want him to think I was hiding him, but it never felt right to me. Before I knew it, we had become an item in the media.

When the news broke, Angel was really hurt and upset, and he immediately allowed his jealous mind to think I had been cheating on him with Lorenzo way before we even broke up—which was not true. He sent me a bunch of text messages, "I can't believe you're doing this." "If you didn't get back to me, now I know it's probably because you were already seeing this guy." No matter what I said, he didn't believe me. No explanation was good enough.

There was another factor at play: Angel and Lorenzo weren't friends per se, but they ran in similar music circles. To the point where, I later came to find out, we had even sat at the same dinner table once. Lorenzo had tagged along that night with his friend Abner Mares, the first boxer Angel had signed in the boxing division of Del Records. Abner was trying to get Lorenzo signed to Del Records. I honestly don't remember that night, but Lorenzo said he did because he had noticed how Angel was feeding me and how that irritated me.

Obviously, Angel also remembered him, hence the sudden suspicions that something had been going on while we had been together. He thought I knew that they had met each other and took my dating him as a low blow on my part. Ugh, it was a total shit show, and the miscommunication was killing me. I never meant to hurt Angel, but I was also tired of having to explain myself to him, over and over again, when I did nothing wrong. I only wish I had had the chance to talk to him about all of this before it hit the media, but that was beyond my control.

As the heat of the moment subsided, Angel finally calmed down and said to me, "Okay, if this is the person you want to be with, that's fine. But honestly, I think he's a liar, he's a drug addict, and he's a cheater." I chalked up his warning to jealousy and tossed the comment aside. My tío Juan had said something similar when he first heard I was dating Lorenzo. "Look, I asked around about this guy and was told he's a really cool guy, very talented, and he is, but they say he loves to party and he does coke." That shocked me, so I straight up asked Lorenzo about it one day soon after this, while I was in my closet folding my gym clothes. But he denied these allegations. He swore on his father's life it wasn't true. And I believed him. This was September. His dad died, out of the blue, in October. I'll never forget that.

With Angel's and my tío Juan's comments still nagging me, I googled "How do people act when they're high on coke" so I could recognize the signs if what they mentioned was true. Sure enough, during that first trip to Vegas, they were all there: his nose was runny, he'd sniff and touch it a lot, his eyes were red and super open, he could drink all night and party until six in the morning and no one could keep up with him (and I'm talking about a man who wasn't great with alcohol), and he was slightly more egocentric and edgier, with spurts of energy that came out of nowhere.

Red flag, red flag, red flag! Yet somehow, I managed to shrug it all off. He was charming and loving and made me laugh. He supported my music career and celebrated me showing off my curves rather than asking me to cover them up. I think I also chose to look the other way because I couldn't face being alone. It's likely what I needed the most, but I didn't have the guts to deal with that sense of emptiness. I preferred to put a Band-Aid on my heart than face that pain.

In retrospect, despite our lows and differences, Angel gave me a stability and comfort that I wouldn't feel again for a long while. The media knew we had been together all those years, but they respected him enough to leave us alone and not turn it into a spectacle. I will be forever grateful to him for his support and love during such critical moments in my life. Those years helped shape the woman I am today.

Now it was time for a new beginning with a very different man, one who would also play an important role in my life but who would eventually shatter my heart.

May our faith in the future be far greater than the false illusions of the past.

8

MY BODY IS MY TEMPLE

*T*hose first few months with Lorenzo had me walking on air. He had that butterflies-in-my-tummy effect on me every time our eyes met. And, although I was still trying to guard my heart given my recent breakup, he was winning me over with his undivided attention. It was so refreshing to be with someone who actually heard what I had to say, and who also understood my career since he was in the same industry. I liked that he was confident and adventurous. He'd take me to Six Flags on a whim, and as a natural-born planner, I loved how he just lived in the moment. I also appreciated his swag and Prince Charming game, that we shared the same type of energy, and that we could roar with laughter together.

I honestly didn't know where it was going, and I didn't want to overthink it either. I was just enjoying the ride in that sweet honeymoon phase we all experience when we're first getting to know a love interest. Plus, deep down, I wasn't ready to jump into something new so soon. I was still carrying the sadness and toxicity of my previous relationship; it was heavy on my heart. Trust issues were front and center, and that made me feel a little jaded in the love department, but I also really wanted to find *the one*. As I worked through these thoughts with my therapist, I realized that what I was really striving for was balance. I didn't want to be in a controlling relationship. As an independent woman, I didn't need to be taken care of financially, but I didn't want to have to take care of anyone either. I wanted a hardworking man who also desired to be in an equal partnership, where we could walk hand in hand in the same direction, cheering each other on as we set out to fulfill our dreams. And what I really craved was emotional support and a man of faith. Check, check, check: Lorenzo seemed to fit the bill.

All I could clearly see were the pros, the good, the positive—I couldn't deal with more hurt, more drama. I was in healing mode, and although I should've given myself the alone time to recover, I thought what better remedy to mend a broken heart than exploring a new relationship with the person I thought was the man of my dreams? My fear of commitment hadn't magically disappeared. But the heart wants what the heart wants, no matter what my gut was trying to tell me, and my love blinders were on tight.

This man was showering me with compliments, feeding my mind and spirit, and celebrating my body—he loved my curves and I was loving every ounce of the attention. Every time he saw me, he'd say, "You're so beautiful." He'd grab my face and kiss me passionately. With Lorenzo, I felt really sexy. He'd grab my ass in public and caress my body; we had no problem being affectionate in public, and I loved that. There was no shame in my cleavage or my booty. He loved when I put on a short dress, and if I showed any hesitation, he'd say, "Fuck yeah, wear it, who cares? Even if guys look at you, you're with me." I think it made him feel like a bigger, better, and cooler man. My curvaliciousness was celebrated, and for someone who grew up with body image issues, this meant the world to me.

That yearning to look like the girls in the magazines didn't really go away when I hit young adulthood. I went from trying to be like those stick-thin models, which had nothing to do with my body type, to breathing a sigh of relief when Kim Kardashian first hit the scene. She had it all: the big booty, the tiny waist, and the large tits. I loved her voluptuousness and could see myself in her body type, except for the breasts, but that could be easily fixed with a little plastic surgery. I got my first set of breast implants in 2011. My mom warned me beforehand: "Don't do it. You're going to regret it." But I had a vision and wanted to see it through. It turned out I didn't factor in my short stature. That first pair of double Ds were humungous, way too big for me. Regret set in. I didn't want to admit it at first, but Momma was right. That's why the next year, I decided to go under again and have them reduced to a large D. I stayed at that size for a few years, but as my weight went up and down and back up again with all my yo-yo dieting and emotional eating, my breasts required a lollipop reduction to give them a little extra oomph. I thought it was all good, but when I began to make more TV appearances, I noticed that the top-heavy look wasn't very flattering on me. That's why, in 2016, amid my recent breakup and my budding romance, I said, "Fuck these implants." I wanted my nice little humble titties back, so I got the implants removed, had a little lift done to my original girls, and went on my merry way.

I liked my current look, with my big hips, small waist, and smaller boobs. Did that mean I stopped thinking about breast surgery completely? No. If I've learned anything over the years it's that loving your body is a journey in and of itself. I prefer to acknowledge my thoughts rather than sweep them under the rug and pretend everything is fine. That's why I've made a point to be super open about the struggles and joys that come with embracing what God gave us, as well as the surgeries I've undergone. I've received endless flak for my weight fluctuation over the years, but, as a result, I also became somewhat of an unofficial ambassador for curves. I started to receive comments filled with gratitude on social media about my openness and honesty, but it really hit home during that same year I removed my implants, when I was invited to speak at the Ultimate Women's Expo.

I was there to promote my Be Flawless lip line, so I jumped at the shot of talking to the crowd—even though it also gave me the jitters. I didn't have a big speech prepared; I just walked on that stage and let my instincts move me through the moment. When the women in the audience started asking questions and speaking up, I realized that what I was casually sharing about my story was actually inspiring them to embrace and believe in themselves, and that almost brought me to tears. I had finally taken a step toward what I feel is my essential mission, to help and inspire and empower others, and I couldn't have been happier.

Despite the many ups and downs, everything felt like it was slowly falling into place by the end of 2016. I was with a guy I really liked (dare I say loved?), I had participated in my first public speaking engagement, Be Flawless was thriving, I was working on my second album, the healing was happening, and the changes were leading to new doors of possibilities. Until my first real health scare decided to knock on my door at the start of the new year.

It happened one night in January 2017. I was jolted awake at three in the morning by a stabbing pain in my stomach. I usually have a really high tolerance for pain and tend to tough it out until it passes, but that night it was absolutely excruciating. I honestly thought I was going to die. I stretched my arm out to my night table, grabbed my phone, and quickly dialed Omi's number. "You need to take me to the ER." Once we were on our way, I said, "I don't want to die in the car." She tightened her grip around the steering wheel and started to run red lights as she sped over to the nearest hospital. Doubled over in pain, I walked in and was examined, only to be told a while later that my extreme discomfort was due to a cyst in my left ovary. Given what I felt, I could've sworn he was going to say it had exploded inside me. "It turned over on itself, that's what caused the pain," the doctor explained. He recommended I get it removed eventually, but it didn't call for an emergency procedure, so I was sent home with some painkillers and lived to see another day.

Up until then, I had always been on the fence about having kids, thinking, *If I'm meant to become pregnant, it will happen.* The truth is that, shy of giving birth, I am already a mom in many ways. I basically raised Johnny and Jenicka, and I worry about them more like a mother than a sister. I put my life on hold to help my mom with them, and with Jacqie and Mikey too. I watched how she struggled as a single mom, and then I took the kids under my wing once she was gone. But that day at the hospital really shook me. *Maybe I should consider freezing my eggs,* I thought. I didn't know how many good eggs I had left, but I figured if I froze them, I'd have that option available to me should I ever consider taking matters into my own hands. So I started doing research to see what steps to take and if it was the right move for me.

Meanwhile, things were going strong with Lorenzo. We'd basically been navigating a long-distance relationship since he was based in Texas, so by the spring of 2017, he expressed that he was ready to make it more permanent. I freaked out for a second thinking that he was about to propose, but then breathed a quiet sigh of relief when he clarified that his idea was to move to his own apartment in LA so we could be closer to each other. Knowing that his whole life was in Texas and he was willing to uproot himself to be closer to me made me feel so special that I suddenly blurted out, "Why don't you just move in with me and Johnny?" I figured

I needed more space, Johnny needed a bigger room, and Lorenzo needed a place to live, so why not? We giggled a little nervously and agreed to go house hunting and see where that took us.

We had fun with the idea of playing house, but when it came time to choose a place, something in my gut was holding me back. A year earlier, I had moved in with Angel only to break up and move out in less than a month. What would guarantee Lorenzo and I could actually make it work? On top of this, Jacqie was in the process of separating from her husband, and Johnny had just graduated from high school at sixteen. I needed to provide him with some stability and guidance. It was a lot. I had already put him through a hellish situation with my previous attempt to cohabitate with a boyfriend, and that ended with us living in a hotel for a few weeks before moving into a new rental. I needed to be more careful this time around; I wanted to protect him. I did love Lorenzo, and I did see a future with him, but I realized I needed a little more time to figure this one out.

One day, while I was in my bedroom folding my clothes, Lorenzo walked in and asked, "What's going on?"

"Nothing, Lorenzo, why?" I said.

"Talk to me," he said.

"I'm just frustrated."

"You always do this to me. You block me out and then I can't tell you anything. You're the one that's always like, 'Let's talk, let's talk.' Well then, let's talk now, come on."

We sat on the bed and I said, "I know that I love you, but I just don't know, I don't know. This is a huge step for me."

"It's hard living out of a suitcase for work. And then I come here and live out of a suitcase as well. I'm doing all this for us," he pressed on.

"With Johnny, I have the huge responsibility of taking care of his heart. I've already put him through something so difficult with my last relationship."

Lorenzo kept grabbing his forehead, seemingly exasperated.

"And that's not your fault," I continued. "But these are real-life things that happened in my life, which play a part in this big decision."

He just stared at me with impatience written all over his face.

"I've already been through the whole moving in, moving out," I said. "Not only that, you're coming from a completely different state!"

"Yeah, don't you see that I'm trying?"

"I do see that, and I appreciate it, but at the end of the day, on me it's heavy—"

"Then don't tell me these things, don't say, 'Let's try to look for a house,' don't take me house hunting, don't get my hopes up."

He wasn't getting it.

"I'm not getting your hopes up," I replied, irritated. "It's something I want to do, but at this moment, I'm feeling a little unsure."

"That's the problem, though," he answered.

"There's a lot of things going on."

"That's the problem; it looks like you're going in the right direction and then you hit the brakes."

I just closed my eyes and took a deep breath. I didn't feel we were understanding each other at all.

"Honestly, I can't be doing this anymore," he suddenly blurted out.

"You can't be doing what?"

"It's crazy. We go up and down—just figure things out, Janney, and give me a call," he said, standing up from the bed and grabbing his stuff.

"Oh, so now you're going to walk away," I said.

"Yeah, it's just . . . I can't. I'm taking off."

"You're leaving?" I said in disbelief.

"Yeah, I'm leaving," he said, slinging his backpack over his shoulder.

"And you think that's going to make things better?" I said.

"I don't know. At least you'll get your thoughts together. I'm a phone call away."

I can't begin to tell you how many unresolved issues this brought to my heart. The most important people in my life had abandoned me in some shape or form: my dad, my mom. Losing her in the middle of such a crisis in our relationship almost broke me. And those scars made me want to push people away before they could be close enough to hurt me. That was why I ran hot and cold sometimes. I preferred to avoid any situation that could potentially turn painful—it was my defense mechanism. When Lorenzo and I finally regrouped to talk all of this out, I let my guard down a little and we made up.

Now it was time to revisit that damn cyst before it killed off more of my eggs. Questions flooded my mind, *What if I become sterile? What if I can't have children?* Up until then, procreating had been exclusively my choice. I didn't want anything to take that away, so I began to seriously consider freezing my eggs to keep my options open. Since, down the line, this decision could potentially involve my boyfriend, I decided to discuss it with Lorenzo. He wasn't crazy about the idea, "Are they going to be science babies?" He didn't think his mom would be cool with it. But at the end of the day, it was something I wanted to do for myself. So I went ahead and booked an appointment with a fertility doctor at the Southern California Reproductive Center. When I arrived, I was seen by Dr. Ghadir. He performed an ultrasound, and that's when I found out that my cyst had gone from the size of a walnut to that of a five-centimeter orange. My heart dropped. I stared at the doctor as he explained that given this size, surgery would be tricky. If they removed too much of the ovary, I could lose a lot of eggs, but the cyst needed to be removed, so I could no longer put this off. I was scared.

The day of the surgery arrived, and Omi and my friend Ellen took me to the clinic. I couldn't help but think, *What if I don't wake up?* It wasn't like I'd never had general anesthesia before, but my previous experiences had all been cosmetic surgeries for my breast implants. This one was different. It involved my health, my fertility. *What if I lose my ovary and half my eggs?* I was scared and I really missed my momma.

Lorenzo was busy with work, so I didn't think he was going to make it, but as I waited for the doctor to come see me, he made a surprise appearance. Seeing him warmed my heart. I was so used to disappointment that having my boyfriend show up for me really gave me immense comfort. Lorenzo's presence helped lighten the mood and made me smile through the fear and anxiety that were clutching my chest. I finally went under, and when I woke up on the other side, my friends, Lorenzo, and Johnny were there, and I was fine. The cyst had come out clean, and my ovary was still functioning.

I thought that would be the end of it, but the following year, right before one of my shows in Mexico, that familiar pain came back with a vengeance. There was no time to go home, so I made an appointment with a local doctor and we scheduled a surgery to remove another cyst. I haven't had any more issues since, but I put the idea of freezing my eggs on hold. My body needed a break.

At this point, I'm not sure if I want to go through the egg-freezing process. I think I would prefer to let nature take its course, if I ever decide to give it a try. To be honest, if I don't have children, I know I will be okay. I have my sibling-kids and my wonderful nieces and nephews, who all fill my heart with love. I also still feel as though I only recently managed to take flight and to focus on my own life and career, and I'm enjoying this road so much that I'm not sure I want to backtrack to raising more kids. In any case, the door remains open. What will be, will be.

Honor your shape,
honor your health,
honor yourself.

9

ENTRE BOTELLAS

When Lorenzo and I first started talking, he said he wasn't sure if he ever wanted to get married again and didn't know if he wanted to have more kids, and I thought, *This is perfect.* After seeing my mom suffer through three failed marriages, I wasn't too keen on saying I do either. Yet, as our relationship progressed and managed to survive its first big fight and major breakup, I didn't shy away when we started talking about moving in together again and the possibility of marriage. What made me open up to the idea wasn't anything he did or didn't do; it was more about me. I was finally ready to take this step. I was ready to compromise and adjust my life to allow another person in it. I knew he had his flaws, but I chose to be with him anyway. He gave me a sense of peace that made me feel like we were in this together. And I loved him. I hadn't felt that type of strong connection with anyone before, so I kept telling myself, *Whatever comes our way, we'll be able to figure it out because love is on our side.*

At the start of that year, I had cut out a picture of a random yellow house from a magazine, pasted it on my vision board, and wrote, "I want my house. I don't want to rent anymore." So we started house hunting again; I was on a mission. My list of requirements was specific: I needed good parking space to fit my cars—I had three at the time—I wanted a nice backyard because I've always loved to host get-togethers and parties, I needed at least four bedrooms, and Lorenzo wanted a pool. I was the one buying the house, but since Lorenzo and I had decided to move in together, I wanted to take his needs into consideration too. And so the search began. We went to Glendale, Woodland Hills, Calabasas, Toluca Lake, Studio City, Sherman Oaks, Tarzana—yeah, this wasn't a one-and-done deal. I was on the hunt for about five months, until my dream home finally manifested itself.

My realtor had said there was a house I should check out in Sylmar. We drove over one afternoon, and after I opened the gate door and began to walk up the entryway, watching my step on the incline, I looked up and gasped. "The house is yellow."

"Your vision board," said Omi, who was with us that day.

"Yes," I said, thinking, *It's a sign.*

"That's a good thing," said Lorenzo. "This is nice."

When the realtor opened the double front doors and we walked inside, a very familiar energy washed over me. My jaw dropped, and I smiled. It reminded me of my momma's house in Encino. I felt like I was meeting *the one.*

"Oh, I like it . . . high ceilings," I said.

Then we went into the kitchen.

"Aw, this is where the Riveras hang out, right here," said Lorenzo.

So true. The kitchen is everything in our family.

"I love it," I said. "It makes me want to cook."

"It kind of reminds me of your mom's kitchen," said Omi.

"It's like a baby version of my mom's house," I replied, moved.

The kitchen and dining areas immediately drummed up images

of Christmas and Thanksgiving celebrations. It was the first house where I could actually see myself living. I was over the moon. When we walked upstairs, the realtor showed us a small room that needed work, but I knew it would be my future glam room.

"Every bedroom has a bathroom," said the realtor, "so you won't have to share."

"Hide and poop, we could play hide and go poop," joked Lorenzo, always bringing the humor to any situation.

Johnny's room was perfect because it was on the other side of the house, which gave him a little independence.

Then we walked over to the master bedroom.

"Yeah, the king's master bedroom," said Lorenzo.

"The queen's," I corrected him, and he chuckled.

"There's room for both of you in here," added the realtor.

It had two walk-in closets, a large bathroom en suite with a tub, which I loved because I'm all about self-care, and a balcony overlooking the backyard.

"Look at the pool, babe. It has a slide, a waterfall, rocks," said Lorenzo.

"I love that sound," I said, referring to the trickling water. "I want to wake up to that every morning." It was like a mini oasis with towering palm trees and all. I was hooked.

To the side of the pool was a playground area, and I could already see my nieces and nephew and Lorenzo's daughter having a great time out there. Sure, I noticed a few things I would upgrade or change inside, like the floor, but I kept thinking, *Oh my god, this is perfect.*

Then the realtor took us to what she called the "back back," another area at the back of the house with a double lot, which had plenty of room for my cars, and a basketball court right next to it with the Lakers logo painted on the ground—as an LA girl, I loved the Lakers. The entire property was enclosed by two gates, which made me feel like we'd be safe in there.

It was a little out of my price range, but as I finished the walk-through, I knew I had to figure out how to make it work, because this house was perfect. I felt it in my heart; this was my home.

There was an ongoing bidding war with four offers in front of me, but I didn't care. "I want this to be my house," I said to Lorenzo. Later that day, I spoke to the owners, I offered above their asking price, and I worked my way up until they said yes to me.

I was so excited; Lorenzo and I could finally move in together. I was able to visualize us in that house together and it made me happy. This would be the first home I would buy for myself, a true milestone in my life.

In the months leading up to finding my dream home, Lorenzo and I had organically begun to talk not just about moving in together, but also about marriage. At first, it was coming more from him.

"I want everything with you," he said to me. "I want to be with you for the rest of my life. I want to make you my wife."

But when we started house hunting together, it all felt more real, like the possibility of taking that next big step was now within our reach.

"Well, if we're going to live together, and we love each other, why not get married, if you're serious about it?" I said to him, after leaving one of those houses I already knew was not the one.

"Okay, so how would you want your engagement?" he asked.

"I would love for my whole family to be there, my siblings, my grandma, my grandpa."

It was all casual talk between us, and the way it was unfolding felt natural, good. We had agreed to live together, and we'd also agreed that the next step would be marriage. Now the ball was in his court. But then, the summer came and went and the fall of 2017 was upon us, and nothing. I went from hesitantly talking about these possibilities to wondering, *Why the heck hasn't this guy dropped the big question yet?* It was making me antsy, so I talked to my friend Ellen about it.

Ellen had witnessed our relationship from day one and I shared everything with her, so one day, while we were hanging out at my place, I mentioned my concerns.

"He says he wants to marry me, but he hasn't asked, which is so weird. I just don't know. . . . You would tell me if you knew, right?"

"Yes, but I'd want you to be surprised too," she'd said.

When I expressed my worry again only a few days later, she finally said, "He's had the ring for you since December 2016."

"Wait, how do you know that?" I said, totally taken by surprise.

"Because he showed it to me once and told me," she replied. It seems he'd been carrying the ring in his backpack just waiting for the right moment to pop the question.

"What the hell, why didn't you tell me?" I asked.

"Well, because I didn't want to ruin it!" she said, and rightly so. "But now that we're talking about it, I've gotta be honest with you. I know you're a wonderful woman, but it makes me a little uneasy to know he's had the ring for that long and got it so soon after meeting you. You guys made it official in September and he had a ring by December. I can't help but think, are his motives pure?"

"No, he's a good guy," I said, waving away her worry.

"I don't know. I feel like he's fake," she said, honestly.

"Wait, so you're saying that he doesn't love me or like me?" I asked, a little offended.

"No, you're amazing, why wouldn't he want to be with you? It's just that, at first, he wasn't sure if he wanted to get married again and have more kids, now he does—I don't know. It's just a little sketchy to me."

I'm actually relieved he didn't go through with it in December because I would have totally freaked out. I'd only just broken off my relationship with Angel six months earlier, so that was definitely the last thing on my mind. However, by the fall of 2017, I felt ready to take this next step. Little did I know, he'd already set the wheels in motion.

A few weeks before the big day, during a *The Riveras* shoot, Lorenzo took Mikey, Jenicka, and Jacqie out to lunch. Once they sat down, he began acting a little strange—probably from the nerves—until he finally came out with it.

"So, you know, we've been looking at houses, Janney and I, so we found a place that we like. That's why I'm here to meet with you guys," he said, nervously looking down at the table. "The thing is, I want to ask her to marry me . . ."

"Ey," said Mikey.

Jacqie gasped and put her hands on her face.

Jenicka laughed at Jacqie.

"Jacqie's gonna cry," said Mikey.

"Really?" asked Jacqie with a huge smile plastered on her face.

"I'm serious," he said.

"You really want to go through with this? You can run away, dude," joked Mikey.

"You like her that much?" asked Jacqie.

"I love her, yeah," said Lorenzo softly.

"You like us that much?" asked Mikey. "Because you know you're marrying us too, right?" He wasn't wrong.

"No more privacy in your life anymore," continued Mikey.

"Yeah, you know, the first time you guys have sex after you're married, we're gonna be there," said Jacqie, messing with him. He laughed nervously. "That's how tight we are," she added.

He told them he'd also talked to my tío Juan and my tía Rosie.

"Wait, why didn't you ask me first?" asked Mikey.

"He's asking us nooow," said Jenicka, speaking for the first time at the table.

"I am my sister's keeper," said Mikey protectively.

"It's not about you, it's about them," said Jacqie. Then she added, "You're going to take care of her forever?"

"I'm going to take care of her," he replied.

"He's had a crush on her for, like, forever," said Jenicka.

"Even on her worst day. You're not going to change?" continued Jacqie.

"I feel like she's the one," he said.

"Okay, wait," said Jenicka. "You *feel* like she's the one, or you *know* that she's the one?"

"I know that she's the one," he answered.

My siblings grilled him good. Then they sat there and planned some of the engagement day logistics. The stage was set.

It was a sunny October afternoon. I was in Jacqie's car, and we were driving over to Temecula Valley Wine Country. I was told we'd be getting together with friends at this winery and that would be our location for the day. So I didn't think much of it. I figured it was just another workday filming *The Riveras*. Lorenzo had told me earlier that he had to go to Piolín's radio show to promote some music. I was a little bummed because I would've loved for him to come with us, but it was fine.

Meanwhile, back at the winery, all of my close friends and family had gathered with Lorenzo and his family inside one of the venue's rooms to sit and wait for my arrival.

"Hey guys, we're screwed," said Jenicka suddenly. "She saw the picture that grandpa posted and liked it."

Grandpa had published a photo of himself and Mike captioned: "A surprise for Chiquis." When I saw it, I knew something was up.

Tía Rosie quickly came to the rescue and called us to try and cover their tracks.

"Baby, so, you guys didn't know we were surprising you guys. We were going to try and make peace with the family. We got everyone together, a lot of us together, and for once we wanted to invite tío Lupe. And we talked to Lupe for a little bit, but it didn't go too too well. So he left, but you guys should still come," explained Rosie. She insisted we should make the most of it anyway.

I didn't completely buy the story—I've always had a sixth sense that awakens when something is off—but I went with the flow.

After being in the car for so long, I was relieved when we finally arrived. Wine was exactly what I needed to unwind. We walked through the winery's main entrance and over to an outdoor tasting room, where some of my family was "casually" waiting for us. I said hi, sat down at one of the tables, and asked, "What happened?"

"I think it was probably too much for him," said Rosie.

Rosie tried to explain it all away, but I was still suspicious that they weren't telling me the whole truth. I knew something was up, but I couldn't pinpoint what it was.

"You guys are scaring me. I feel like you're not telling me something," I said, a little emotional. Everyone was acting super weird, but I just let it go. I figured we might as well enjoy that we were all together, so we went ahead with the wine tasting. Then we all got up and strolled over to the venue's large veranda to take in the beautiful view of those earthy Riverside County hills lined with bright green vineyards and dotted with trees. It was a stunning day, without a cloud in the sky, and the height of the sun's golden hour. We couldn't have asked for better weather.

"This is kind of like our life, a panorama," I said, relaxing into the beauty of the landscape and stretching my arm out ready to start philosophizing. As my eyes dropped to the road below, I suddenly noticed someone on horseback approaching us from the left. "What the hell . . ." I said, totally taken aback once I realized the rider was actually Lorenzo. He started waving at me and I waved back, but I was so confused. As I began to walk over to meet him, my extended family and close friends began to pour out of the large wooden doors to my right.

"Oh my god, what's happening, hold on . . . is it what I think?" I said, as my heart pounded and tears slowly filled my eyes. My knees were locking in place and the butterflies were causing a hurricane in my stomach. Mikey came over and hugged me, and I looked at him and said, "Hi, brother." Then I began to take a few steps back and uttered, "No, no, no." I was so overwhelmed. Then Jacqie walked over to my side, and I asked, "Is this real? I feel like I'm dreaming." I took a few steps forward and said to everyone, "Why didn't you guys tell me, I could've brushed my hair?" They all laughed.

Lorenzo dismounted the horse and walked over to me, and I said, "Hi."

"Hi," he replied.

"Oh my god, Lorenzo," I said, nervously covering my smile.

"Janney," he said as he grabbed my right hand.

Amid the flurry of emotions, I whispered, "It's the other hand." By then I knew.

"I just want to say that I want to spend the rest of my life with you," began Lorenzo. "They say marriage is hard, but I really can't think of anything harder than being without you. So I think this is probably going to be the easiest thing. And I want to ask you in front of all your family and everyone else: Will you marry me? I want to spend the rest of my life with you."

I said, "Yes!" still in disbelief.

While he slipped the ring on my finger, a mariachi band began to play in the background. We kissed and embraced, and then I fell into the arms of my friends and family. I was thrilled that they were all there, but then a wave of disappointment briefly crashed my mind. *Fuck! I wish the cameras weren't here.* I really wanted it to be just family, something completely organic and private, without the pressure of being filmed for our show. When the cameras are around, you can't help but overact a bit or tense up. It's just different.

A few days after that fairy tale–like proposal, I realized that the one behind the magic, the person who had Lorenzo talk to my family beforehand, booked the venue, invited my family and friends, and came up with the idea of having Lorenzo ride in on horseback like Prince Charming had been none other than Edward, one of the producers of *The Riveras*. The show actually paid for everything— I was an executive producer, that's why I found out. The engagement was staged. I know Lorenzo was planning to propose. He probably mentioned this to Edward, and they hatched the plan together. Lorenzo can be spontaneous, but he's not a man who takes the initiative, which is likely why Edward took over and pushed to get it done—and he did a fantastic job. I don't blame Edward. He created a showstopping moment that generated extra ratings, but I didn't want my entire life to be staged—that's another reason I was reaching my limit with reality TV. I wish Lorenzo would've realized that I didn't need the vineyard or the knight in shining armor riding in on a horse. I just wanted something intimate, genuine, a memory that was ours for the keeping.

Even though knowing this made me feel weird about the engagement, I never spoke to Lorenzo about it because I didn't want to come across as ungrateful. *Maybe it's me,* I thought. *Maybe I'm overthinking this. Maybe I shouldn't feel this way.* I finally got out of my head, brushed it all aside, and tried to focus on the silver lining. I was excited about the idea of getting married. Yes, there were things that worried me about him, but I thought this might be the answer: moving forward with the relationship and getting married. Because I loved him. Because I was ready to be with that one person. Maybe this meant he was ready too. Maybe that's all he needed to change, to stop partying, to start focusing on his goals. Maybe things would really start looking up now.

And they did, on the career front. As I digested the fact that I was once again engaged, I got news that I was invited to the Latin American Music Awards. For the previous two years I had attended as a presenter, but this was the first time I was invited to perform on live television, with none other than Spanish singer-songwriter Natalia Jimenez! She had released a tribute album singing twelve of my mom's songs a little less than a year earlier, and I was thrilled to receive an invite to sing "Los ovarios," one of my momma's songs (and one of my favorites) that really spoke to my experience of facing all the bad-mouthing and hurdles in this industry. I was so excited.

As I prepped for this show, rehearsed, and chose my outfit, I was also dealing with the dilemma of how to announce our engagement to the media. I was promoting the upcoming release of my second album, *Entre botellas*, so I didn't want to spill the beans at the Latin AMAs and have that news overshadow all the hard work I had put into my music. The other important event we had lined up as a couple a few weeks later was the Latin Grammys. I thought maybe I could just show up with my ring on, but Lorenzo's band was up for a few nominations, and I didn't want to steal their thunder either. So we decided to keep it under wraps for the time being.

In the past two years, I had visualized myself taking this particular stage one day as a singer, as a performer, and it was finally coming true. And the timing couldn't have been better. That year I had been doing two to three shows a week, which was a lot, but all that practice and experience meant that I was ready to bring my A-game to the performance. My voice was stronger than ever and so was my confidence.

On the night of October 26, 2017, when the cameras panned over to us, and Natalia, in her long fuchsia dress with gold detailing, sang, "Qué alboroto traen conmigo," I was in pure ecstasy. I was onstage with a monstrous vocalist, whom I deeply admired, and I didn't feel shy, I didn't feel less than, I didn't feel insecure. She was so sweet and wonderful, and she made me feel like one of her equals. As she finished her verse, I jumped in with mine: "Nadie te quita ese puesto, donde tú sigues triunfando." Our voices joined in the chorus, and I was having so much fun I didn't want those minutes to end. That night was a triple blessing: I was finally on that stage, performing with someone I adored and admired, and we were singing my mom's song . . . the best of all worlds.

It was mid-November. Lorenzo and I had just flown out to spend a few days in Las Vegas for the Latin Grammys. Clearly, this is a party town, so we went out the first night to catch a Bad Bunny concert at one of the high-end clubs. I was drinking but not that much—I remember the night clearly—Lorenzo got wasted. The second evening was a repeat of the first, and I was getting a little annoyed. I never liked it when Lorenzo went on his drinking binges. But when I tried to talk to him about it, and said, "You're drinking too much. Could you please just have some water." He'd come back with, "Come on, Janney. Loosen up. We're out here having a good time. Just relax, let it be."

I hated that he made me feel like a party pooper, so I went with the flow those first two nights, but by the third one, right before we headed out, I said, "Look, I have a long weekend of work ahead of me (and he did too), so I'd love it if we didn't stay out too late tonight." I wanted to create a united front as a couple so that when it was time to go, we'd already be on the same page.

"Sure," he said, agreeing to the plan, but when we were at the club, that understanding and supportive guy was nowhere to be found. I went along for the ride, but when I realized he was on another binge, I leaned into his ear and said, "Hey, babe, I think we should get going."

"Noooo, you're always trying to control everything," he whined. "Let's have fun!"

"We have had fun, and we had an agreement," I said, sitting down on one of the club's sofas.

"Stop trying to be my mom," he said.

"I'm not trying to be your mom, dude. But we have to be responsible. Yes, I understand we're in Vegas, we're with friends, we're celebrating, but don't overdo it because then you get sloppy, and I'm afraid you're going to get in trouble."

"You don't have to worry about me. Stop taking care of me; you're not my mom. Why don't you just be my girl?" he pushed on.

"I am being your girl, but there are certain things that I don't like."

I couldn't trust him. Anytime he stayed out later than usual or went away on a trip, I always thought he was going to do drugs. It would keep me up at night. Sometimes it almost felt like he was cheating on me with the coke.

"Oh, you just want to go with your fat-ass friends," he said. There he went with his coke-induced aggression again.

"You know what, fuck this," I said, as I got up in his face and then turned around and left.

My friend Helen and I had to bum a ride from a woman we barely knew, but we made it back to the hotel in one piece. I took off my makeup and climbed into bed, knowing I needed to rest, but it was impossible. I kept tossing and turning, checking my phone for a text, waiting in the silence of the night for a call, but nothing. I could've been lying hurt in the street, and Lorenzo would have been none the wiser. That lack of concern really got under my skin.

On the day to day, we had a great time together, we were good friends, but when it came to real-life stuff, I wasn't sure we were on the same page. He was spontaneous, while I was a planner; he had great ideas but oftentimes didn't see them through, while I created action plans that I set out to execute and finish. At times, I wondered, *Are we fit for one another? Had I looked the other way too many times?* I didn't want to lose my kindness, but I didn't like the feeling that I was giving more than I should either. I've always had an issue with setting boundaries—it's still a work in progress—and now it was creeping into my relationship. The abandonment issues I started carrying as a teenager turned me into a people pleaser. I was afraid that if I stood my ground, those I loved would leave. And that's what was happening with Lorenzo too. I didn't want to lose him, but I knew I had to get my priorities straight so as not to lose myself in the process.

At nine in the morning, I heard the door unlock and watched as Lorenzo tumbled in totally shitfaced. Didn't he know I had to fly out at eleven? Was he doing this on purpose to avoid the discussion that would inevitably follow this episode? I was so irritated and upset. Then it hit me: *Oh my god, is this what my future will be like?* As I watched him snoring through his hangover, I thought, *I can't do this, I just can't.* I took off my engagement ring and wrote on the hotel notepad, "Thank you, but no thank you," and I left the note on the desk. He stirred awake as the bellman rolled my luggage out of the room and said, "Janney, where you going?" but he didn't get up from the bed. He barely moved. So I just left.

As I tackled this tidal wave of emotions and concerns, the show had to go on. My second album, *Entre botellas*, was set to release in March 2018, so the photoshoot was in the books, and no matter how downcast I was feeling that November, I had to see it through. In a way, the timing couldn't have been better. The title of that album was meant to symbolize bottled-up emotions. For a long time, I felt like I'd been floating underwater unable to come up for air. That's why I wanted to be in a pool on the album cover. I wanted people to feel sadness when they saw it—a sadness that wasn't hard for me to portray that day because it was actually front and center in my heart. I honestly felt like I was on the verge of a nervous breakdown.

A few days before the shoot, as Omi and I were driving home from running errands, I said, "I think I need to go to the hospital." I was absolutely depleted and full of sorrow. I honestly thought that if I went to the hospital, I'd be able to rest. All I really wanted to do was curl up in a ball under the covers and sleep it all away. I was tired of always having to be so strong. Instead of the hospital, Omi pulled over to the side of the freeway, and I just cried and cried and cried and then yelled and let it all out. I had been bottling up so many emotions for so long that, at times, I actually felt like I was drowning. And you can see it in that album cover. The sadness in my eyes, that wasn't acting, it was the pure and raw truth.

Lorenzo apologized and we made up. A few days after our Vegas trip, and after a lot of thought, I invited him to come over to my house, and we sat down in the living room to talk.

"If you don't control this alcohol thing, it's going to mess up your life," I forewarned him with authentic concern.

"It's social drinking," he replied, dismissively. Then he added, "You don't trust me?"

I trusted him in the sense that I didn't think he was out there being a ho, but I was losing trust in his word, which is equally serious. If you say you're going to do something and then don't follow through, once, twice, three, four times, that eventually wears the other person down.

"I'm not lying about something crazy," he said. "I just feel like you bash me too much."

It wasn't just the Vegas blowup, it was the lack of follow-through and the "white" lies he kept spinning to cover his ass and justify why he hadn't texted me back one night, or why he got home so late another day.

"I don't have time to put up with bullshit. I know what I want. And I don't want a man who can't tell me the truth," I finally blurted out.

"I apologized already," he whined, puzzled.

There was a clear lack of communication—he just didn't seem to get where I was coming from.

"You know, Janney, you act like I'm out there fucking bitches, but I'm just drinking and talking, and usually when I'm drinking I'm talking about you. Ask everyone, ask my cousins, ask all the people who were with me," he said.

"But why, though? Why do you feel the need to drink all night? You knew I was upset and we were fighting, but you didn't come after me to try and fix things."

"I know, but I was with my cousins and we were in Vegas, the city that never sleeps. I wasn't doing anything wrong." He always pointed the finger back at me, like I was the crazy bitch for thinking that he was cheating when he was acting like a saint all along.

"Look, I just want you to put more effort into this relationship. If you're really ready to be married, you need to stop doing this stuff," I said.

"Okay. I'm going to stop drinking, I promise you," he said, never admitting that he also had a coke problem. "You know I love you. I love you so much. At least I'm not cheating on you. I'm just drinking. I'm sorry, Janney. I'll prove it to you. Just give me one more chance."

It wasn't the first time we'd had issues because of his drinking and it wouldn't be the last. He liked to party—my tío Juan and Angel were right.

Although I was skeptical about long-lasting relationships because I hadn't had that example at home, I really did want to get married, but I also knew it was a huge step, and I wasn't about to take it lightly. I already had my bag of commitment issues to deal with, and these red flags were getting too big to ignore. It broke my heart to take that ring off, but I could no longer ignore what my gut was trying to tell me. I needed a breather, I needed space, and we both needed time to figure out if we really wanted to go through with it. Time was still on our side to make the right decision.

Before making any final decisions, we decided to go to couples therapy. I went in focused on talking about the two big issues that were holding me back from truly committing to him wholeheartedly: his excessive drinking and his inability to keep his word. It wasn't like he was drinking every day, but when he did, he was binge drinking to the extreme. He'd follow it up the next day by saying what he thought I wanted to hear, just to please me, to cover up his fuckups. He'd stop the argument in its tracks by looking into my eyes and telling me how much he loved me. Then came the kisses. He'd kiss my lips and my neck, and do everything in his power to get me horny, which would inevitably lead to sex. He followed that up with a dose of laughter, and with all the tension orgasmically gone, I'd cave and say, "Okay, fine, I forgive you. Let's give this another shot." But his words began to mean nothing to me because he never followed his promises through with actions later.

After greeting our therapist and sitting down on the sofa across from her, I opened our couples session by saying, "From the beginning of our relationship, I think the biggest issue that we've had is . . . his binge drinking."

"When you say 'binge drinking' what does that mean?" asked the therapist.

"Well, I don't drink every day," said Lorenzo. "But when I do it, I just do it to the fullest. She doesn't really drink at all, so, you know, it's a huge difference, so maybe—maybe for her it's too much."

I mentioned that I had spoken to his mom, and that she'd had similar issues with her husband. She said Lorenzo's dad was never unfaithful, but that she felt he drank too much. It got so bad for her that she decided to leave him, taking the kids and moving from Mexico to Colorado for a year. She was determined not to go back to him, but he followed her, stopped drinking and smoking, and became a changed man. I couldn't help but see the parallels between his story and Lorenzo, and that happy ending gave me a small ray of hope. I then described the Vegas blowup to her.

"Why does his drinking upset you so much? What's happening for you that's making you so fearful?" asked the therapist.

"Because he lies," I said without hesitation.

"When I do mess up," said Lorenzo, "she has a strong personality, so I'm gonna have to hear it for a good while, you know. And I start questioning myself, *Am I good enough for her?* So I'd rather lie."

"What's the thing that started and created the fear around you being honest with Janney?" the therapist asked Lorenzo.

"She doesn't have to be with me, it's easier, because she's a busy woman, she has a lot of things going, so maybe it'd be easy for her to move on to the next, and that kinda scares me because I do want to be with her," he said.

Funnily enough, what he didn't seem to understand is that the very mechanism he was using to stay in the game with me was actually pushing me in the other direction.

"Has she ever done anything to make you feel justified in that fear?" she asked.

"She has been engaged three times, that kind of scares me too," he said, avoiding the question.

"Have I done anything to make you feel that way?" I asked him.

"No, not really."

"Yes, I've been engaged three times," I said to the therapist. "I guess now that I come to this relationship, my tolerance is very, very low . . . It's just so fucking frustrating. He needs to come back and just be honest, that's it. Believe me, I don't think I'm being irrational," I said with tears welling up in my eyes. "I'm just at a point where we've been together for a year, and if this isn't going to work, I'm okay with walking away."

I had reached my limit. I was tired of protecting him, trying to make him see that what he called "social drinking" was a much bigger issue. I could no longer continue to push him to be better.

"I already raised four kids," I said.

"Just trust me," he said. "When someone trusts me I become a better man."

Wait, how could I do that if he didn't fix his drinking problem? We were caught in a loop that was going nowhere, and rather than helping, the session was beginning to aggravate us even further. It was clear we had to compromise, somehow meet in the middle, but neither of us knew how to get there. We were totally stuck, and that feeling just made me want to bolt. I was thirty-two years old and didn't feel I had any time to waste. Either we worked it out and stepped up for each other or we let it go.

As the year came to a close, everything he did began to irritate me. I was also angry because I felt he'd robbed me of something that had initially been genuinely exciting: planning our wedding. Nevertheless, we continued to talk. One night, when we'd gone out for dinner, I told him that the only way I could start trusting him again was if I saw his words reflected in his actions. And I wasn't willing to settle for anything less.

"Lorenzo, I don't give you problems. I don't hide my phone, I tell you where I'm at, what time I'm coming home. I'm a woman of my word, and I do my best to be that way. I'm trying, and you've given me a lot of reasons to want to run away. And I just want certain things to change before we figure out where this is going, if it's going anywhere."

He just stared back in silence, then said, "It hasn't been the easiest. You're a great girl, everything I've always wished for in a woman, so I'm here and I want to fight for us."

I heard his words, but it was hard for me to believe him. If you want to fight, then fight for us! I felt like he didn't look at me the same because I was no longer that loving, giving girlfriend, and because I was calling him out on his shit, and that was really discouraging. I know I wasn't looking at him the same way either. It was hard. I felt like I couldn't speak my truth.

So by the start of 2018, we put moving in together and the engagement on hold. We said we'd try until trying was no longer an option, but I honestly thought that was it. I hated the idea of losing him, but I'd already lost so many important people in my life that I knew I could handle it. There was still love in our hearts. The question was, could we find our way back to each other?

Then came February 14, 2018. He was in Mazatlán for work,

so we clearly weren't going to be spending that Valentine's Day together, but I thought he'd at least show up in some other way. The hours ticked by. I stayed up that night, waiting for him to text or call me, seriously worried that something might have happened to him . . . nada. When I finally got ahold of him, I said, "What the fuck, dude? What happened to you?"

"Oh, something happened to my phone," he replied. "Someone ran it over, I swear to you!"

"Okay, so are you coming home already?" I asked. We were still trying to work things out and hadn't completely canceled the idea of moving in together.

"No, I'm going to stay," he said.

I thought he remained in Mexico an extra day for work, but later that night, I saw in his stories that he was partying it up big-time— his work had wrapped a day earlier. That was it. I'd had enough. I opened our message thread in my phone and, in a fury, typed, "I'm fucking done," pressed send, and blocked his number.

> We are commanded to forgive, but trust is earned. Like a building, it takes seconds to destroy and months, if not years, to rebuild.

10

THE CRAZIEST THING I DID FOR LOVE

After our February breakup, Lorenzo and I didn't talk for more than a month. At first, I thought there was no going back, but as the weeks crawled by, my heart ached for him. I began to post little clues on Instagram and Snapchat, like Jesse and Joy's song, "Me dueles," knowing he'd likely see it and understand I was speaking to him through those lyrics. Then, in March 2018, I traveled to Mexico City to promote the upcoming release of my sophomore album, which Lorenzo had helped me with a lot by coming to the studio and providing encouragement and singing tips, and also recording some vocal tracks. It just so happened that he was also in the city at the same time, so he DM'd me: "Can I take you out to dinner?" I was in such a vulnerable spot, missing him and also hurting after a big fight that had distanced me from Omi (thankfully, only temporary) and my best friend Ellen (unfortunately, not so temporary), that I caved and said yes.

We met up at a Japanese restaurant. I was wearing a sleek red coat and he was looking sharp in a blue businesslike suit. Sitting at that table across from him after so many weeks apart, I thought, *Fuck, I love this guy.* It was like we picked up right where we left off, chatting, joking around, and laughing, which made me question why we broke up in the first place.

"Janney, you're the woman who taught me how to love," he said to me that night. "Women that I've been with before never put themselves as high as you do. You want me to open the door for you, give you flowers, and you want to be loved the right way, and I've never had that."

I just stared into his eyes and let him speak, eager to hear what he had to say.

"Yeah, I've never needed to do the things that I do for you. You want to be courted, while I'm used to women coming after me. So, with you I have to put in extra work, and I'm not used to that."

It wasn't that bad, was it? I wondered, as I listened to him, hoping to justify the blast of emotions and desire capturing my heart.

"But I feel that sometimes it's just never enough," he said, tears filling his eyes. "Sometimes I think that I don't deserve you. You're just a great woman. I don't deserve you."

It almost felt like he had an ability to cry on command—he'd often resort to tears during our fights. Were they real or was he just a great actor? I'm not sure, but they were working. I thought, *Well, I get it, maybe I do expect too much from him.* I do have high standards.

"I'm sorry, but I want to be treated the way I treat you," I said. "I go out of my way. I'm always paying attention to the details, and I need you to do that too."

"Okay, I will," he promised. "I was just never taught that. With you everything has been different, and shit like this really gets to you."

"Yeah, because I want to be treated like a queen," I replied.

As we finished our dinner and were close to asking for the check, I finally said, "Okay, fine, let's try this again."

The Craziest Thing I Did for Love

When he opened up like that, when he became vulnerable and showed a willingness to change, I was once again hooked. Our talk felt so sincere that my heart urged me to give him another shot. Sometimes, it comes down to an honest apology: it's the key that unlocks the possibility of forgiveness in my heart, and, once again, he managed to open that door. I honestly thought we could make it work this time. Plus, I was in love with him, there was no denying that.

"I still want to marry you," he said, as he handed back the ring I had returned a few months earlier. "Please wear it."

I agreed, on one condition. "It's tainted by last year's pain, so you need to have it blessed first."

Once he did that, I put my engagement ring back on, and by that summer, he slowly began to move in to the home I had recently purchased. Neither of us was ready to give up on the other just yet. Our story clearly had more chapters to play out. However, to be honest, my doubts were still strong that year. Whenever we talked about our past breakups, and I linked them to his drinking, he'd make his usual excuses—*I don't drink every day, it's just social drinking, I like to have fun with my friends*—and then disarm me by tickling me and saying, "Come on, babe, don't be mad anymore." Or he'd say something totally out of the blue, like, "Look at that bird," which would distract me from the conversation, and then he'd hit me with one of his jokes and make me laugh. He was so good at deflecting arguments that I didn't even realize it was happening. He has a way with words, I feel he knows how to place himself in a story, and understands what others need to hear so that they end up feeling bad for him. They see him as the victim of his circumstances—I've seen him do this with his parents, with the media, hell, he even did it with me; by the time the conversation is done, everyone is like, "Poor Lorenzo." I see all of this clearly now.

But back then, when I tried to point out what needed to change for us to work, he'd say, "You know me, Janney. You know my heart."

"Yeah, I guess I do," I'd reply, somewhat confused as to how we'd arrived here.

"Janney, you've forgiven worse things in your life, like your dad and stuff that happened with your mom. Why can't you forgive me?"

"Fuck," I'd say. "I guess you're right." And I'd fall for him all over again. Then he'd do something dorky and make me crack up, and that was it. We kept going, even though our issues remained unresolved. I think love sometimes really is blind.

The months flew by that year. There was still friction, but we continued to do our best to listen to each other, to work things out. It was confusing. He was still my best friend. Despite our differences, we continued to laugh together. We also had special bonds that made me feel like I could be my authentic self with him—part of the reason I fell for him in the first place. We were both Mexican-American, we both spoke Spanglish, I felt like I could talk about anything with him—what was going on with my family, my deepest thoughts—and he got me. Even when I left the house wearing mismatched socks or a onesie, he'd say, "Oh my god, you're so freakin' cute. Fuck it, let's both go to the store in our onesies!" I loved all of that about him. So I latched on to those peaks in our relationship and pushed forward.

I never really dreamed of getting married as a little girl, my big thing had been my future quinceañeara. I wanted a big, poufy, sparkly dress and an awesome party, but, as I told you in *Forgiveness*, that never happened because my mom went ballistic when I didn't tell her that we had been let out of school early and I was hanging out with friends. Her punishment: cutting my long, soft, silky hair down to two inches from my scalp and throwing me out of the house. I spent that summer living with my grandma. My birthday came and went like any other day, with no big party, no special dress, and no call from my mom.

So, when the time came to finally start planning our wedding, I felt it was my chance to fulfill my quinceañeara fantasy. I wanted it to be perfect. Lorenzo and I envisioned a Mexican wedding, something beautiful yet also relaxed, where we could celebrate our love with our friends and family. As we considered different venues, we thought, *How about if we have it on a ranch?* There was this private ranch not too far from us, where my mom used to go when she needed space to relax, and I knew the owners. When I reached out and asked if we could have our wedding on their property, they said yes. I was thrilled to get their okay, because it meant I'd have another little piece of my momma near me on that special day. I missed her so much.

We had secured the land, and now we needed to build the venue from scratch, electricity and all, and customize it to our liking. I hired a wedding planning team, and we got to work on the details. We also decided to hold the ceremony at Westminster Presbyterian Church to celebrate the tradition of our union in a sacred space.

Juggling work and wedding planning left little time for much else that year. As I continued the *Entre botellas* tour to promote these songs and keep the momentum going, a new opportunity landed on the table: Fonovisa, the Regional Mexican division of Universal Music Group, wanted to sign a deal with me, and I said YES! After producing and releasing my first two albums through my own record label, I couldn't have been more excited about this opportunity to work on my third one with such a prestigious company. I was entering a new stage in my career and couldn't wait to see what I would accomplish with such backing.

All plans were now in motion and, as we rang in 2019, the countdown to our big day began. I wanted my wedding dress to look like cream, so I chose a heavy ivory silk fabric, but I also wanted some lace details on the top to give it that traditional Spanish style I was aiming for, just enough for the skin on my shoulders and arms to elegantly peek through. The mermaid silhouette I chose let me tastefully show off my curves and feel like a true Spanish princess. The second dress—because you know one wouldn't have been enough for this clothes-loving chingona!—had more of a hippie vibe. It was also ivory and super lacy, almost like one of my abuelita's classic tablecloth toppers or doilies, and I paired it with some comfy cowboy boots so I could dance the night away at our reception. My sister Jacqie came with me to see the fabrics, but that was mostly for the reality show so I had someone to interact with.

Between finalizing my dresses and meeting with the wedding planner to continue to check off our to-do list, I also began to record my third album, *Playlist*, which was due to release the following year, in May 2020. To hype up the fans with what was to come, we decided to wrap the first single, "Anímate y verás," early and premiere it on June 27 with a music video. So as our wedding day drew near, I was also in the studio putting the finishing touches to this song, which was being produced by renowned Regional Mexican music composer Luciano Luna. This matchup sent me to cloud nine, and the timing felt perfect. I was at a point in my career where my voice had matured, and I had the experience I needed to make the most of this amazing opportunity.

Once the recording was finalized, it was time to figure out the video's story line. I was in my office talking with my manager, Richard, whom I call Mr. Bull, brainstorming different themes when Lorenzo, who was sitting there with us, came up with the winning concept: a waitress at a coffee shop is in love with one of the regulars and finds a way to gather the courage to ask him out by slipping him a note with the place and time to meet her that night. When he arrives at the designated dive bar, he discovers the waitress is actually onstage belting out this song and he's instantly smitten. We loved it and ran with it.

We'd have to shoot the video on three locations: the coffee shop, the dive bar, and the soundstage for the Chiquis glam shots that would be weaved among the main story's scenes. This also meant I had to have a hunky guy play the part of my love interest.

"You go ahead and choose the guy," I told Mr. Bull that day, in front of Lorenzo.

"Do you want to see pictures?" he asked.

"No, I don't care. You go ahead and choose him."

The morning of the video shoot, Mr. Bull texted me a photo of the guy I'd be working with.

"Cool," I texted back, then I showed the model's headshot to Lorenzo. "Babe, this is the guy I'll be working with today."

"So you are going to have a model in the video?" he asked.

"Yeah," I said, taken aback, "but you knew this already."

"No, you didn't involve me. You didn't tell me."

"But you knew the plan. It was your freakin' idea, and we went ahead with it. I wasn't even involved in choosing the model."

"Well, I'm not going," he said suddenly.

"What?" He was supposed to go with me to the shoot that day. "Are you fucking kidding me?"

"Yeah, I'm not going. How do you think I'll feel seeing my girl with some random guy?"

"Lorenzo, I don't even know what to say. I had to go through this with you a few months ago. This is something normal. You said it yourself when I was with you at your video shoot and I was upset. I'd feel more comfortable if you were there."

I had flown to Mexico to support him during the shoot of his song "Imperfectamente perfecta" only a few months back, because it was his first recording as a solo artist. But he gave me no warning that he'd be canoodling with a model on the set, rubbing noses and holding her, while she was in bed wearing a baby doll, no less! We got into a huge fight that day due to this lack of communication and respect, but our blowup didn't stop him from recording that video. Up until then, I believed that, as a couple who was engaged to be married, it was something we'd logically discuss beforehand—or at least get a heads-up before I got there—but that didn't seem to be the case. So, I took it to mean that models or actors of the opposite sex in our videos were now fair game. My video was much more innocent than his, but he suddenly freaked out and didn't even want me to rub noses with the guy. I wasn't planning on kissing him regardless, and I didn't, but this double standard was not flying with me. Now I wonder if he thought I would choose him to be in the video and that's why he was so upset.

"Okay, I'm going to send you the locations anyway," I said, thinking that maybe he was in a mood because it was early in the morning. The whole situation really bugged me because I hate when people say they're going to do something and then back out at the last minute. We had plans. I had been super excited about this day, and I knew I had to deliver my best video yet, given my new record deal. The pressure was on, and I had to deliver no matter what.

There I was, six weeks prior to our wedding, on the set of my first shoot for Fonovisa, without my fiancé by my side. Another broken promise. But I did my best not to let his funky mood ruin this day for me. Nothing was going to stop me from enjoying the moment. I was determined to make it fun, cute, and flirtatious. And it was working. I was feeling young and sexy and ready to turn some heads, oozing the kind of thicker-woman-owning-her-curves sex appeal that Regional Mexican music, with its classic extra-hot-

and-slender divas, wasn't used to. I was ravaged by some of the critics because of this, just like my mom was in her day. "Why is she wearing a tied-up shirt and showing her stomach?" they'd say. Wait . . . why not? Being larger than a size four doesn't automatically cancel our power of seduction. Rather than shy away from what I had to offer, I embraced it. I loved representing a curvy, sexy, confident woman in my genre, and nothing was going to keep me from continuing to do so.

The shoot was a success, and as happy as I was with this accomplishment, I had a dark and pesky little cloud hanging over my head. The long day of work had gone by without even a peep from Lorenzo. He didn't show up, he didn't call, he didn't text. Nothing. I was upset and annoyed, so once we wrapped the shoot, I reached for my phone and FaceTimed him, only to find him drunk out of his fucking mind at some random guy's house.

"What the hell?" I said, super pissed off. "I'm working my fucking ass off and you're nowhere to be found, even though you knew the locations. And you picked a fight with me in the morning, and now you're drunk off your ass." I was so furious.

"No, babe . . . no, wait. We're talking about business, and this guy wants to invest in me."

In that instant, the same thought that I had had back in our Vegas hotel room more than a year earlier popped into my mind again, *Oh my god, is this what my future will be like?*

When I got home, I called my pastor and said, "I can't do this. I can't marry him."

But my pastor repeated something he had said to me on other occasions when I ran into conflict with Lorenzo, "He has a good motor. He's a good guy. The outside of the car can be fixed. We can help him. But his motor, his heart, is good."

I listened attentively because I felt he had a good motor too, but my doubts were still present. "I don't know, something's telling me I shouldn't marry him," I replied.

Pastors Mom and Dad suggested we meet with them to get some guidance, and they were the ones who kept me from running that time. We managed to mend things yet again, then two weeks before the big day we got into another fight, this time about the prenup. He made a scene and refused to sign it. I know this can be a touchy subject, but I needed to cover my ass. I was old enough to know that shit happens, and if you're not rightfully protected, a separation or divorce can easily turn into a huge nightmare. He took the document and held on to it for the following two weeks. When we were only a day away from our wedding, and I realized that he was totally ignoring my request, I said to him, "If you don't sign this, I'm not walking down the aisle." That little wake-up call made him put pen to paper and sign on the dotted line.

As if all of this back-and-forth wasn't enough, we were faced with another obstacle: his ex-wife had decided not to allow his daughter to come to the wedding. Even though we weren't on the best of terms, I did everything in my power to convince her to let her daughter attend, and she finally agreed.

Meanwhile, work didn't magically stop just because I was planning to say "I do." My first live performance of the year was happening at San Diego's Viva la Música festival, and that had me slightly on edge. It had been five months since I'd performed live, so I was a little fearful, but my siblings, their kids, and my abuelita drove down with Lorenzo and me to cheer me on. I loved having them all there, but it was a little crazy and hectic, which didn't help calm my nerves.

I sat down so that my stylist could finish doing my hair, and when I got up, my tight black pants ripped right along my butt crack. My heart skipped a beat, but hey, the show must go on. After my team safety-pinned my booty back into the pants, I took a swig of tequila with a friend who'd stopped by to say hello. Then I formed a circle with my team for a quick prayer before heading out toward the arena's stage. Taking in the hum of the expectant audience, I grabbed the mic and sang out "Que se te quiteeeee" a cappella before I stormed the stage, feeding off the adrenaline rush that hits performers during their opening tune.

As soon as I heard the audience singing along with me, I was in the zone, performing, making jokes, and working the crowd. There's really nothing like that connection, that vibrating energy between performer and audience. They filled me with the confidence and light I needed to get up there and give them my all. The stage felt like home. I had missed it.

As I got into my groove, there was a song up next that Lorenzo and I were going to perform together, but he got caught up watching the show from the bleachers and totally forgot. I couldn't believe it. He beelined it through the crowd and onto the stage, barely making it in time. What the hell? His nonchalant ways were fine in certain scenarios, but in cases like this one, it irritated the hell out of me.

Doubts, doubts, and more doubts continued to hound me as we entered June. So much so that during my celebratory escape to Las Vegas with my girls for my birthday-turned-bachelorette weekend, I couldn't help but express that I was still worried Lorenzo might not truly be ready to get married. We still had unresolved issues, and I felt he had some more growing up to do, yet I vowed to do everything I needed to be a good wife. "If it doesn't work out," I told my friends, "it's not going to be because of me." I think they were taken aback that I was going in ready for the possibility of divorce.

My friend Vanessa had already expressed her concerns early on in my relationship. "This isn't the guy for you," she said to me over drinks one night, during one of our many heart-to-heart talks. "I feel like he isn't who he says he is. I think he's using you."

"Look, this is my life and I'm going to do what I want," I replied. We bickered a little, like besties who are more like sisters do.

"You're right," she said in the end. "It is your life. As your friend, I just have to tell you what's on my mind."

By the time the last week before tying the knot came around, I was so stressed out about how messy everything was between us that I wanted to throw in the towel and just cancel. My soul felt heavy. Deep down I knew I shouldn't go through with it, but I thought, *Fuck it, I'll make it work. I can change him. I'll help him. We'll figure it out.*

Our wedding was the talk of the town. The media was constantly mentioning it on their shows and in their publications, speculating when and where it would take place because I had decided not to sell it to any outlet. I wanted to keep that sacred day for us. I didn't want to have to worry about broadcasters and what they would or wouldn't say about us—what we were wearing, what we were saying, and so forth. I didn't want to be judged that day. I just wanted to be, to enjoy my family and friends, to soak it all in without any pressures. So I kept the date from being released to the public and asked all the guests to sign NDAs for this sole purpose. The plan was to eventually share some behind-the-scenes footage and the final wedding video, but I wanted it to be in my own time and through my own platform. At least that's what I had planned.

Three days before the wedding, the shit hit the fan. Someone leaked our evite invitation to the media. It was splashed across screens of all sizes. I found out like everyone else did, on national TV, and the show that had the audacity to "break" this story didn't even bother to blur out the location's address. If you ask me, that's malicious intent. I was fuming and crying. How could they do that?

This was not the price anyone should pay as a public figure. It just goes to show that no matter how we treat the media, many of those outlets would turn things around to benefit their shows without even giving it a second thought, no matter the emotional damage they may cause. Sure, my life is pretty public, but I have the right to some privacy, especially when it comes to a blessed moment like this one.

With my emotions at an all-time high, I stopped for a moment and thought, *Wait, whoever leaked the invite had to be part of the wedding*. We'd been so careful, and we had almost managed to pull it off. Sure, there's always a chance something might leak, but I never would've imagined the media would go and publish the date, time, and address with such indifference and disregard.

What were we going to do now? My first reaction: let's change the ceremony's location. My team and I immediately got to work and reached out to countless possible venues. I was even ready to give up on getting married in a church. But finding a new venue for the ceremony with such short notice, and with guests traveling here from near and far, was impossible to coordinate. Meanwhile, Lorenzo kept saying he was sorry. (But it wasn't his fault, right?) I was so stressed out I felt like my head was about to explode. The only other option we had was to beef up our security, so I agreed to hire ten additional guards to give us the extra protection we'd need at the church. We also ordered several big black umbrellas, because I wasn't about to give these assholes the satisfaction of getting a shot of me in my wedding dress. We also had to forgo releasing two doves at the end of the ceremony because we could no longer freely access the exterior of the church without being persecuted by the media. Nevertheless, we would make it work somehow—I refused to let them get the best of me and ruin my day.

June 29, 2019, finally arrived. After a late evening with Vanessa and Judy, who spent the night with me, I woke up in my room in a gorgeous hotel in Pasadena only about ten minutes from the church. It was around seven in the morning, half an hour before my alarm was set to go off, and the sunlight was streaming in through the floor-to-ceiling windows, promising a stunning day. Feeling a little antsy, I quietly sat up in my bed, trying not to wake my friends, and prayed for a little while. *Oh my god, this is real. This is really happening*, I thought. *I'm going to get married and my momma's not here. I'm not too sure if this is the right decision. I miss her guidance, her mother's instinct.* I was so afraid that I was making a mistake. I wished she was there to walk me down the aisle. To stop my mind from reeling out of control, I placed my headphones in my ears, put on a little meditation music, and read my angels book, but, as much as I was looking forward to the ceremony and celebration ahead, my momma's absence pierced my heart. I thought a shower would help shake the feeling of sadness, so once I was in the bathroom, I put on one of my favorite worship songs, "Tú estás aquí" by Jesús Adrián Romero, and as I started singing along, I felt like I was actually singing to Momma, and tears started flooding my eyes. The sentimental crying quickly turned into straight-up sobbing. *I don't know if this is right. I don't think this is what I should be doing. I love him, but what's my life with this man really going to be like?*

I let the shower wash away the remains of my salty tears, put on my robe, and finally left the bathroom, only to find Vanessa waiting for me outside. "Are you okay?" she asked.

"Yeah, I'm good," I said, pretending everything was fine.

"I heard you crying, but I gave you time," she said with concern in her eyes.

"Yeah, I miss my mom, and I don't know if I'm making the right decision," I confessed.

"Look, I don't think you are," replied Vanessa, in her signature straight-shooting way that I love. "If you want, we can cancel—"

"No! How in the hell am I going to cancel my wedding?!" I exclaimed.

"Okay, no worries. If this is what you want to do, I'm here to support you."

Everyone was already there and everything was set up and paid for; it was too late to turn back. I just couldn't bring myself to do it. In hindsight, I can't help but think of my mom's wedding day with Esteban. Two weeks before she walked down the aisle, we were sitting in her office during our weekly meeting, bickering about her wanting to invite my ex-boyfriend, Hector, to her wedding, when I finally got the nerve to speak my mind.

"Momma, I really don't think you should marry Esteban."

"Why?"

"Because you don't love him." I actually really liked Esteban for my mom. I thought he was a great guy, and I felt comfortable leaving her in his hands. I thought she'd be well taken care of. But I knew she was still communicating with her ex Ferny, and that even though their relationship had been like one of those thrill rides at Six Flags, she still loved him.

"Well, what do you want me to do now? I'm too far in at this point. I can't back out. I know he's good for me, and he's good for my kids."

"So you're not getting married for love?" I asked.

"No, I'm too grown for that shit," she replied. And that was the end of that.

So, I swallowed my words, followed her lead, and smiled for the camera. I was so hard on my momma that day for going through with that circus when she wasn't really feeling it, and there I was doing the exact same shit almost nine years later. I should've had more dignity, I should've not cared about what people would think, and I should've said, "This is not right for me and I need to stop this." But I didn't.

Instead, I snapped out of it, pushed these thoughts back, and smiled through the unsettling emotions until I was once again in the moment, enjoying the prep with my wonderful bridal party. After my hair and makeup were done, and I carefully slid into my custom-made ivory wedding dress, Jacqie came up to me with a ringing phone in her hand and said, "It's Dad."

"Oh shit," I muttered, overwhelmed.

I've talked to my dad on the phone a total of three times. The first call happened in the summer of 2016, while we were filming *The Riveras*, after Jacqie had reinitiated contact with him and visited him in prison. She was happy with her newfound relationship; they were speaking regularly, sometimes even twice a week. It still made me uncomfortable. One day, while on one of these calls, she mentioned to him that she was driving over to my place, and he said he'd call back once we were together. She sprung this on me as soon as she walked through the door, and I didn't even have time to react before the phone started ringing. The last time I spoke to him had been in court ten years earlier, when he was on trial for sexually abusing Rosie and me, and he didn't even look at me.

My chest hurt as we stood by my kitchen counter and Jacqie answered on speaker. Mikey was sitting in the living room quietly watching us. So many things were crossing my mind as we waited for the prison to connect the call. *Am I supposed to be talking to him? Is this okay? Am I betraying my mom?* Then Jacqie said, "I'm here with Chiquis," and I just looked at her. I was wide-eyed and in full panic mode. I had forgotten that I had a dad. She passed the phone to me and insisted, "He wants to talk to you."

I was practically hyperventilating. "Hello," I said shyly, not knowing how to begin the conversation, and trying to push the phone back to my sister. He said hello back, and I replied earnestly, "This is really strange, I wanted to speak to you, but I don't know what to say." He eased me into a conversation by asking how my business was going. His voice sounded different, yet I quickly recognized his low-pitched, soft-spoken tone. My stomach was doing somersaults. I had spent more than half my life without him, digesting the fact that he was no longer around, but when I heard him on the other end of the line, I thought, *Oh my god, that's my dad. I have a dad.*

For a moment, I forgot about everything that had happened and why he was calling from prison, and I started to fill him in on my life—it was so bizarre. How could I trust him after what he had done to me? The situation was becoming way too overwhelming, and just when I felt I couldn't chitchat any longer, I was saved by the operator: "You have sixty seconds remaining." I yearned for that parent, the one who would give me advice, but he hadn't been in my life for twenty years, and we were skipping over crucial steps that needed to happen before we could get to this point.

After we hung up, I honestly didn't know how to feel. I didn't like that he had decided to pop back into our lives after my mom had died. Was it because he was afraid of her? Or was it because now that she's not around, he thought he could manipulate us into having a relationship? It was working with Jacqie. But I couldn't reconnect with someone who abused me and, from what I had heard, continued to stand by his reasoning that what I said happened, what he did to me, was actually just something my mom had put in my head. Would he be able to admit the truth and finally apologize? These were all questions I hoped to ask him one day, if the opportunity presented itself. I was ready to have that conversation with him, to open old wounds and go there. I was ready, but he wasn't.

The second call from him came a few months later. This time

Jacqie wasn't there to mediate. He called on his own free will. I actually missed his first few attempts, but then finally answered. "Hola, mija, ¿cómo estás?" he said—he only speaks Spanish. It was another very on-the-surface type of call; he just wanted to know how I was doing. I honestly didn't even know how to respond. It was almost like talking to a stranger. That call probably lasted five minutes, if that.

Then about a year after his initial contact, I decided to go see him in prison. But he wanted to see Jacqie, without me. It took me so long to get to that point, to gather the courage to face my abusive father again, to give him the benefit of the doubt, to see if he had repented, to allow him to speak, only to be rejected. I didn't get it. After doing the work and trying to let my guard down ever so slightly, my protective shield went up again in full force, and I wasn't sure if I could ever bring it down again.

When Jacqie came back from that visit, she explained that he was upset about something I had said in an interview about his sentencing, but he continued to avoid talking about what he had actually been sentenced for in the first place, and Jacqie didn't seem to press him on the matter either. There are probably very few people who will ever understand what it's like to take the stand and testify against their father and then have to deal with the public backlash of being called a liar by him and his family. Why in the hell would I lie about such a traumatic event in my life? Why would I willingly scar my memory with such scenes? This is one of the reasons I've always had the urge to be extra honest and demonstrate that I have nothing to hide.

The third and last time we talked was on my wedding day. He told Jacqie, "I want to talk to your sister, I want to pray for her. It makes me sad that she doesn't have one of her parents there." Jacqie asked me what time would be a good time for him to call, and I said after getting my hair and makeup done. Jacqie was my maid of honor, so she was in the room with me, and she held up the phone as the call came through.

My heart was pounding beneath my wedding dress as we waited for him to come on the line. He asked me how I was feeling, and I took big, deep breaths to try to control the tears that were threatening to burst out of my eyes and ruin my makeup. He congratulated me and gave me marriage advice: "As they say in church, it's a challenge, right? The key is mutual respect, that's what makes a marriage." He wished me all the best, and then Jacqie asked him to lead us in a prayer.

The crazy thing is that I am no longer angry at him. I don't want to waste any more time experiencing the pain of my past. I'd simply like to have that face-to-face conversation one day. I think it's necessary for my soul—and his too. I see myself saying, "Hey, what's going on? So, are you ready to admit to what you did to me? Are you going to apologize?" That's all I really need. Sensing his remorse and receiving his apology, that's what would really give me enough peace to begin to consider giving him a chance to right the wrongs and start fresh. I honestly don't know if I'm right or wrong as far as allowing him to have such easy access to me, but I want him to know that I'm not mad at him, that the door is open and I'm ready to have this sincere exchange. Without it, there's really nothing to talk about; all the other calls we've had have felt somewhat superficial and empty.

I felt so vulnerable after we hung up with him. It was a lot, too much, but I managed to compose myself and went downstairs to the white car that awaited me. As we drove over to the church, the excitement of the big day started to build in me. I looked down at my mom's diamond-encrusted butterfly ring, which had been recovered from the accident's wreckage and I had chosen as my "something borrowed." She usually wore it for interviews or meetings, but not so much at her shows. Even though I wasn't a diamond girl like my momma, wearing this ring on my wedding day felt like I was carrying a piece of her with me. Then I glanced at the heart locket carrying two pictures of my momma, which I had hung from my bouquet of white peonies so that I could hold her near my heart. This was it. There was no turning back now, no running away, no bolting. It was a beautiful day. I was about to walk down the aisle to join the man I loved in holy matrimony and begin the rest of my life, and in that moment, I was honestly happy.

When we arrived, the media frenzy was in full effect. I knew it would be intense, but I didn't expect it to be that overwhelming. I had made such a huge effort to keep this moment private, even forgoing large offers (more than $200,000) from different media outlets just to keep this event as intimate as possible. That's also why I refused to add it to the reality series. This wasn't a show, this was one of the most important days of my life. I didn't want to hold an event that included cameras, gossip, or having to be extra cautious of what we did or said for fear of it being taken out of context. I didn't want to work on my wedding day. I yearned for this to be our sacred moment, one filled with peace, just for the two of us and our loved ones.

As the driver parked the car in front of the church's majestic entrance, all I could see were bodies. It felt like a stampede was rushing toward us. My jaw dropped as I watched the chaotic spectacle unfold. It wasn't just the media. Since the location had been nationally broadcast, there was also a big gathering of fans who'd come from near and far just to be a part of the event, to catch a glimpse of us—some had been camping out there since the crack of dawn. It was insane. Anxiety started to set in as I wondered how the heck I would make it to the actual church in one piece. The security guards opened the black umbrellas and created a tunnel for me to step into as I exited the car. There was pushing and shoving as cameras tried to get the money shot, and I felt like I was on the verge of a panic attack. I cried so hard when I finally entered the church that I scared my grandma. Then I took several deep breaths and pushed past the initial desolation and fury. They would not ruin this for me. No one would.

I closed my eyes, connected my soul with the presence of God and my momma's energy, shook off the craziness, and locked arms with my grandma as we began to walk down that angelic aisle. A third of the way, she passed me on to Mikey. He walked with me for another stretch and then delivered me to Johnny, who accompanied me to the altar and gave me away to Lorenzo.

Many people have wondered why I didn't ask my grandpa to walk me down the aisle. The truth is that, although I love him very much, I've been sad about my abuelito for a long time. I don't agree with how he handled things with my grandma when they divorced. After forty years, he just stopped taking care of her. That hurt. I respect him and admire what he did for our family, but I've always been closer to my abuelita. She helped raise me. She was there each time my mom and I were on the outs. She never turned her back on me. And without my mom to do me the honor, it felt fitting to ask her and the two most important and steadfast men in my life: my brothers. As much as I wanted a traditional wedding, in this particular detail, staying true to myself came first.

When I joined Lorenzo at the altar, we started giggling with excitement as we walked up to the pastor. My heart felt at peace. The ceremony was beautiful and touching. Since we both envisioned a traditional union, instead of writing our own vows, we decided to give a short speech to each other at the reception. We exchanged our I do's and sealed our wedded bliss with a kiss. Then the pastor presented us as Mr. and Mrs. Lorenzo and Janney Mendez and, with intertwined hands, we walked up the aisle, celebrating with our family and friends and smiling wide. We didn't know what life would have in store for us, but in that moment, all the doubts and fears had melted away and we were genuinely happy.

I had to surpass all the obstacles in my path to know I was ready.

11

TIME TO OUTSHINE THE SHADE

Toxic voices are everywhere: trolls, cyberbullies, thugs, shade throwers. Nowadays, no matter where you turn, especially on social media platforms, it's easy to spot those bad apples. They're the ones who take out their problems on innocent bystanders, the ones who grab a positive post and give it a negative spin. I wish we could wave a magic wand and get rid of these voices from the world. If that were the case, who knows, maybe my momma might still be with us, maybe my family would be more united, maybe we'd all be happier with who we are and what we have to show for ourselves. But that magic wand doesn't exist. So we have to figure out how to deal with this poison ourselves. We have to learn how to identify toxicity before it inflicts harm on us to the point of no return. We have to learn how to distance ourselves from it, ignore it, and sometimes even call it out.

Two days after our wedding, the media went after Lorenzo and me hard. Aside from their anger for not being officially invited to our big day—which led them to crash our ceremony—there was also an incident between one of the security guards and a camera-man. The media used that moment as an excuse to eat us alive, with talk about boycotting the entire Rivera family from their outlets. It had gotten so out of hand that instead of enjoying our first week as newlyweds, Lorenzo and I felt the need to go on Instagram Live and set the record straight. I wasn't about to let them get away with the mistruths and rumors they were spreading. Not once did they stop to think who started all of this. Who leaked the invitation? Who deliberately didn't blur out the date, time, and location on national TV? Who basically invited everyone to crash what was supposed to be a sacred and intimate moment that we had originally planned to hold in private?

Look, I get it, if you're a gossip reporter and you get the scoop on a hot story, it's your job to share it with your audience. But was it really necessary to show the time and place? No. It's that simple. That was malicious and not okay. I wanted an apology. Lorenzo and I had always gone above and beyond with the media. We were never disrespectful. So when they blamed the altercation between the security guard and the cameraman on us, that was the last straw. WTF? We weren't even there. I would've stepped in and tried to de-escalate the situation if I had been present. I always face the music and accept responsibility when called for. But this accountability did not fall on me. I was determined not to let them draw us into this cesspool. That's why we spoke up, shared our truth, and then moved on.

Toxic voices can come in all shapes and sizes. They can be resentful media conglomerates or spiteful people. Clearly, this is not my first rodeo. Some of the people who were around my mom as she rose to fame did her more harm than good, planting seeds of doubt in her mind that made her second-guess herself. Although she was strong, intelligent, and independent, she also allowed herself to be misled by what other people said. For instance, if someone from within her circle told her that a host on a TV show had started some crazy rumor about her that led to outrageous headlines, rather than do her due diligence and check out the episode in question to see exactly what was said, she'd immediately react and storm over to the show's producers to tell them off. Many times the producers would say, "Wait a second, have you actually watched the clip?" That's when she'd realize the headline that spun her into a frenzy was just clickbait. The actual piece didn't merit her reaction. This happened a lot. Her impulsive streak often overpowered her. I watched this play out with her time and again, and I learned that reacting before taking the time to actually see the piece in question only leads to more drama.

There are so many qualities that I admire about my mother, but I'm very intentional about certain traits that I do not want to emulate. Like being impulsive and letting myself get carried away by toxic voices. I fervently believe that this played a role in the demise of our relationship. That's why when people within my circle of friends, family, or coworkers say someone isn't good for me, I acknowledge and store their advice, but I need to get to the bottom of it myself first.

How am I supposed to believe what is said about others after having experienced firsthand all the lies that have been said about me? In my eyes, you are innocent until proven guilty, but I will tell you what's up if something is bothering me. It's a constant battle between my mind and my heart, and sometimes it ends up biting me in the ass, but I stand by it. There's no denying that a lot of people told me Lorenzo wasn't good for me, but my fear of falling for toxic voices pushed me to follow my heart and figure it out on my own. Is this the right way? I don't know. It's my way, based on my past experiences. I don't want to live my life suspecting everyone is out to get me. I'm very intentional with being spiritually connected and remaining as aware as possible with regard to the people who surround me. But don't mistake my kindness for weakness. Once I realize someone is toxic, I will take measures to distance myself. I'm pretty good and quick about cutting off people who are harming me.

Sometimes, it's not just toxic voices we have to worry about, but toxic environments as well. The music industry is amazing, but it can eat you alive and spit you out in the blink of an eye if you don't put in place the necessary precautions to protect yourself. I've seen what it can do to people. It can be quite a dark place if you're not spiritually aligned. It affected my mom's mental health, and, at times, it has affected me too.

In the early days of my career, the pressure was on. Comparisons with my mom abounded, and I had to fight to be seen as a singer embarking on her own path. It really began to take a toll on me. In my music genre, if people aren't drinking at your shows, you're not successful, because the venues that hire us make their main revenue off alcohol sales. The songs themselves are also geared toward drinking; it's the nature of this style of music. When I first hit the stage, I was considerably shy and insecure, so I began to depend on liquid courage to get through my shows. As the months went by and the performances grew more frequent, I started drinking for the wrong reasons, not just to give me a boost of confidence but to numb my pain, and I didn't like it one bit. That's why, by late 2017, I decided I needed a break. A break from drinking, a break from toxic environments, a break from social media, and, ultimately, that break I took from Lorenzo. I needed time to get my head and heart straight, to cleanse myself from the toxicity that had seeped into my life.

When I finally emerged from that self-imposed retreat, I got a much better handle on how to take a swig of tequila onstage for fun, as part of the performance, without it turning into a crutch that would help me get through the show. The temptation to step over that line is there, but knowing I share a more positive part of myself with the audience when I retain that control helps keep me focused. Drinking to cover up emotions can easily lead down a road of no return. That's why I'm intentional about staying connected to God. That spiritual alignment keeps me on the right track and helps me course correct when I start heading down any shady alleys. We have a responsibility with the music we make. I take extra care with the words that I choose to sing because I know they hold power. We have to be a light in the midst of the darkness.

I tried to share all of this with Lorenzo. I explained that one has to be spiritually and mentally prepared before pursuing a career as a solo artist, because it requires discipline and accountability. Contrary to being in a band, when you're a solo artist, everything falls on you. The weight of it all is much heavier, and if you happen to have a weakness or show signs of a problem with alcohol or drugs, it will likely only become exacerbated in this industry. You have to have a handle on your shit. And that's just the start. I don't think he got it at the time. I was hoping to guide him, but I now realize this is a personal journey. Each of us, on our own, has to face our demons and find our true path. To do this, I've made a point in the past few years to surround myself with people who bring me light. This cannot be forced. I don't want people who are just *with* me; they need to be *for* me. There's a huge difference. A lot of people can be *with* you and hang around you, but they're just taking up space. Those who are *for* you are the ones who are interested in your well-being and higher good.

This goes for social media too—another incredibly toxic environment, one that can easily poison our mental health and confidence if we aren't careful. First, there are the comments. The good usually outweighs the bad, but sometimes those negative comments can really sting, especially if you're feeling vulnerable. It's not easy, but since this is part of my job and I use my platform to promote my music and my businesses, and to share my thoughts and parts of my life, then I have to make a conscious effort on the daily to focus on the long list of positive comments. I want to bring light to my followers, instead of reacting to the cyberbullies who hide behind the anonymity provided by their screens. And that's just the first battle, one I don't always win.

Social media can get real dark. If you get caught up in how other people allegedly live, it can take you down a black hole. *Why don't I look like that? Why can't I have that house?* It's important to remember that most of it is either staged or it shows only one side of the story (usually the best side). It's a grand façade. Some influencers might not have enough to pay their rent, but they turn around and charge a $5,000 bag just to keep up appearances so not to lose followers. I know many influencers, and I also know about the tears that are shed behind the scenes of those posts, where they are seemingly living their best lives.

There's a lot of clout on these platforms, but there's also a lot of pressure to post and stay relevant (fun fact: a lot of the cars and the things featured in influencers' posts aren't really theirs to begin with!), and it can take an obsessive turn if you're not careful. I remember once, when I was checking someone's profile, I suddenly thought, *Why does this girl get so many more likes than me when I have more followers?* Yes, I fall prey to these doubts too. If you're scrolling down your feed late at night, it's easy to become overwhelmed by a sense of anxiety that makes you question if you're doing things right, if you should try to imitate some of what you see to pique people's interest.

When you start posting solely for likes, you can easily lose yourself in the process. I've had moments when I've had to check myself before publishing a post because of this. What does society expect from me? What should I do? How should I look? *Fuck that!* I'm quick to stop these thoughts when I get sidetracked. I ask myself, *Wait a second, am I posting to please my followers and get more likes or am I staying true to my essence?*

We're flooded with this sense that we're expected to be perfect, lead perfect lives, and always be happy, and anything less is unacceptable. When I find myself swimming in the deep end of this pool of unhealthy thoughts, I take a break. If you follow me, you've seen it. Sometimes it's for a month, sometimes a week, sometimes a day. Disconnecting from the social media madness and reconnecting with my tangible reality is what keeps me sane. It's my lifeline. It's how I've learned to cope when I get wrapped up in these toxic spaces. This helps me hit the refresh button to avoid becoming one more online robot who mindlessly follows the herd.

I think it's amazing that we can use our platforms to reach so many people, but with it comes great responsibility. I can be a little bit of everything, but at the end of the day, I always remember I have a mission and a purpose, and I need to make sure the substance I communicate is in line with that purpose. I can't allow myself to get lost in that emptiness. An ass picture will get more likes than one of your face with a nice smile and a positive quote. That says a lot. People want to see more ass, more tits. It scares me for the younger generations, actually for all of us. We can easily get lost seeking people's approval, but it's so much more attractive to just be yourself.

What drives me to be so raw and honest on social media is the need for people to know that, at the end of the day, the real beauty lies in our imperfections. Yes, I'm on television, and yes, I have material things (that I worked hard to get, btw), but I'm not always living my best life. I cry. I have bad days. I make mistakes. And that's okay. I'm just another human trying to make sense of this world, just like you. I want to use the platform that God has given me to touch hearts, to reach out to those who are going through crappy days or heartbreaking moments and let them know that they're not alone. When I'm honest and speak up about the difficulties I face in my path, it is so well received. What comes from the heart, reaches the heart; it's as simple as that.

At the end of the day, the people who follow you and like your posts will continue to do so, and there will be others who will drop off. It really doesn't matter. There's more to life than follows and likes. There's more to life than gossip. Bullies can suck it. Use your voice to speak up, to share your truth, to outshine the shade. Don't let toxic voices dictate how you live your life. When dealing with life's bullshit, focus your attention on what's meaningful to you, and keep moving forward. That's what got me through the wedding day fiasco and every other misrepresentation I have had to suffer in the media, and even within my family. My voice, my truth, and my faith set me free.

> *Never allow anything or anyone to dim your light.*

12

HAPPILY EVER AFTER?

I married Lorenzo because I felt like I could be myself with him. I did it because we could talk and laugh and dance together. I did it because I thought we shared the same values. I did it because I believed we could help each other grow. I did it for love.

Lorenzo loved me too. I know it. And he had honestly tried to step up and be the man I needed. But after we tied the knot, things changed. He changed. It almost felt like I was discovering another side of him. I think he had been forcing himself to be someone he's not, and once the deal was done, he didn't have to force it any longer because he was my husband and now I had to put up with him, no questions asked. His problems were now my problems and there was no way out. He never said this verbatim, but it's what I interpreted through his actions, or lack thereof. The little things that made me fall deeper in love with him before we were married—like when he massaged my feet out of nowhere—just stopped. I knew things could change in a marriage, and we could grow apart, but I never thought it would happen so quickly. Wasn't the first year supposed to be marital bliss?

I'd go out of my way to tell him he was handsome, to boost his confidence because I had a feeling he felt inadequate. He had a lot of debt, so I helped him pay off his car and his credit cards. I wanted to help him get a fresh start. I figured what's mine was his, and I was eager to see him succeed. Work had me busier than ever that year. If it wasn't a performance or a recording, it was a meeting for the revamping of Be Flawless, or sitting down to review the pages of what would later become my second book, *Chiquis Keto*. I was thriving and loving it, but when I got home, my husband would say, "Oh, you don't have time for me." This really worried me. I grew up thinking that men who are with busy, independent women usually end up cheating to combat that sense of inferiority. So I went above and beyond to compensate for my busy schedule. I'd wake up and make him his coffee. I complimented him often. I made sure to keep him satisfied. And I cooked for him, even when that meant making two meals because I was sticking to a strict keto lifestyle. I went out of my way to be a good wife, while also handling the needs of my growing career.

Meanwhile, he was sitting around at home playing Fortnite and Clash Royale. The disparity was so obvious that even Vanessa would say, "What thirty-three-year-old guy spends his day playing video games?" This would spring me into defense mode. "Just leave him alone," I would say. "As long as I know that he's there and not doing anything bad, I'm fine with it." Red flags be gone. I covered up with excuses what I knew deep down was not right. And I'm not saying he had to go out and become the main breadwinner. I just wanted him to have a plan, a vision, the ambition to get off the couch and go work for his goals, or to simply take out the trash without having to be told, like a little boy.

Two months after the wedding, I found out through my social media manager that at our reception, Lorenzo and some of his friends were partying way harder than I thought. He said he saw Lorenzo and his friends offering coke to the other guys. I had made him promise that he wouldn't do that. Disappointment settled into my heart. I began to silently drag around the weight of it all, and it was so painful. I know how to put up with a lot. I have a high tolerance for other people's issues because I try to empathize with them, forgive them. I believe in second chances because none of us are perfect. A relationship requires love but also compromise. It means every day we wake up wanting to make it work because we choose to be with that person. But it's a two-way street. Each person has to do their part. It took me a while to realize this. Instead, I began to carry our load of problems on my own and suppress my emotions. Maybe we were just adjusting to married life . . . maybe I just needed to give him a little more time . . . maybe I was being too hard on him . . . maybe . . .

That summer, we had a trip to Israel planned with his mom and sister, but I wasn't feeling it. Something urged me to stay home, but I didn't want to disappoint his family, so we hopped on a plane—first stop: Greece. That week was a blur of fights and misery. *What am I even doing here?* Then we flew to Israel. I had been looking forward to this for months. I had heard it was a magical place, but it went beyond my expectations. No matter what you're going through, it's hard not to connect to that land on a spiritual level. The tension between us began to ease, and we decided to get baptized together in the Jordan River, to cleanse our souls and start fresh together. His alcohol and drug issues had begun to take over his life, so to celebrate our new beginning, inspired by Jesus's forty-day fast after his own baptism, I said, "Why don't we do a forty-day cleanse?" He totally agreed, and relief washed over me. Maybe this was our shot to press the reset button on our marriage.

Back home, we continued to stick to our cleanse. We both gave up alcohol. I also avoided coffee and was following a pescatarian diet. We were in good spirits and once again getting along smoothly. But before our forty days were up, Lorenzo was called to do a show in Mexico City. I was in the middle of filming the talent show *Tengo Talento* as one of the judges, so I couldn't go with him. But it was fine. We were both working, we seemed to be getting to a better place in our relationship, so what more could I ask for?

On an October afternoon while he was away, I was in my seat on the show's set when an incredibly strange feeling began to course through my body. It was like something was trying to attack me, and I was thrust into fight-or-flight mode. Then it was replaced by a deep sadness. I was told that this cleanse could cause these types of spiritual earthquakes, but knowing this and experiencing it is a different story. I quickly grabbed my phone and texted Lorenzo. I really needed to connect with him. He replied, worried, and said, "Call me as soon as you're out of your chair." Slightly relieved, I wiped away the tears that were rolling down my cheeks, put my phone away, and pulled myself together for the show, unable to completely shake this weird feeling.

When I was done, I immediately dialed his number. No answer. Strange. He knew what time the show ended; he knew my schedule. *Maybe he fell asleep?* I called him again on my way home. Nothing. Then I called him when I got home. Nada. "Lorenzo, what are you doing? Why aren't you answering my calls. I really need to talk to you," I texted. I reiterated that I had never felt like this before and was a little scared. I waited. The minutes ticked by with no reply. *Did something happen to him?* Despite the twelve hours I had just spent working on set, I couldn't catch a wink of sleep. Two of my friends came over and spent the night with me in my room because I was afraid to be by myself. I finally dozed off at five in the morning and woke up at nine-thirty to the sound of my ringing phone.

"Why didn't you answer my calls?" I asked Lorenzo when I picked up.

"I failed you."

My heart dropped. *Shit, he cheated on me.*

"What do you mean, you failed me?" I said.

"I'm on my way home."

"Wait, where are you?"

"I'm here. I just landed. I'm in an Uber on my way home," he replied.

Then I started to get pissed off. "You saw my messages, you saw my missed calls, and you got on the fucking plane without so much as a text to me?" My worry turned to fury.

"Yes," he said. "I'll be there soon."

Those thirty or forty minutes it took him to get from LAX to our home felt like days. My mind was reeling and my emotions were through the roof. So I called Pastor Dad.

"Oh my god, I think he cheated."

He tried to calm me down, urged me not to jump to conclusions. I was so scared, but I left it in God's hands.

Lorenzo walked through the door looking totally depleted, as if he hadn't slept a wink. And he reeked of alcohol.

"I failed you," he said again.

"Did you cheat on me?"

"No, I didn't. I failed you, Janney," he repeated and started crying. "I'm sorry."

"But did you see my messages? You knew I was going through something."

Yes, he did see my texts, my missed calls, but instead of answering, he flipped his phone over and decided to talk to me later.

Something shifted in my heart that day. *I can't count on this asshole.* I couldn't count on him for money or for stability, but I married him anyway, thinking he would at least take care of my heart. *This isn't going to work*. That was the first time this thought crept into my mind since our wedding.

He not only disregarded my feelings that day, he also broke our pact. We were just one week shy of the end of our forty-day cleanse. Seven days, that was it. But he didn't make it. That's what he meant when he said he'd failed me. This brought to light another thing that had been bothering me for a while: he couldn't finish what he started; he couldn't keep his word. These issues were part of a bigger problem: his addiction.

We'd been down this road before and had even reached a point of acceptance. He acknowledged he had a problem, but then he put it all on me. "Oh, why are you tripping? This is a disease. You need to help me. Call rehab for me, call counseling."

"No," I replied firmly during that conversation. "Those are calls you need to make." He expected me to take him by the hand and lead him to recovery, but that's not how recovery works. "No, Lorenzo, this is your journey," I tried to explain to him time and again. "If I do that, then you're going to resent me later. This has to come from you." He never understood that. He interpreted it as a lack of support, while all I was trying to do was help him.

That day in October was a before and after. It wasn't just that I couldn't count on him, I honestly had the feeling that he cheated on me while he was away. I kept replaying what he'd said about the night before in my mind. If he was awake all night with his friends and I was telling him I had been overcome by such a strong emotion and needed to simply hear his voice, why avoid me? I wasn't even mad at that point. And now that he was back, something shifted in his demeanor. I can't pinpoint it, and I will likely never be able to prove it, but my sixth sense was tingling, and it was hard to ignore.

As the weeks trudged along, I had to dim my light to make sure he felt okay, and that began to eat me up inside. When you're with the wrong person and you ignore all the cues, the energy of that constant sadness and quiet tension sucks you dry. Then came our White Party in December. I invited people from the music industry, a lot of my friends, his friends, and cousins. It was supposed to be our end-of-the-year bash, a moment to celebrate and relax. And he did it again. He offered someone coke at our party . . . in our house. I was furious, embarrassed, and felt so helpless.

The next day, we were supposed to pick up his daughter together, but he decided to stay home because he didn't want to deal with my anger, so I went with his friend's wife instead. During our ride, I felt so overwhelmed that I brought it up to her. "You know what, I never talk to you about this, but I'm miserable. I'm married to a little boy. I am married to a little boy." I kept repeating that last phrase because it was suddenly sinking in. I didn't care if she told her husband. "I am miserable, I am sad, and he is eating me up alive. I don't know what else to do. I keep trying and he keeps disappointing me." I even talked about the drug issue with her. She let me get it all off my chest and then said, "I totally understand. Why don't you tell him to go to rehab, give him an ultimatum? I know he loves you so much."

I needed to vent, but I was also looking for reassurance. *Is it me? Am I the one fucking it up somehow?* My own issues and insecurities came into play, but they were exacerbated by his reverse psychology. Somehow, he always managed to blame whatever he did on me. His go-to phrases still resonate in my mind: "You're so controlling. You're so jealous. You're so insecure. You need to stop taking out your insecurities on me." He mind-fucked me so much that I started looking at myself differently in the mirror. I began to wonder if he was right. No one had ever shaken my confidence like that in my life. Maybe it was because I actually cared about what he thought, and I loved him. This mental back-and-forth was driving me insane.

Throughout the holidays, I began to bring up my sadness and disappointment with my friends, planting little seeds to be remembered later. They still recall how miserable I was. But I was married, so I felt I had an obligation to make it work. I also loved him deeply, more than anyone before.

January 2020 came along—new year, new us, maybe? I wasn't convinced, but I was trying. We sailed through that month with our usual big blowups followed by stalemates. This was my best friend, someone I connected with on another level. I could be my raw self with him, and I didn't want to give that up. So I kept turning a blind eye to our unresolved issues, hoping something would eventually click and we'd finally figure it out. Yet, as the weeks passed, I became quietly devastated. I couldn't count on him, and that worried me for the long haul. Lorenzo was signed to a record label, but he wasn't happy with how it was going. He complained that they didn't listen to him or take his ideas seriously. He said he wanted to be an independent artist, but he wouldn't come to terms with the fact that this path takes a lot of money. I was already helping him a bit, but I didn't have hundreds of thousands of dollars to invest in this gamble. I encouraged him to take action, but he did nothing. I found brands that were willing to work with him, but he turned them down, saying, "I'm a musician. I don't do brands," and I'd end up looking bad with these companies. The problem was that his career wasn't his main source of income, so he had to figure something out to bring some money into our household. That's why, when he brought up having kids, I'd say, "How are we going to have a baby if you don't even know what you want in life?" Getting pregnant meant putting my career on a standstill for nine months plus the time it would take to get my body right again. How could I do that without him pitching in financially?

Then March 2020 hit. The world was brought to its knees because of Covid-19, and life came to a screeching halt. We didn't quite grasp the gravity of the situation at the time. I think most of us thought we'd be home for a couple of weeks and then everything would go back to normal. Masks and social distancing weren't even a thing yet. So, we decided to make the most of our time at home by throwing a small house party. Things went south real quick that day. Lorenzo got wasted. He was doing coke in the back of the house, and once again he offered my friends some lines, which they turned down. When you're married, there are certain things you don't share with everyone in order to protect your partner, so his coke offering really brought his problem out in the open and put me in an awkward and embarrassing spot.

Once the party died down, and most of our friends had left, the remaining little group went inside to hang out and unwind. As we were chatting away, someone came in through the back door. We looked at him, puzzled. "Everyone left me behind!" he whined, clearly drunk. He was someone we knew who had been at the party, but I couldn't help but wonder where he'd been while we were saying our goodbyes to the rest of the guests. Was he in the back of the house? In the office? A friend of ours, who was still there, was also a little concerned, so he said to Lorenzo, "Why don't we go check and make sure he didn't take anything." Lorenzo, who was still coked out of his mind, didn't know we knew this guy, and instead of playing it cool, he lunged at him like a monster. I immediately jumped to my feet and stopped him, saying, "Relax, he's fine. Just let him go." The guy quickly stumbled out the front door without saying a word, but Lorenzo went after him again. "Leave him alone!" I screamed.

"What the fuck were you doing in my house?" yelled Lorenzo, getting up in his face.

The guy was wasted and didn't understand what he was talking about. The next thing I knew, Lorenzo took a swing that landed the poor guy straight on the floor. I was furious. He'd lost it. We were in quarantine, and we weren't even supposed to be having a party. What if someone recorded him? He was drunk, high on coke, and he'd just hit one of our guests, who didn't even fight back. I couldn't believe it. I started hitting him to make him snap the fuck out of it. Then I dragged his ass inside the house, and now I was the one who lost it. One of our friends quickly stepped in and pushed me away, because I was ready to get in Lorenzo's face and let him have it. Meanwhile, the guy outside finally managed to peel himself off the ground and leave, while nursing his busted lip.

As if that wasn't enough, Johnny had witnessed everything and exploded. He started yelling at Lorenzo, "Calm the fuck down, dude!"

"This is my house!" yelled Lorenzo.

"No, this isn't your house!" replied Johnny.

"Stop, Johnny," I pleaded. "Please, just let me handle this." I always wanted Lorenzo to feel comfortable in the house, to know that it was his home too, but he had an issue with it because I was the one who bought it.

Even though Johnny had never really liked Lorenzo, he respected him and was cordial because of me, but he wasn't able to hold back that night. After all, he carried the responsibility of giving me away at the altar, and he took that to heart. On our wedding day, he gave Lorenzo his most prized possession, and he expected him to take care of me as such. That night, Johnny was beyond disappointed. He was hurt, something broke for him right then and there, and after he snapped, he stormed off to his room.

I sat down on the couch, miserable. The first three weeks of quarantine had been so blissful. The three of us had such a nice time; we were getting along great, cooking together, hanging out, and watching movies. We really bonded as a family. I thought we were finally getting somewhere, and then it all just went to shit.

That's when Lorenzo went in on me. He started screaming, "How could you defend that guy?" I was done. I had no fight left in me. So, I apologized. "I'm sorry that I got upset. I'm sorry that I hit you." He was so drunk and high that there was no reasoning with him, no room for a logical conversation, so I figured I should just patch things up and we could talk later. It was a temporary fix, but it worked. We all calmed down and went back to chatting, when suddenly, Lorenzo got up and pulled his pants down in front of me and the two couples who were still there with us. I didn't know where to look. It was so embarrassing. Coke turned him into a little buffed-up devil with no filters and no limits, and I hated it.

Eventually, I decided to call it a night. I said my goodbyes and went upstairs to my room and fell asleep. At around three in the morning, that same night, I woke up and something made me check the security cameras. When I did, I noticed Lorenzo was trying to sneak out of the house. He knew where the cameras were, of course, so he was tiptoeing out the side door with a friend. Why did I wake up right then and there? I don't know. But I stormed down the stairs, fuming, and reached him as he was climbing into his friend's truck. I made them both get out of the truck and gave them an earful, like a mom with rebellious teens. "You guys aren't going anywhere; we're in quarantine."

"But we're just gonna buy beer."

"No!" I ripped each of them a new asshole, and they came inside.

"You always tell me what to do!" screamed Lorenzo. But I ignored his whining and walked them to the studio at the back of the house.

"Stay in here. You guys aren't going anywhere," I said.

A switch flipped in Lorenzo, and he sprung into attack mode again. But this time, I was the target.

"Lorenzo, sit down," I said, trying to keep calm. But he came at me, wrapped his hands around my neck, and started to choke me, and then he spit in my face. Johnny watched everything go down from his bedroom window, which had a clear view of this area of the house, so he rushed down with a big barbell in one hand, ready to charge at Lorenzo to defend me. That's when Lorenzo let me go.

"Johnny, please," I yelled. "You're gonna make it worse. Stop, Johnny, please. He's drunk. Stop."

Then Lorenzo turned his eyes on Johnny, ready to fuck him up too, but Johnny went back to his room. Then I grabbed a vodka bottle and threw it at the wall. Lorenzo finally took off and didn't come back until later that morning.

I was in pieces. I honestly thought that was the end. But when he came back, what followed were his waves of excuses. "I was drunk. I didn't know what I was doing." Blah, blah, blah. Funnily enough, he never admitted that he'd been coked out of his mind. He'd always deny it, then say, "Yeah, but it was just a little bit. But I never buy it; they give it to me." There was always a solid reason behind the magical appearance of coke. It just happened to be there. *Yeah, and you just happened to snort it,* I thought.

"Okay, then you need to stop drinking," I said. "I'll do it with you." We agreed to do another cleanse together. And we forged ahead yet again.

Alcohol and coke are like best friends. They balance each other out so you can continue to consume both of them all night long, so I figured if we took one out of the equation, he'd be clean from the other too. I also figured that, knowing his problem with drinking, I had to step up and stop drinking with him, stop feeding into his disease. I knew what he did to me was not okay, but I accepted his excuses, hoping this was the rock bottom he needed to finally get his shit together.

That was March.

April was our dry month. A sudden sense of peace and quiet followed our tsunami. We had fallen back into our pattern, trying to make it work, feeling better, reconnecting. But it was a false sense of hope. The calm before the next storm.

I had organized a Cinco de Mayo party at home, but was thinking of canceling it because, even though I wasn't the one with the problem, I wanted to support Lorenzo and help him stay sober. I had heard what my sister Jacqie and her friend had said to me, "If you know his problem, then you need to be a better wife." I didn't want to add fuel to the fire. But I didn't cancel. Maybe a part of me wanted to test him. Maybe it was just that I needed to let loose and have some fun after more than a month of quarantining at home. Regardless, that party was the beginning of the end.

Rather than fret over his behavior and worry about what he was up to when he went to the back of the house, I simply ignored him. I'd basically thrown in my towel. I no longer gave a shit anymore, and that bothered him. When he grabbed the mic to sing with the grupo we'd hired for our gathering, he shoved it in my face "playfully," but, really, he was trying to pick a fight. He knew I was upset. I remained standoffish with him, which made him come over even more to give me a kiss and show off his love for me. Then he dedicated songs to me, which felt fake, like a front to make our guests believe he was a good husband. My level of annoyance was through the roof. *Just leave me alone,* I thought. *You know that we're not okay. You're fucking with me.* He did this so much that I reached my limit. We could be on no-speaking terms at home, but then he'd comment on one of my posts, "Oh, my sexy baby," and add heart emojis. I wouldn't respond because we were in the middle of a fight, but then who looked like the crazy, bitter bitch in public? He was great at faking through his funk, which is what he was doing at our party.

This was irritating Johnny too. He and Lorenzo hadn't been on good terms since March. The tension was thick at home. Quick to react to Lorenzo's foolishness, Johnny went upstairs and came down wearing his 27 hat (which was Angel's logo) just to mess with him. When Lorenzo saw him, his demeanor shifted. He stared Johnny down, and I immediately noticed that Lorenzo was ready to pounce. I sprang toward him and quietly, yet fiercely said, "Don't you do that, because if you do, it's something I will never be able to forgive." The tension left his face, and we enjoyed the rest of the party as best we could.

May went downhill from there. We were fighting a lot, and Lorenzo was in and out of the house. He and Johnny were no longer on speaking terms, and I felt stuck in the middle, trying to reconcile my son with my husband, all while attempting to figure out what to do about my marriage. It weighed heavy on my heart. "You need to fix things," I'd say to Lorenzo, to which he'd respond, "Well, he doesn't like me." And that would inevitably lead to another one of our blowups. And then he left. He was gone for the last two weeks of May, out of the house, out of sight. I thought it was finally over, but then he asked if we could talk in person. We met at a sushi place. I purposefully chose a public space to de-escalate the situation, because I didn't think he'd like what I had to say.

"I want a divorce," I said, looking him straight in the eyes. I was very respectful and calm. "I know you love me. I love you too. But I want a divorce."

He was super pissed but kept his cool. Then he said, "I'm going to stay in the back room because I'm still married to you. I'm not leaving the house until you divorce me." He added that he wasn't going to return my car either, because "I'm your husband."

"Okay . . ." At that point I didn't care about the car. I wasn't going to call the police, like some friends suggested. He needed it, and I had another one. It was fine. I wasn't out to destroy him. I just wanted to end this toxic relationship. It wasn't doing either of us any good.

The day after I told him I wanted a divorce, he partied the night away. Someone recorded him completely wasted, and it was splashed across all media platforms. I think that was a mini wake-up call for him. He realized that if he didn't get his act together, the public would come down on him hard. That's when he decided to check himself into rehab.

I found out through a friend. *Oh shit, he's really going,* I thought. It was a step in the right direction. To be honest, it gave me a sliver of hope. You don't stop loving someone overnight. I saw him through the window when he came over to pack his stuff, and I went downstairs to help him.

"I know we're not together," I said, as I folded some of his shirts and put them in his bag, "but I want you to know that I support you. I'm here for you. I'm very proud of you." I was truly moved. Could this be the fresh start we needed? Had the tide finally turned? When his friend came to pick him up, we said a tearful goodbye, and, moved beyond words, I let down my guard and we hugged.

Those first two weeks while he was away in rehab, I really missed him. I cried a lot; it was almost cathartic. Despite the suffering, I felt so much peace knowing that he was somewhere safe. It also gave me the opportunity to reconnect with myself. It helped me realize, *Okay, I can be alone.* But I won't deny it, seeds of hope were planted with his decision. *Maybe he'll come back different. Maybe we'll be able to make this work.* I still loved him a lot.

Each day I prayed, I meditated, and I made sure to support him in his journey to recovery. I helped pay for this treatment to make sure he could go. I answered every call he made from rehab. My phone was basically stuck to my hand at all times because I wanted him to know I was there for him, that I wasn't doing anything bad, and that I wasn't taking advantage of him being away. I aimed to give him peace so that he could focus on himself. Each time we spoke, I assured him, "I'm fine, you don't have to worry about me." I wrote him letters. I sent him a care package with clothes and books. I talked to his counselor. I did what I would've liked to experience had I been in his shoes. Unlike what he said a few months later in an interview, we did talk, I was there, he wasn't alone, and I supported him through and through.

Then June 26 came along. It was my birthday, and I needed to get away. So I rented a house in Ensenada and invited my girlfriends. I wasn't planning a girls gone wild trip, far from it. I just needed some quality time with my friends, a much-needed breather from my current reality. As I started to relax into the weekend vibe, my phone rang. It was Lorenzo.

"You're with these girls, and I don't know what you're doing," he said, flipping out. "You're drinking too much. I'm worried about you."

"Wait a second," I replied. "I know you're in rehab and you're trying to fix this issue, but I'm fine. I'm a responsible woman just celebrating her birthday."

I knew he was feeling insecure because I was out, but I was just spending time with my girls at a house overlooking the sea. I wasn't the one in rehab; I wasn't the one with the problem. How could celebrating my birthday be a bad thing? And why call me to make a scene and ruin it for me?

Then he said, "I want to get out early. I want to celebrate our wedding anniversary together."

"Lorenzo, no. You have to complete your stay. You have to see this through. You have to finish something. This is important to me too. As much as I'd like you to be here for my birthday and for our wedding anniversary, for me, as your wife, it's important to see that you are finally starting something and finishing it." I kept trying to get this point across, but he was obsessing over what I was doing in Ensenada. "I'm with my friends. I'm answering your call. The only guy here is JP, Helen's husband. Other than that, it's just us girls. Lorenzo, please."

That just triggered one of our now classic fights, and, while we were in the thick of it, I thought, *Oh no, he's still the same person. He's just been disguising it.* We hung up, and I did my best to shake it off. I was determined to enjoy the weekend regardless of his hissy fit.

Once I got back from my birthday getaway, he convinced me to pick him up at the recovery center three days shy of completing his full month. I drove over carefully, making deliberate turns to make sure no one was tailing me. The last thing we needed was a media circus. When I confirmed that the coast was clear, I entered the center, which was thankfully far removed from the street. I was hoping to have a calm conversation with him. I wanted to say, "Look, I'm with you, but you still scare me. I'm still worried. I think you still need to work on yourself. I think we should still be separated." I had it all planned out, but when I saw him it all flew out the window. He seemed like a changed man. It stopped me in my tracks. We hugged, got in the car, and drove to San Diego. I had booked a hotel room down there because I thought it was a neutral space that would serve us better at this crossroads in our relationship. No one knew about this except for my assistant. I told everyone else in my close circle that I was going to a different location. I lied because I didn't want to risk the media getting wind of where we were. We desperately needed this quiet time together to talk things out and figure out our next steps. It was an intimate and private moment, and I wanted to keep it that way. I was so adamant about this that, during our drive, I kept checking to see if anyone was following. Nada. The coast was clear.

Meanwhile, Lorenzo was talking up a storm, about his spiritual awakening at rehab, his life plans, and how inspired he felt. And I slowly went from thinking, *I don't want to be with you* to *Oh my god, this is all I've ever wanted, for you to have a plan.* I couldn't believe my ears. I thought something had finally clicked within him. I would no longer have to tell him what to do. He now had a plan for his life, for us, and for the future that was lucrative, could bring us financial stability, and would also help with his sobriety. My heart swelled with joy and relief.

He wanted to open a rehab center and launch a related clothing line. Inspired by his enthusiasm and change, I was all in. We'd been down this road before with no luck. He knew I had a certain amount of money I wanted to invest, and, in the past, when I had suggested we do a business together and asked him, "What kind of business would make you happy, would make you feel good?" he said a bar and grill. "Lorenzo, how am I going to open up a bar and grill for you if you have a problem with alcohol?" Those conversations always ended with a fight. This was the first time I said, "Fuck yeah. I'll invest hundreds of thousands of dollars in this. I believe in it. We'll be partners, and we'll bring in the friend you made at rehab." It was an idea that finally made sense. He was so enthusiastic that he started wondering if he should give an interview to announce this plan, but I suggested, "Write a book first." He could use that to get into all the details of his journey and how this idea came about. It would also give him time to continue to work on his sobriety, while we began to drum up a business plan and work on the opening.

Happily Ever After?

I was hyped up, happy, I couldn't believe this was finally happening. We reached San Diego and the good streak continued. He was once again the sweet man I had fallen in love with. He even set his phone aside and wasn't taking any selfies (and he's a selfie queen!). He woke up at seven each morning and got on his knees to pray. He spent time outside reading his books. And I just observed him in awe. Those first two weeks were absolute heaven. *My prayers have been answered*, I thought. The look in his eyes, the way he was expressing himself, the way he was so patient with me if I felt a little sad or a little worried that this was too good to be true, it was everything I had hoped for and more. If I needed reassurance, he was there. He didn't get angry; he was so patient. It was beautiful.

Then it happened. He insisted we go out. I really didn't feel like it, but I did it for him. He was jumpy, worried about his outfit. "It doesn't matter," I said. "We're just going downstairs to sit on the beach." I watched him get dressed up, but I didn't bother to put on any makeup or anything. Why? It was just us. When we were walking by the ocean, I saw him: a paparazzo, camera in hand, snapping away at us. *What the hell?!* My heart sank. The last thing we needed were headlines splashed across the media saying we'd reconciled (they had already caught wind that we were on a break).

We scrambled back to the hotel. Upset doesn't even begin to cover it. He tried blaming my team for the leak. The same team who zipped their mouths while he was in rehab and publicly called it "a spiritual retreat." The team who said nothing about his alcoholism and his use of coke. Why would they leak this? I still think it may have come from his side. They had details no one could've known, like how we'd hugged when I picked him up at the rehab center. No one should've been able to see us there, yet somehow they were able to describe that hug. I don't know, maybe he thought the pressure from the media saying that we were back together would push me to not go through with the separation. What he didn't know was that he was shooting himself in the foot by pulling that maneuver and trying to take control of the narrative. I'll never know for sure if it was him, but, in retrospect, there was more than one occasion since we'd known each other where the media conveniently showed up when least expected. This is me speculating now, but it's also where my head went even back then.

Now that our location was discovered, we packed our things and headed back home. That's when we tested positive for Covid-19. Trying to put a positive spin on this downward spiral, I thought, *Maybe fifteen days just by ourselves at home, with no one else around, will help us come full circle.* We nursed ourselves back to health, and Lorenzo continued to hang on to his sobriety. It was a positive sign in my eyes, but then he started to slip in his recovery. He wasn't reading his books as much, and I was once again the wife pushing him to do more to stay on track, yet he was making small yet crucial changes, like sharing his location when he left the house, so that we could work on building back our trust. And I appreciated that immensely. Now I needed him to make amends with Johnny.

Once we were Covid negative again, Johnny came back to the house, but he made it clear that he wanted out. I kept telling him, "He's different, just give him a chance." But Johnny wasn't buying it. He stopped talking to me; he'd walk by and ignore me just to make his point. It broke my heart to feel Johnny so distant, but I also thought Lorenzo deserved another shot since he was putting in the work.

When I talked to Johnny about this recently, he said, "When the fight happened in March, I didn't like the feeling I got at all. It's when I finally saw Lorenzo for who he is. Then I started to put other pieces together throughout April, May, and June. And by July, when you got back from San Diego, I kept thinking, *How the fuck does she not see it? It's right in front of her face.* And I wanted to tell you, *You're fucking things up; you're fucking things up again.*"

But he didn't, not in those words. He did say he thought Lorenzo was a master manipulator. It was a possibility, I couldn't deny it, but I still thought we had a shot at saving our marriage. Then his old habits started creeping back into his daily behavior. I continued to be patient. I spoke to him lovingly, saying, "Lorenzo, I don't want you to get mad. I want you to be okay. But I'm seeing little things that worry me. You don't have a sponsor. You haven't gone to any of your meetings. You're not reading your books anymore. This is all the stuff you told me you had to do now, but you've stopped doing them. You aren't even praying as much." No matter how careful I tried to be with my tone, my demeanor, and my words, it just blew up in my face. He'd get defensive, I'd point out I was trying to be a supportive wife, and then a fight would follow.

I wanted to bring up the Johnny issue with him again because I knew that, as the days went by, Johnny was more open to the idea of talking, so I approached Lorenzo and said, "I think you should text him, I think you should try."

"But what if he ignores me?"

"I know you're afraid of rejection, but this is important to me. This is my kid. I need you to be okay with him."

"He's not your kid, he's your brother." He always liked to point this out, and he followed it with, "I wouldn't care if you didn't talk to one of my sisters."

But he didn't have the same close bond with his siblings that I shared with mine. He didn't raise his sisters. I raised Johnny and Jenicka. Yes, they're my siblings, but I took care of them like they were my kids. When my mom passed away, Johnny was only eleven years old, and I stepped back into his life after a few months of separation and picked up where I had left off. So, yes, he's my brother, but he will always be my kid too. And Lorenzo couldn't play dumb with me because he knew this from the beginning.

When the "he's your brother" argument got him nowhere, he'd revert to "I don't feel respected by him." To which I would reply, "Respect is not just given, it's earned." It was a never-ending loop that got us nowhere. I hated being stuck in the middle. I wanted to save my marriage, but this was my kid we were talking about. When he had issues with his daughter, I did everything in my power to help them patch things up because I knew how important it was to him. But when the tables were turned, all he cared about was himself. It was very selfish.

July and August were transition months. I was hoping his changes would stick, and I was waiting patiently to see if we could make it work. Then Lorenzo began to worry about his career. He saw a video on social media of a well-known banda singing at a party and his face fell. He asked me, "Do you think people forgot about me? Do you think I'm no longer cool? Am I getting old? Does being married make me look older?"

"What are you talking about? No." It seemed like he wished he was there with them instead of at home with me. He denied it when I asked, but it was written between the lines and I was reading him clearly. Things got worse after that.

He'd finally landed a job at a radio show but was frustrated with his schedule. He didn't like having to wake up at a specific hour to go to work. He preferred getting up and doing whatever he wanted with his time. But he was getting paid, so he did feel a little more financially secure. I had also gotten him three brands to promote, so the checks were coming in for that too, which helped feed his confidence. He said he felt powerful when he had money, so I naturally figured this income would make him feel good and help with his sobriety. Yet, no matter how much I helped him get ahead, no matter how many ideas I shared, or what I did to push him forward, he'd say that I didn't support his career. I was tired of all the whining and did my best to let it slide, but it came to the forefront yet again when I bought myself a Cartier bracelet. It was a gift to myself, something I bought with my own hard-earned cash, but it bothered him.

"You deserve it, of course, but that money could be used for other things."

"Like what?" I said, bordering on defiant. "All the bills are paid, I just paid off your mom's truck in El Paso, and all my credit cards are paid. So, if I want to buy myself a treat, I think I deserve it—"

"No, you deserve it, but I just feel like you don't support my career."

"Well, what do you want?" I asked, annoyed.

"Oh, I don't know, maybe you could like give me a loan. I don't want to depend on you. I want to be free."

"Okay, wait, but you're married, so you can't really be free or independent because marriage means we do things together."

He conveniently did not acknowledge this last phrase and kept pushing for me to give him a loan, so he could invest in his career and record a high-quality solo album. I had signed with Universal a year earlier, so that I didn't have to invest in my singing career for a change. As much as I loved his gifted voice and believed in his talent, I knew what a huge risk it was to put all that money into making an album. It's a big gamble, because there's no way of telling if it will be a hit or a flop, and I knew how much hard work and effort it takes to push for even a little bit of success. Plus, with unresolved addictive behaviors, I didn't think he was strong enough to deal with such a cutthroat industry on his own. I really wanted him to focus on his sobriety and getting himself okay mentally, emotionally, and spiritually before diving back into this career.

"Lorenzo, you're switching shit on me. The only reason I decided to get back with you is because you had a plan, because I felt safe." I had caught a glimpse of that sense of stability and security that I had been yearning for, and that inspired me to stick around. Plus, I'd already agreed to invest my money in his rehab center idea. Two weeks after we talked about it, I had opened an entity for it. He was a 50 percent shareholder with me. I was all in. It was for a good cause and would hold him accountable in terms of his sobriety. But he started backpedaling on this, saying he wasn't sure he wanted to write a book or commit to talking so openly about his sobriety yet. He wanted to leave the door open to having a drink with me down the road and not be judged by anyone because of it. So he suggested we start with the clothing line instead of the center.

"How are you going to start with the line when there's no mission behind it?" I laid it out for him: "Your book comes first, then the rehab center, then the clothing line." He could say all he wanted about my issues in our relationship, but business is my middle name. I've proven time and again that once I have a vision, I do everything in my power to manifest it.

Yet he continued to pull away from that business idea. So then I laid out a plan for him that included music. "Come out with the center and clothing line, get a real handle on your sobriety, then release a badass album and we'll push it." As a businesswoman, I didn't feel it was feasible to invest in an album first, based on where he was standing.

"Well, that's the problem," he said. "You're seeing me as a business and not as your husband."

OMG, there was no way of getting through to him. I was looking out for him. I never said I wouldn't support him, but I wasn't about to put my money into something I didn't think was well planned.

"Lorenzo, I'm a businesswoman, I've worked so hard to get where I am. And when it comes to such a big investment, I've learned the hard way that I need to be smart. I need to set aside my emotions and see if I think the plan is feasible. From a business perspective, I can see that you're not disciplined, you're not responsible, you're not a man of your word, and you have an addiction problem. So why the fuck would I invest money in you? Because I love you? Because you're my husband? And then what?"

I was brutally honest, but he kept repeating the phrase that worked best for him, "You have to support me as my wife." That's what he meant when he later began to say in interviews that I didn't support his career. Really? Guess who paid for the "No me medí" video he shot back in February 2020? Guess who paid for hair and makeup? I even directed the photo shoot. And what was he doing on set while filming that video? Drinking and doing coke. That's where I drew the line and when I decided to stop investing in his career because it was almost like investing in his addiction.

Up until then, no matter how mad we got at each other, we didn't stop wearing our wedding rings. But as this conversation unfolded, he took off his ring for the first time. For three days, his ring finger was bare. He also chose to stay in the guest room. I was working, so when I got home from my twelve-hour call each night, we'd have these long and exhausting conversations.

Our feelings were raw and exposed, but we were going nowhere. Then he suggested couples therapy, and I said, "I'm not going to call the therapist or counselor. If you really mean it, then you do it." I was so sick of always taking the initiative. I needed him to take charge and show me he meant what he said. Nothing happened. He never called.

During one of our last conversations, I suddenly sensed he was one foot in and one foot out of the relationship. I hadn't felt that before with him. It was like he was trying to say that he wanted to leave, feel free, liberated, but he didn't have the balls to verbalize it.

Meanwhile, I started thinking, praying, and searching for an answer, for the right next move. I was giving myself time. Then he was asked to go to Arizona with the radio show he was working on, and he planned to merge that with a stop in El Paso to visit his family. It was the first time he'd be flying without me post-rehab, and I was feeling insecure about this.

"You can't go to Arizona without me," I said.

"What do you mean? I don't like how that sounds or how that makes me feel. I want to feel free—"

"I don't trust you yet. We're not there."

He went anyway, of course. He had to for work. But when he got back, he was acting different. His attitude had changed. One night, when we got intimate . . . we couldn't even finish.

Then, he confessed, "I feel that my career would do better if I weren't with you." I'll never forget that. I went to my office and prayed. Then we talked again.

"What do you want to do, Janney?"

"Look, Lorenzo, I love you very much, and I want this to work, and I think that I've shown you this, but I don't feel like you want to be in the relationship anymore." The conversation was long and drawn out, and by the end of it, I said, "I think we should go our separate ways."

"Okay, Janney," he said, looking me straight in the eye without arguing to the contrary. He kissed my forehead, grabbed my hand, and added, "Let's pray together. I'm always going to love you. If this is what you want, I'm going to respect it. But could you just tell me again why this is happening? And this is your decision, right?"

"No, this is our decision," I replied calmly, "because you're not willing to do the work I need in order to trust you again. You haven't gone to your meetings and you haven't made amends. I've been telling you to—"

"No, no, no . . . I just wanted to know why. I respect your decision. I just wanted to know, so that when people ask me, I know how to respond."

I was absolutely drained and barely had the energy to react to this last infuriating comment.

"I'm not doing this," I said and went to my room. Within the hour, he started packing his belongings and putting them in a truck he'd rented.

As I watched this unfold, I decided to leave before he was done because I couldn't handle seeing him go. I met up with a friend for a bite to eat and tears began to streak my face like incessant rain. Then I got a text from him: "Something's telling me that I shouldn't leave, that I should stay."

"I don't know what to tell you," I replied.

No answer.

I got home to find everything that he possessed gone, even his Listerine; and his junk drawer was empty too. *He really took everything,* I thought in dismay. It was so final. He didn't waste a second. I guess that's what he really wanted after all.

I stepped into the shower, hoping the water would help wash away my grief, and then I noticed his body wash was also gone. It was a calculated move. And the message was clear: he wasn't coming back.

Despite it all, my hopeful thoughts were relentless. *Maybe he'll stay at a nearby hotel. Maybe he'll call to say he's going to therapy.*

Maybe he'll say that he wants to make this work. Maybe he's just gathering the strength to fight for me.

The next morning, Omi, who didn't know what was going on between Lorenzo and me, casually said, "Hey, Lorenzo is in Arizona." Meanwhile, I had received a text from him with a picture of his hand; he was wearing his wedding ring, "Nunca te voy a soltar. Te amo. I still have hope for us." Why was he wearing it now that he was gone, when he hadn't worn it for the past few days? And why was he in Arizona again? My gut felt something was off. Was there someone else in Arizona? I was so tired of questioning his actions. I sent him a long message expressing my disappointment, and then I changed my number.

Given how this was going, and knowing he'd likely go to the media soon, on September 16, 2020, I decided to post about our separation: "With a heavy heart, I'm informing you through this platform that Lorenzo and I have decided to separate. It was a mutual and difficult decision, but necessary." I went on to express our need for privacy and thank everyone for their support. I was done with the speculation. I needed to control the narrative, and I didn't want to give him the chance to flip the story like he'd done before. I made clear that we were both accountable. My idea was to treat the situation with the respect it deserved, without pointing fingers, without hurting anyone.

Lorenzo lost it. Looking back, maybe he thought he'd tap out for a month or two, do his thing, all the stuff I wasn't comfortable with, and then come back to find me waiting for him with open arms, but the veil had finally been lifted—there was no going back.

Some of my friends were a little offended because they didn't know this was going on, but I didn't have time to consider their feelings. I had to act. The last thing I needed was to look like a fool if he was caught red-handed in Arizona. The media would've had a field day. Unfortunately, this post opened another can of worms with my family.

We were just about to launch a mini quarantine tour with my tío Lupe, called Gira en el Campo, when I announced my separation. Juan and Rosie reacted like I had done this to them on purpose. They said it was awful timing because now the media would ask about our separation instead of the upcoming concerts. Jacqie agreed with them. Instead of asking me how I was, they said they thought I'd acted selfishly, that I could've waited, but what they didn't realize is that I had already waited too long.

Don't let the red flags come back to haunt you like I did. If something feels off from the start, don't ignore it. Listen to your gut. As women, you know that feeling we all get when we think, *Hmmm, this is questionable*, well, you better believe it's fucking questionable! I had that instinct in my past two relationships and chose to ignore it. That's me giving people the benefit of the doubt, or thinking, *Maybe it's me?* When my insecurities kick in, I start making lame excuses only to later find myself wrapped up in shit I had spotted from the start. When people show themselves for who they are, when they reveal their true essence, we should never look the other way.

> *I stopped expecting and started accepting.*
> *I stopped pretending and started expressing.*
> *I stopped forcing and started releasing.*
> *Relief.*

13

MAD ABOUT TEQUILA

I was filled with doubts after Lorenzo left. *Am I not worthy of him staying? What did I do wrong? Was this the right decision? Did we give up too soon?* But every time one of these questions entered my mind, his actions solidified my decision. We were not right for each other. Our relationship had been broken for longer than we liked to admit, so by the time we officially separated in September, my focus was on cycling through the pain that comes with love gone wrong as gracefully as possible and setting my sights on the future. I needed a light at the end of the tunnel to help pull me through the darkness. Enter Mr. Tempo.

The first DM I received from him came on October 7. And it was strictly business. For a long time, I've been approached by different people to do my own liquor—whisky, tequila, vodka. And I always said no. I figured my obligations to my mom's tequila had to come first for the sake of my siblings. And that's what I did for a while, until her tequila started to go down a road I didn't feel was the right one.

I've learned the hard way that in order to thrive in business, I couldn't make emotionally based decisions. I couldn't continue to promote something I didn't believe in just for my mom or siblings. No matter the product, if something isn't done right, then I have to rethink my role. I felt the quality of my mom's tequila was declining, and the marketing wasn't up to par. I had suggestions and solutions that were falling on deaf ears. That's when I started to draw a line: fix the problem or don't count on me for promotion. I was at this tequila crossroads when Mr. Tempo approached me with a business proposal that caught my attention. We met at the opening of his new restaurant, exchanged numbers, and set up our first business meeting.

"I really admire your hustle," he told me. "I've been watching you for a long time. I think you have great engagement. And I would love to help you come out with your own tequila. Actually, I already have one. I'd love for you to be the image of it."

He poured me a shot, and I took a sip. It was my favorite type of tequila—cristalino, aged and filtered to remove the color it picks up from the barrel and turn it into a crystal-clear wonder—and it tasted amazing. I also liked the name he'd chosen, Reina del Sur, though it carried with it some controversy given that it's the alias of the infamous Mexican narca. But he assured me he had the rights from the actual Reina del Sur and the go-ahead to make it happen. I was still a little hesitant about the implications of the name.

"Why don't you ask Kate?" I asked, since Kate del Castillo played La Reina del Sur in the TV series.

"Because she has her own tequila." He then added that he felt I was the right fit.

"Let me think about it," I said. I needed time to figure this out, and I wanted to talk to my family before I agreed to any deal involving tequila. Then I added, "As you know, my mom has her own tequila. If you can help me get my mom's tequila on its feet, then that could open the door for me to have my own." I asked him for his honest opinion about it.

"As a tequilero and someone who has done a lot of research, I'm sorry, but it's just not up to par." He said the bottle wasn't convenient for bartenders because it was too heavy, and he gave me excellent feedback on what he thought was missing and what needed to be changed.

Funnily enough, a lot of what he said was what I had already suggested to my family. I wanted to make women the target audience for my mom's tequila, put money behind it, change the name, get artists involved in the promotion, and rerelease it in December with her picture on the bottle. And now I was talking to someone who had the same marketing vision, as well as contacts at restaurants, and I figured it could be a win-win for us both.

"Okay then, help me get there," I said, enthusiastically.

"Sure, well, one thing at a time."

As the days passed, we continued talking about this and other possible business ventures. But we never signed a contract. We were just floating ideas around, good ones at that. Then things took an unexpected turn. He confessed that he liked me, that he'd had a crush on me for the past five years. There had been a lot of guys who started reaching out after I announced my separation from Lorenzo—even some of his acquaintances and friends. The attention was fun, a welcome distraction, but with Mr. Tempo there was also undeniable chemistry. He was older, had kids, was divorced, and was a businessman. He said he would take care of me and whispered everything a woman would dream of hearing: "I want everything with you. I've never felt this so quickly with someone. You're what I've always wanted. I want to take care of you. We can build things together. Imagine us traveling the world and opening up restaurants . . ." And I was toast. I sincerely thought, *Oh my god, he checks off all the boxes of what I want in a man.* Plus, I was starving for affection and intimacy. All I wanted was to be hugged and loved.

My sex life while married reached a point where one night, about a week before we finally called it quits, when we were climbing into bed after a party, I was feeling horny, and I made my moves on Lorenzo, only to be received by "I feel kind of full."

"No worries, grab my vibrator."

"You want me to grab it?"

"Yeah, I'm horny and you're not doing anything about it."

So he handed me my vibrator and while I was lying there, naked and playing with myself, he was right beside me scrolling through his phone.

In disbelief, I stopped and asked, "Are you going to help me? At least kiss me, touch me, something?"

Ah, I feel full, I recall that he repeated.

I had never felt so undesired in my life.

So when Mr. Tempo came into my life and showered me with compliments about my beauty and strength, he unknowingly fed my self-confidence, and that admiration and desire made me fall into his arms. I suddenly realized there was life beyond my heart-wrenching separation. He made me feel like a desirable woman again. So instead of stopping myself right then and there to think things through, I ran with it and let my guard down. The chemistry was out of this world, and I was vulnerable and in need of that type of attention—I just wanted someone to make me feel loved. And that's what I'm guilty of. Lorenzo and I had legally split on September 16, so after that it was fair game. Whatever I did with my pussy from then on was my business. Was it wrong in the religious world because we were still married? Perhaps. But at the end of the day, I was no longer his problem and he was no longer mine. He didn't even have my number. I wasn't doing anything wrong. I never cheated on him. What I do regret is allowing myself to fall so quickly for someone new. As a public figure, I should've been more cautious. As a woman, I should've known I needed time to heal.

When the cameras caught us kissing, I was absolutely devastated. My heart couldn't take another media debacle. I was later told it was a setup, but that Mr. Tempo had nothing to do with it. With time, I had a feeling that maybe his publicist hired someone to take pictures of us without his knowledge. Whoever was behind this sold the pictures to the gossip show *Suelta la sopa*, which means they made money, and that made the publicist look good in the eyes of his client.

Mr. Tempo was sick to his stomach when he got wind about the leak. He was in the middle of doing interviews about his tequila, so I gave him the green light to address it in public. He defended me, but the outside optics didn't do us any favors. Everything happened too fast. I chose to trust him, but I didn't know if I could trust the people around him. Then I found out he was with someone at the time—of course he didn't tell me that. He later explained he had a girlfriend, but it was rocky. *What the fuck!* So I suggested we put a hold not only on our fling but also on our business talk. I needed to get divorced and get my head in order.

However, by the end of October, I was la puta of the story. Since I'm a woman, having a little fun after my separation was still frowned upon. The attacks were relentless. The media latched on to the marriage certificate like we were living in the 1920s. I'm sorry, but we were in 2020, what did they expect? So I was supposed to wait around for a paper that legalized my separation while he did whatever the fuck he wanted? I have two words for them: double standards. If I had been a man, this scandal would've been handled differently. Men are never called whores for having an affair. They're reprimanded and then everyone moves on. I was furious that this had become a scandal, I was furious at the media's reaction, and I was furious at Lorenzo for using it as an opportunity to play the victim in the public eye and act like he was the innocent party in all of this.

"I never cheated on you, and you know that," I said to Lorenzo as this all unfolded. "And not because I was so in love with you. It's because I'm in love with God, and I'm too afraid of disappointing him. Now it's fair game. You can do whatever you want, I don't care. And so can I."

Then I had to deal with my family. My plan had been to talk to them first before making any decisions regarding the tequila venture and signing on the dotted line. But when that kiss was leaked to the media, and Mr. Tempo put me out there by talking about our idea of partnering for the tequila, that was a game changer. I was really upset with him, but I don't think he knew better. My mom's fans started saying, "OMG, her mom has a tequila, how could she do this to her!" Yeah, and so do a bunch of other celebrities. There can be more than one celebrity tequila on the market. Still, they called me a bad daughter, and my family was really upset.

Out of common courtesy to my tío Juan and tía Rosie, I reached out to address what was being said in the media, to explain that, yes, I was in conversation about a possible tequila partnership but nothing had been set in stone. I suggested we have a meeting so I could tell them where everything stood. Rosie was very bothered by the situation, and I got it. This is not how I wanted to handle this delicate issue. They immediately viewed the possible venture as a threat and took serious offense that I hadn't looped them in. I tried to explain that my idea was to help my mom's tequila too, but once my family gets offended, it's hard to get through to them. They latched on to the "conflict of interest" phrase, but I still stand by my thinking: There's no problem with my mom and me having tequilas out there at the same time. The proof is in our makeup lines. I have one, my mom has one, and my sister Jenicka was thinking about having one, and we are all coexisting in the market just fine. Each of us has our own following, our own audience, and own customer base. It hasn't affected our bottom lines, but I felt that my aunt and uncle were too stuck in their ways to see the bigger picture.

I was also sick of them playing the mom card. I know my momma better than anyone else, especially when it comes to business. She and I worked side by side; we created her empire together. I know what she would like, her take on quality, I know what she would expect because I helped her build the foundation of what would become her legacy. That's why I also knew her original plan for her tequila: "We're going to start this tequila and make it so good and make so much noise that Patrón is going to come and buy us out." That's what she said to me when we were first planning this venture. To grow it exponentially and then sell it off; that was the goal. It's what my mom wanted. In order to do that now, some major changes had to happen. But I felt my uncle and aunt completely disregarded my ideas. It was a delicate situation I wanted to handle with care, but after their constant rejection, and the Mr. Tempo madness, I realized we'd never see eye to eye on this, so I decided to step away.

As a businesswoman who graduated from the University of Jenni Rivera, I've done so much and worked so hard to get to where I am today, on my own, that I can't afford the luxury of associating my brand name to merchandise that isn't up to par with my standards. Period. My momma has been gone for nine years, it's not her business anymore, it's theirs, and I don't have any obligation to be a good daughter to them. I've finally matured enough to understand that I no longer need to bend over backward for their approval. At the end of the day, what's on the line is my image and my integrity, not theirs. My followers trust me, and I will not risk losing that hard-earned relationship. If I promote something that isn't up to par with my standards and my followers realize this, they will drop me like a bad habit. That's the way this business works. It's cutthroat. One minute you have a huge customer base and the next they're gone. Then what?

It was a hot mess, and the time had come for a cold shower. I now realize that Mr. Tempo and I should've focused on our business ideas and not mixed it with pleasure. I still believe they would be very lucrative, and although he and I have distanced ourselves for obvious reasons, I've remained in touch with his business partner because I respect their entrepreneurial sense. There is no contract. At the moment, I'm just giving it time, but the door remains ajar. I will say, though, that that brief encounter with him woke me up from my heartbroken misery for a quick minute to show me that there are men out there who have their shit together. They do exist. I didn't have to rush anything. My time would come. I had to simply remain connected, diligent, and intentional, so that I could really start the healing process and emerge as the best version of myself. I would survive and once again start to thrive, but there were still a few deep potholes in the road ahead.

Some people aren't strong enough, wise enough, or mature enough to handle you or what you have to offer them. That's not your problem, though; that's theirs to figure out.

14

RECOVERING EMOTIONAL CARBOHOLIC

I cannot wait for the day when I wake up and realize I no longer love you." I emailed that to Lorenzo as my heart fought to
understand how I hadn't woken up from this unhealthy relationship sooner. Despite the media circus, his interviews, the blatant
lies—like the times he said I didn't support him in his career—I
still missed him. My heart wanted one thing, my vagina wanted
something else, and my mind was trying to get those two on the
same page but they refused to listen. The hurt was deep, and I felt
as alone as I did in the fall of 2012. Déjà vu, and not the good kind.
I was once again estranged from my family and the media's favorite
target while suffering through an impending divorce. But I bit my
tongue and swallowed all the shit that was being said because I
didn't want to react impulsively. I needed to process it in my own
time. My truth would come out eventually in these pages, so I held
on to that, knowing that I was doing the right thing. Meanwhile, I
turned to my ultimate comfort: food.

I know people who stop eating when they're sad—well, that's
not me. I'm what you call an emotional eater. Chowing down my
feelings has been my go-to since I can remember. For someone

who tends to put on pounds easily and has gone through hell and back on more than one occasion, this has been a recipe for disaster. Through every heartbreak, every loss, and every tough moment, my one and only constant companion has been food. It's never let me down. As a kid, when I was scolded, the first thing I'd do to soothe my pain was turn to food. My stepdad Juan would bring me snacks when I was in trouble and put them under my pillow to comfort me, hiding it from my mom because she was obsessed with weight loss.

The first time I became aware I was carrying a few extra pounds was when I was ten years old. I noticed that I was chubbier than the other little girls in class, and I wasn't the only one who noticed. My mom immediately put me on a protein diet, and that was just the start. The weight would fall off, I'd gain it back, then my mom would put me on the next diet of the month: the soup diet; the Zone diet; you name it, I did it. Her intentions were good: she wanted to help improve my looks and my confidence, but it was doing a number on my self-esteem. Yo-yo dieting became the new constant in my life, but it didn't stop me from eating my feelings. I just got better at hiding it to avoid getting an earful from my mom. I began to have a love-hate relationship with food and my weight. Every time I thought I had it under control, life would throw a wrench and I'd fall back into my old ways.

Because of this, when I was grieving my mom many years later, I turned to tacos and enchiladas and anything that reminded me of her so that I could feel her presence. I didn't like going out much because people were starting to recognize the kids and me, so we'd stay home and watch a movie, and I'd order a pizza. The pain was so deep that no amount of food could fill the void she'd left behind, but eating brought me the comfort nothing else did—it meant instant relief, even if only temporary.

I did the same thing when I broke up with Angel. The French

fries, the ice cream, the pizza, the cheeseburgers. I felt so shitty that I just wanted to eat, lie in bed, and make it all go away. Comfort food had become my addiction. Throughout the ups and downs of my relationship with Lorenzo, I also ate. Many times, I didn't even realize when I started piling on the weight. My wake-up call usually involved catching a glimpse of myself on TV or in a photo someone else had taken, and that's when it would hit me: *Oh shit, I guess I don't look that good.*

As I inched closer to my mid-thirties, I realized that I had to make my health a priority. I was sick of this yo-yo dieting, of not feeling comfortable in my own skin, of hiding my arms in long-sleeve shirts, cardigans, jackets, and dreading the damn scale. I had tried every diet under the stars, but what I needed was an overhaul of my lifestyle. Enter my new trainer and now close friend Sarah Koudouzian. Growing up, my mom forced me to do exercise so much that it became a chore, something I kind of dreaded. I didn't get the thrill of it, until now. After a few years with Sarah kicking my ass in our sweat sessions, I can honestly say, if I stop exercising for a while, I actually miss it. But I knew that no amount of exercise would do without a diet. When I asked her for advice on that front, Sarah made me dump my scale and then introduced me to the world of keto. I finally found something that included food that was bursting with flavor, which immediately made me feel a rush of energy and all-around goodness. I personally know that the only way I can stick to something for the long term is if I feel like I'm not missing out. That's why combining healthy eating with flavorful choices is where it's at for me. I also love that I can always find something that fits my needs on the menu of any restaurant, so eating out isn't off-limits either.

One of the keys to long-term change on this front is to adopt a healthy way of eating that fits your palate. It has to sit well with you and make you feel great. I love keto, but as time has gone by, I've also realized that vegetarian-leaning meals sit even better with me. So I'm learning how to do keto with a vegetarian and pescatarian edge to adapt to what my body is asking for. There's no one way or the highway when it comes to food that is good for you. We each have to figure out what works for us.

Another thing that has helped me is to do away with the word *diet*, which carries such a negative connotation in my life. Diet triggers thoughts of restrictions, a fad, a temporary fix. It reminds me of bland, boring, unfulfilling food that leaves me hungry. Getting rid of that word and instead adopting a healthy lifestyle allowed me to flip a switch. Now I've figured out how to feed my body what it needs, rather than just what satisfies me and my emotions momentarily, while also allowing myself a guilt-free day of indulgence.

But, of course, I'm still a work in progress. Old habits die hard. While going through my separation with Lorenzo, that trusty crutch didn't magically disappear. I turned to a Western Bacon Cheeseburger and a side of Crisscut Fries from Carl's Jr. to smooth the edges of my shattered heart. Pain debilitated my willpower. I couldn't think straight, let alone choose healthy foods. I reached for what I knew would ease my suffering. When you feel like your world is upside down, that instant upper is addictive. The issue here is that I can't give up food. It's not like drugs or alcohol, where you can sober up and never have it again. It's vital, so the focus lies in repairing that relationship with food.

This time around, I was much more aware of how what I was putting into my body would affect me in the long run. I knew it wasn't good for me, and it was clear that I had to find my way back to better choices to break with my emotional carboholic downward spiral. And I had faith that I would. But I also learned to be kind to myself while I was down. I forgive others all the time, so I've learned to be more forgiving with myself when I slip up too. I allow myself to fall and then say, "No, Janney, you have to do better for yourself," and then I focus on the next meal to get back up again. I don't like that post-binge sluggishness; it's awful, and it makes me want to go back to healthy food so days no longer turn into months of mindless eating. I've managed to break that cycle, and that sense of accomplishment is what continues to inspire me to do better.

I've also learned how to exercise my willpower and say no when it comes to food. I may really want some pizza on Wednesday, but now I push myself to wait until Sunday, my indulgence day, so that I can enjoy it guilt-free. This newfound willpower became addictive with time. *Wow, I can do it!* When you find balance in one area of your life, it's easier for the other areas to follow suit. Learning how to say no to unhealthy eating has also taught me that it's okay to say no in other areas of my life in order to preserve my mental and emotional health. I was able to say no to toxic relationships, no to my family, and no to my marriage when it reached its limit. There were times after we separated where I really missed Lorenzo, and a hug would've been amazing, but I said no. I knew that, just like the cheeseburger I was craving, he wasn't good for me. If you're not serving my higher good, whether you're a relative, a friend, a husband, a lover, or food, then I will say no to you. That willpower lives within me. When I claimed that control, I suddenly felt liberated.

After that, it all comes down to finding your groove, your balance. I have control over certain things, like food, working out, and choosing the people in my circle; and then there are the things I want to control but can't because life is a bitch sometimes. In those instances, I have learned to let things be. When I couldn't trust Lorenzo, I was overcome by a feeling of needing to know where he was at all times because I was afraid he'd self-destruct or do something that might harm me. Now I understand that, just like I can't control the weather, I can't control other people's actions either. I have to trust the universe and God and put the Serenity Prayer in practice by truly living one day at a time and making the present my greatest gift.

My focus now is not so much on my weight, but rather on my body, mind, and spirit, because I want to live a long and healthy life. And to do that, I have to say yes to myself. I figure if I do that time and again, God will eventually reward me with the wisdom to make the right choices for my future. When I feel good, there's no stopping me.

> *"God, grant me the serenity to accept the things*
> *I cannot change;*
> *the courage to change the things I can;*
> *and the wisdom to know the difference."*
> —SERENITY PRAYER

15

FAMILY: IT'S COMPLICATED

*P*art of the downfall I suffered in the second half of 2020 wasn't just the end of my marriage, it also had to do with my family. I felt like it was 2012 all over again. It's no secret that I have a complicated relationship with some of my relatives. First and foremost, I love them. But sometimes I don't like them. Things got tense with my tío Juan and my tía Rosie when the tequila scandal broke. Meanwhile, my uncle Pete, the pastor of the family, decided to criticize my handling of my relationship in interviews without even reaching out to me first to find out what was really going on. Then my sister Jacqie suddenly shut me out, even though she promised she'd never turn her back on me again after 2012. I felt so hurt and alone, like everything was all coming down on me at once. Did we not learn anything from the past eight years?

No. Rather than uniting after my mom's passing, things slowly went downhill from there. I got a lot of pushback when I first began my singing career. Sure, my family went to my first concert, but I always felt very judged, especially by Rosie and Juan. As my career grew, instead of being happy for me and supporting my dream, I was met with their indifference. It seemed like they suddenly saw me as the enemy, as the competition. It was insane. I wasn't out to take her place. I just wanted to follow a plan I had actually first discussed with Momma herself about launching my music career. It was time to carve my own path, but some of my family wasn't having it. I remember my tío Juan made me feel terrible. Just recently, he launched a new singer on his record label and posted a story saying, "Yes, I like how she sings better than my niece, yes." Was that even necessary? From the beginning, they really disappointed me, but no matter what everyone said, I knew that my momma supported this dream, and I was determined to see it through.

I loved my tío Juan. He had been such an important figure in my life. I will be forever grateful for him, because he was the only one in my family who stood by me when my mom stopped talking to me and disinherited me in the fall of 2012. He believed me. I will never forget that. But by taking my side, his relationship with my mom suffered, and when she passed away, they weren't on good terms because of it. I think deep down he resents me for that, even though he probably isn't aware of it. And I believe that played a major role in the decline of our relationship. I saw this clearly for the first time in 2014, during a signing he and I were doing in Chicago for my mom's tequila. I had just flown in, exhausted from the nonstop work, and when I met up with him, I realized he was drunk. He started talking shit, and I was just trying to go with the flow, until he said something insulting about Jenicka and I reacted without thinking and replied with a comment about his daughter, which sent him into a rage. Suddenly, he threw his phone and charger at me with such force I had to quickly duck, and they hit the wall behind me and made a hole. That's when I realized how much pent-up anger he had toward me. It was sobering.

The last thing I wanted to do was go to the signing after our fight, but I felt it was my responsibility. I had to do it for my momma. So

I stood there, hugged her fans, and put on my best happy face. "I don't know how you can be so fake and just smile and pretend that everything's okay," he said to me. How could I not? Those people who had been waiting in line for hours didn't have to bear the brunt of our dysfunctional family. It wasn't their fault. I wasn't going to ruin their moment because we couldn't stand each other. He reeked of alcohol and was livid, but I just ignored him the entire time.

A couple of days later, the phone rang at six in the morning. Angel picked up. It was Juan, and he was drunk. "Why is it that God blessed this little girl with so much love?" he said to him, referring to me. Angel passed the phone to me and Juan continued, "I came to realize that God blessed you with grace and favor, and your mom is sending her love through these people. But honestly, when your mom passed, I thought it would be my time. And here you come without even half my talent, and everyone loves you and everyone wants to work with you, while I've been at this for fifteen years. You're not even prepared; it's so disappointing." They say only drunks and children tell the truth. Something clicked that week, and my relationship with my uncle has never been quite the same since.

Navigating our family dynamic almost feels like walking through a minefield. Just when you think you've narrowly escaped losing a leg, you lose an arm instead. Coming out victorious is practically impossible. That's what I learned when I refused to go on a Dinastía Rivera tour in 2018. "No, absolutely not. You guys hate each other," I said. I couldn't get onstage with them and pretend we were one big happy family when some of them weren't even talking to each other. I didn't care about how much money I stood to lose by saying no, my integrity came first. Selling out was not an option in my book.

After my mom passed, there were things that went down in Mon-

215

terrey, Mexico, that a lot of us don't know about. When my tío Gus (who's always been the black sheep of the family) and my tío Lupe (who's also had a complicated relationship with all of us) came back from that trip, they kept their cool until my momma was buried. Then the issues between them started igniting. Some shit went down, and my tío Lupe and his ex-wife went to my tío Gus's house and she and my cousin Karina had an altercation. Karina ended up breaking Lupe's ex-wife's nose. It was horrible.

So, when I was asked to join the Dinastía Rivera for a performance, it didn't sit right with me. I approached Gus and said, "Okay, now that you're going to do the tour, are you and Lupe going to talk? Are you two going to resolve your issues?"

"No, I'm never going to talk to him again," he replied.

"Well, I don't agree with that. I'm not getting onstage with you guys and pretending like we're this big happy family for the camera and all this shit. You guys go ahead and do it without me."

I wasn't part of the Dinastía anyway, so I didn't think it was a big deal. But then I fucked up. After some insistence from my tío Juan and tía Rosie, I agreed to go on the stage and sing at the Jenni Vive concert on October 31, 2018, to honor my mom. That meant I would be singing with my tío Lupe, whom I hadn't spoken to in four years. It wasn't like we couldn't be in the same room with each other—if we crossed paths, we were always cordial. Plus, he was showing signs of change and was trying to reach out and get closer to the family. In any case, I wasn't opposed to singing with him, it just felt unnatural, but in this instance, I preferred to go with the flow so as to not cause even more problems in our family. I wanted to please my tío Juan and tía Rosie, I wanted there to be peace, I wanted our family to be okay, and most important, I wanted to do it for my momma.

Right before I took the stage that evening, Lupe spoke to the audience and expressed he was proud to introduce someone whom he'd loved as a daughter since she was a little girl. He went on to say he was the happiest uncle in the world. He'd never said any of that to me before, on or off camera. I was so confused, I didn't know how to feel. Rattled, I took the stage and made it through the performance, gaining momentum with each passing song. What I didn't realize then was that by appearing onstage with him, I would lose my cousin Karina, Gus's daughter, in the process. I had remained loyal to both Gus and Karina throughout their feud with my tío Lupe, but in her eyes, I became a sellout when I agreed to sing with him that night. I understand where she's coming from. I didn't do it for him. I did it for my momma. I did it to honor her. But that, together with further miscommunication and misunderstandings regarding other things that people told her about me that weren't entirely true, ultimately cost me my relationship with Karina. She was my closest cousin, and I wish I could've had a chance to talk to her and tell her my side of the story—I never thought I'd get married without her there. Losing her still hurts. We've managed to exchange a few text messages in the past year, but we're far from being as close as we used to be. I'd love to tell her, "Fuck, you were right. This whole time, you were right." My family is fucked up, they are fake. I grew up with the motto "blood is thicker than water," and I believed it. But as I got older, I realized that this was bullshit. People are people. Family can have your back and they can stab you in the back; it has nothing to do with blood.

When Jacqie started talking to our dad again, as I mentioned earlier, it made me feel uncomfortable. I've always been there for her, I helped raise her too, and she knew what that man put me through. But then I talked myself out of those feelings. *I can't be selfish,* I told myself. I know how much not having a dad had affected her. I figured that maybe even something resembling a relationship with him could give her the answers to questions that have hung over her head most of her life—maybe it could help mend her heart. So I pushed my feelings aside. I listened to her when she said she'd only have a relationship with him if he apologized for what he did. Then I watched as she continued to communicate with him, even though that specific apology never came. And suddenly, I had that familiar thought again: *She doesn't have my back.*

When my mom accused me of sleeping with her husband and disinherited me in the fall of 2012, Jacqie shut me out without even giving me the benefit of the doubt. I pleaded with her, "Jacqie, you know me, you know who I am. I would never do something like that." But she chose a side, and it wasn't mine. She never called to see how I was doing. I felt she abandoned me. Then Momma died, and I made a promise to her, as the eldest, to keep my siblings together, and eventually we grew close again. This led to our heart-to-heart talk in 2016 when, a few days before having her third child, she said to me, "I was really mean, and I hurt your heart. I should've known better. I should've brought peace to the situation." She said she knew she should've stood up for me and told Momma she was wrong. But she didn't. However, I learned to trust her again. I understood that she was trying to be a good daughter. "I promise I won't let anyone talk bad about you now. I know I messed up and I know I didn't stand up for you, but now, learning from that mistake, I would never do it again." But she did.

After going through so many more ups and downs with her, after experiencing her taking someone else's side in the family one too many times, I now realize I should've spoken up and let her know how her newfound relationship with our dad really made me feel. I should've said: "Sister, Dad sexually molested me. It affected me in many ways. If you still want to have a relationship with him, you have to know and take into consideration how it makes me feel too." Or "No, Jacqie, I'm not comfortable that you are close to our dad. I think it's showing him that if he can have you in his life, then he can surely make everyone else believe that he didn't molest me. That it wasn't true." I should've. But I couldn't. I put her needs first.

Then 2020 came along and it happened again, and that time I had had enough. I was swimming through shit, trying to pick up the pieces of my broken marriage, dealing with the Mr. Tempo scandal, and I desperately needed my sister by my side, but she wasn't there. Instead, she stood by my aunt and uncle and left me out to dry. Maybe it was because she was too easily manipulated. I will never quite understand what drives her to do this, but this time I had reached my limit. I told her I needed space from her, and she said she felt the same way, that she was tired of being stuck in the middle, always having to choose between our uncles and aunt and me. Sometimes she makes me feel like she chooses them over me. Time and again. Even after apologizing in tears and promising that she'd come to my defense the next time.

It hurts. I'll never understand why. I feel like she takes me for granted sometimes. She and I are okay now. We're cordial, respectful, and we know we love each other, but we're not as close as I'd like. Through therapy, I've come to realize that she's my sister, but that doesn't necessarily make her my best friend. Jenicka and I are friends, we talk about everything and anything, but with Jacqie it's different. She doesn't come to me for deep conversations anymore. Sometimes I feel like she's closer to Rosie and, as much as I would love to have that inseparable sisterly bond with Jacqie, I've learned to respect and accept that I don't, and that's okay. I will always love her regardless.

Now I'm focused on learning how to create boundaries and take care of myself, especially in this family, where jealousy thrives. I experienced it first through my mom. I saw what she had to deal with, and I witnessed her tears. The year before she passed away, I remember how disappointed she was with her family when she got her knee surgery. She said, "All I am to my family is money." No one came to check on her to see if she was okay. It was December 2011, a year before she left us for good, and I remember her saying that she just wanted to give them money so that they would leave her alone. It was toxic for her too. When Lupe was on top, they were against her; when she was on top, they cozied up to her and turned their back on him. I've seen it. I remember it all. And now it's my turn, and it's exhausting.

But I'm doing my own thing, and I'm staying in my lane. I no longer feel the need to prove myself to them so that they can be happy with me, love me, and recognize I'm a good person with good intentions. That has gotten me nowhere in the past. They've always been upset with me for not supporting more of my mom's stuff. And when I tried to stand my ground, they'd go for my jugular: "You're a bad daughter because you don't support your mom's legacy." Wait, I supported my mom and gave her the first twenty-six years of my life. While it seemed to me they fed off her winnings, I was taking care of my four siblings, helping my mom build her career, everything. And because of that, I know that her biggest legacy isn't her songs or her tequila or her makeup line . . . her biggest legacy is her children. No one can tell me I owe her anything anymore. I'm good with my mother. I'm at peace with her. I'm looking out for her kids, making sure all four of them are okay. Even when things are rocky with us, I still have their backs and keep them in my prayers. So when they say, "All you care about is money," to add fuel to the fire, I think, *No, all I care about is earning a living and making sure my younger siblings are taken care of—that's what my momma would want too.*

Despite this, I gave them suggestions on how to handle my mom's businesses, but they didn't want to hear it. In truth, they haven't been my mom's businesses for a long time. Rosie and Juan have been at the helm of that ship for the past nine years. They're the ones behind the brand now, not my mom. And I don't agree with a lot of how they do things. At this point, I wish we could just put all the business nonsense aside and become a family again. I don't want them to turn to me for work and then shun me when I think something should be done differently. I'm sick of it. *Wait, tíos, tía, did you ask me if I ate today? Did you ask me how I'm doing? Did you care about the pain I was going through with my separation and divorce? Were you there for me?* No. No, you weren't. I was crying myself to sleep in November, and just like in 2012, none of them were around. Some things never change.

On one of those days, when I was in the bathroom, weeping and alone, I heard Momma clearly, "Why are you so surprised about our family? I went through this already. This has been going on for years." She's right, I shouldn't have been surprised. But I also think her decision to put Rosie in charge of the estate exacerbated everything. I understand the reasoning: Rosie is frugal and has done a great job managing her own money. What my mom didn't consider is the pressure Rosie would have to endure when taking over a business she really knew nothing about, and how this appointment would damage our family in the long run. I don't think my mom was in the right frame of mind to be making this type of big decision. It should've been assigned to someone neutral, a professional and business savvy estate manager. That would've freed up the rest of us to simply be a family. But what's done is done.

My mom's empire has the potential to be incredibly lucrative, but I believe the decisions being made are emotionally rooted and lack logical business sense, and I believe it's slowly become a sinking ship. It doesn't affect me personally because my mom took me out of her will before she died, so I'm not part of that trust. But it does worry me because it is my siblings' inheritance we're talking about, and I'm afraid there won't be much left by the time Johnny and Jenicka finally turn twenty-five, which is when they can access the first portion of their shares. The second one comes when they're thirty, and the third when they reach thirty-five. That means Johnny still has fifteen more years to go before he has access to his entire inheritance. So when I hear Rosie say, "Oh, he doesn't have a lot of money left," it gives me pause. She likes to blame it on me, that it's all going to cover his expenses. Hold up, I get $2,800 a month for Johnny's food, rent, clothes, and any other essentials. I take care of anything else he may need. That's really not much nowadays. So, when they say I'm spending all of his money, I ask, "How?"

This ongoing situation has driven Johnny to pursue an accounting of the estate. It's actually something he's been wanting to do since he was sixteen. Back then, as his guardian, I stopped him because I didn't think it was a good idea to upset the family. He then revisited the idea with me when he turned eighteen, and I said no. Now that he's turned twenty, he brought it up again, and I asked him to sit on it and pray. He did and was resolute with his decision. "Okay," I replied, "I'll help you with this, I support you one hundred percent. There's nothing wrong with what you're doing, just know that they're not going to be happy about it."

An accounting is completely normal. It should've been happening annually. Up until now, I really didn't feel I had a say because I was shut out of the will, but I finally shook that off this year. I'm still her daughter, I helped build this empire, and I had the right to help Johnny get some answers to the questions that have been bothering him during these last four years. The kids currently don't know how much money is in that account or what comes in and out;

they don't know Juan or Rosie's salary, and they don't know what Rosie's husband gets paid. They're completely in the dark. I've asked my siblings, "How in the hell do you not have access to your account information?" They should be able to see what's going on. After all, it's their inheritance, their money. The purpose of the accounting is to see what is happening with the money that my mom left for my siblings. How much did she leave, how much has been spent, how much has been earned through her merchandise and music, and who's getting paid what in the process? The goal is to make it all transparent. Obviously, it's ruffling my family's feathers. But if there's nothing to hide, then there shouldn't be a problem.

At the end of the day, despite our dysfunctional relationships, I love Rosie, I love Juan, I love my extended family. But sometimes I don't feel they're healthy for me. Will they have my back? No. Blood is thicker than water, my ass. What they forget is that my momma set me on this independent road before she passed away. She pushed me to go live alone, to find myself, to discover my path, my passion. She wanted to manage my singing career. She wanted me to fly, to do my thing. And that's what I'm finally doing, even though my family doesn't like it. Some of our businesses may overlap, but I'm not jeopardizing their income. Do you think I feel threatened if Jenicka or Jacqie come out with their own makeup or skincare line? Hell no! I'm so fucking proud of them! I know they're going to do amazing things, and I hope to support them in any way I can. Because, unlike some of my family, I believe in celebrating one another's successes rather than getting upset because one of us is doing better than the other. There's room for all of us to pursue our dreams and shine.

I've also finally understood that loving them and wishing them well doesn't mean they have to be close to me. Since I was young, I've had issues with boundaries. It all started with my dad. Once

I began to understand that what he was doing to me was wrong, why didn't I just say no? I've asked myself this question a lot. In retrospect, I think I may have uttered it once to no avail. But I didn't want him to get mad at me; I didn't want to disappoint him. I didn't know what to feel or how to speak about it, and I carried that response pattern into my adulthood. When I've had issues with my uncles or my sister or any other relative or friend, even if it was crystal clear that they were wrong, I doubted myself and I didn't speak up. I thought that by pushing my feelings aside, I was protecting them. They came first, even if I felt hurt, even if they were in the wrong. It happened with my mom too. I grew up putting her first, helping her shine, going to the University of Jenni Rivera rather than a real university because I felt it was my job to be there by her side, to help her with the kids, with her business; it's what I knew.

Any time I enter into conflict with the people I love, I tend to put my feelings on the back burner, and I want to figure this shit out because I know it's not healthy. I've just been doing it for so long, it's a hard habit to break. I have to find my voice and the strength to say, "No, that doesn't make me comfortable." I don't want to have toxic relationships, not with my relatives, not with my partners, not with my friends. It doesn't do any of us any good in the end.

On the flip side, I know that the expectations we put on our loved ones versus the reality of what they can give us in return sometimes differs enormously, and that road can also lead to disappointment. I'm learning to be okay with that so I can enjoy what we are able give each other. There's a sense of peace that comes with finally accepting this and no longer forcing unrealistic expectations on my family.

At the end of the day, I want to be surrounded by people who do me good, who ultimately give me peace. I want people in my life who will reciprocate my love, be it in a relationship, with family, or with friends. Rather than the takers who deplete me, I want people who complete me. I yearn for a loving family life, one where there is no shared business involved, where we can just be siblings, and aunts and uncles, and cousins and nephews and nieces, and grandparents, without all the extra drama that does all of us so much harm. I still hold hope that my family will one day turn a corner . . . la esperanza es lo último que se pierde.

> *Let go, and let God.*
> *I don't know what's going to happen today.*
> *I surrender any doubts, any worries,*
> *any fears, and send them to heaven.*

16

SWEET, GLAM, AND SASSY

*W*hen we were kids and my mom asked my siblings and me to consider legally changing our last names to Rivera, I said no. I respected my hardworking Rivera family and was so proud of my grandpa and my momma and everything they'd accomplished, and although I knew (more than anyone) what my dad had done, I also knew there were a lot of things that went down in the Rivera family that didn't sit well with me. Marin was my last name, the one I was born with, the one I identified with, and I liked it. Then, as the years went by, the media began to call me Chiquis Rivera and it stuck, but in reality I am Janney Marin, or simply Chiquis.

Funnily enough, my grandpa thought my name was Chiquis until I was fifteen years old. One day, during that summer I lived with my grandparents when my mom threw me out because she thought I ditched school, the phone rang. My grandpa picked up the receiver.

"Hi, is Janie there?" said a boy.

"¿Quién?" asked Grandpa.

"Janie."

"No, aquí no vive una Janie. She doesn't live here anymore," he replied, thinking the guy was referring to my mom, and then hung up.

227

"Who was it, Abuelo?" I asked, curious.

"A guy asking for Janie."

"Grandpa that's me! I'm Janie!"

"No, you're Chiquis, como que Janie."

"Sí, yo soy Janie!"

He just started laughing, "I can't believe it!"

I understand his confusion. In my family, I've been Chiquis since I can remember. What's more, until I was sixteen, I thought my real name was Janie. It wasn't until I was registering for eleventh grade with my birth certificate in hand that I realized my name was actually spelled Janney. "Why didn't you tell me before?" I asked Momma. "Ay, I don't know, I forgot. I have too many damn kids." Classic Jenni.

But as the years passed, as I was more exposed to the media and I began my own career, my family nickname became an intrinsic part of my celebrity persona. Chiquis faces the camera, she's sweet and bubbly, she takes the shade and outshines it. She's the hard shell that protects my heart. Kind of like Beyoncé's Sasha Fierce, which counters her naturally shy personality and helps her turn into a beast onstage. Chiquis is the one who works and makes it happen. Her world is all about the brands, the glam, the glitz, the glitter. She's my stage persona and my inner Boss Bee. When the media comes at me hard, it's Chiquis who cordially smiles through the darkness, politely deals with the bullshit, and always puts her best foot forward, no matter what. That's what it takes to work in this industry. A lot of people do this to survive. If you don't, you can easily become another Britney Spears or Justin Bieber. You need that outer persona, that hard shell so that the entertainment industry doesn't affect your essence. I learned this coming up—my years working with my mom weren't in vain. When it came to her career and business, she was a chingona through and through. She left her soft, vulnerable side for her close circle of friends and family. I wanted to emulate that as I grew older.

Then something clicked in 2018, after I did my social media cleanse. I had performed seventy-something shows that year and I'd made a lot of money, but it was all taking a toll on me. I realized that I needed to do something to help protect my essence, my sanity, to not get lost along the way. That's when I first separated Chiquis from Janney.

When I remove my glam makeup and peel off my carefully chosen outfits, I let Chiquis rest and come back to Janney, my true essence, my heart. Janney is the homebody, the hippie who doesn't care about social media. She likes to be makeup free, wear her hair in a ponytail, put on a cap, and live in gym clothes. My true attitude is more laid-back, all peace and love. I like to work to better myself. By separating Chiquis from Janney, I was able to reclaim my name and the light that came with it. Only the people who know the real me call me Janney. This is my forgiving side, my inspirational and empowering side. Janney is the author and the motivational speaker; she is my innermost self and my visualized future.

And then there's Valentina. I know, you're probably thinking I've lost it, but just bear with me. Valentina has always been within me, but she was actually born with my second album's first single, "Horas extras." I imagined her as my alter ego, that girl with the long black hair who saves Chiquis from her *Entre botellas* sadness. The name stemmed from a black wig I wore to take on this persona, and it stuck. Valentina Guerrera (yeah, she gets a last name because she is not to be messed with) is a brave, badass chingona.

While Chiquis is the people pleaser, Valentina is like "It is what it is, I'm not going to sugarcoat anything." She's the one who tells me, "Come on, girl, step it up. Stop feeling sorry for yourself. You've gotta be fierce." She's the one who cusses and drinks and takes

Chiquis's show to the next level. Valentina is the unapologetic, outspoken rebel in me. She's my Long Beach and Compton ghetto side. You don't mess with her because she will take her rings off and take care of business. That's exactly why she's the protagonist of my video "Me vale." Unlike Chiquis, who is strong yet much politer, Valentina is a valemadrista who will give you the middle finger, then wink at you and walk away.

I know it sounds crazy, but it really all comes down to separating work (Chiquis) from home (Janney) and the chingona who unapologetically comes to my defense (Valentina). All three of them make up who I am today. These parts of my personality allow me to deal with the media while still holding my head high and pushing forward no matter what they throw my way. It's my coping mechanism, the one that prevents me from losing it when things get way too dark way too quickly.

I think everyone, in some way or another, has these three facets in their personalities. There's your essence. Then there's putting your best foot forward for work, where at times you have to smile through the pain to get the job done because we all need to pay our bills and survive. And then, well, I think everyone needs their own version of a Valentina tucked away in their back pocket in case of an emergency. That's the side that will push you to stand up for yourself and not allow you to get lost in the process of people-pleasing along the way. Chiquis and Valentina are what helped me, Janney, pull through the end of 2020 and make it to the other side in one sweet, glam, and sassy piece.

The best accessory that you can wear is confidence.

17

AND THE LATIN GRAMMY GOES TO . . .

On September 29, 2020, fresh off my separation, one of my dreams came true: I was nominated for a Latin Grammy. It was like God and my momma were saying, hang in there, the good will outbalance the bad. I had been visualizing this moment for years and was overcome with emotion when I heard the news. While recording *Playlist,* I could feel it had a special energy, and I remember saying to myself, "I want a Grammy." I manifested it, but I couldn't have gotten there without my team and the artists who said yes and were a part of my musical journey. My confidence as a woman, as a singer, and as an artist were on the rise, and I'd found my groove. I knew what I wanted: ten songs, in a certain order, mastered to perfection so that they could be seamlessly streamed on any device. I had followed my momma's advice: "When one door shuts, go through the window," and it worked. The perseverance was paying off.

As the weeks went by, this nomination became my beacon of hope, pulling me through the roller coaster that was October, the estrangement with my family, my separation, and the quietly devastating days of November. The day before the big event, I was bursting with mixed emotions.

I missed my momma. I couldn't help but notice the parallels between what I was going through and my mom's experience in 2012. She was also amid divorce proceedings, estranged from some of her family, and even had a knee issue like I did at the time. My mom had won an award for Premios de la Radio that year for best female artist of the year, and now I was nominated for a Latin Grammy. Just thinking about all of this gives me goose bumps. I so wish she could have been there with me, but I know that she was proud. My momma always pushed me to learn from her experiences so that I could do things differently and better than her when my time came. So once she was gone, when faced with any dilemma or crossroads, I always ask myself, "What would Jenni do?" I know the impulsive route isn't the best choice, so I've made it a habit to sit on things and pray about them.

I missed my husband. When he was nominated a couple of years earlier with La Original Banda El Limón, I went with him to the ceremony. And I remember sitting there and thinking, *I'm going to be nominated.* I manifested it that night. Then, while recording *Playlist,* Lorenzo was a wonderful guide in the studio, giving me tips on how to improve my vocal tracks. I would've loved to have him by my side to help me celebrate this accomplishment, but God had other plans. Everything happens for a reason, that's what I kept telling myself.

But I was also so excited. Just being recognized was a dream come true. I made a point to spend some alone time to spiritually align myself. I meditated in the morning. Instead of working out, I rested. I had lunch with Johnny. Then I got a massage. I decided to only do what filled my heart with joy and peace. Then, a crazy sense of calm washed over me during my fitting. Usually choosing what I'm going to wear for such a big moment makes me nervous, but this time around I felt that everything was going to be okay. No matter what happened, I knew that at the end of the day simply being recognized by the academy was such an honor.

On November 19, 2020, I set my alarm for five in the morning, but when I opened my eyes and looked at the clock on my cable box, it said 4:44 a.m. This had to mean something, so I googled it and found that it was connected to an angel message that signifies divine connection, as in, you're on the right path. I smiled; it was a good omen. I tapped on one of my meditation apps and meditated for a little while, then got out of bed and kneeled down beside it, with my angel devotional book in hand, and began to pray. Then I started speaking directly to my mom, which I hadn't done in a long time. "Momma, I'm sorry I haven't talked to you. I know you're busy in heaven"—that's how I imagine her, busy up there—"but you know that I love you. Everything I do is for you. I'm just asking you to help me. You're closer to God." Suddenly, I felt a twinge in my chest and heard her voice within me say, "You got this, baby. It's yours." Tears started to stream down my face because it felt so real. But I shook the thought from my mind—I didn't want to believe it was a done deal because I wanted to avoid suffering the disappointment if it wasn't. I reminded myself that whatever happened would be fine. Just having the honor of being nominated was a huge accomplishment.

At around 5:30 a.m., I started writing my thank-you speech in my Notes app and thought, *God, if I win this, I'm going to exalt your name among everyone because I know you are the reason I got to this point, because of your grace and favor, because you've given me the strength. I promise I will say all glory to you.*

I usually don't like to wake up and read my emails, but that morning I opened my inbox and found one from Lorenzo, which he had sent the night before. It had two videos of us from 2016 and 2017, at the height of our relationship, and a message that said he didn't know how he was going to live without me. I watched both videos twice, but I couldn't get into it with him that day, so I didn't respond.

I then changed into my workout clothes, went downstairs, and rode my stationary bike for forty-five minutes while listening to worship music. I was chugging along just fine until the song "Oceans" by Hillsong United started to play. Suddenly, I felt like God was speaking to me through the lyrics, as if saying, *You've been through so much, especially in the past few months. I'm going to show you that I'm with you. That you are on the right path.* That's what I felt in the center of my chest, and I started bawling. I could hear his voice: *I know you're hurting, but this time I'm going to exalt you among those who don't believe in you and said you couldn't do it. I'm going to show my power through you.* I took a deep breath, and with tears still streaming down my face, I whispered, "I'm going to take it. I'm bringing that Grammy home."

I felt raw, fresh, and at peace as I prepped for the momentous day. Since we were still in the middle of the pandemic, the classic red carpet, ceremony, and after-parties had all been canceled, but that wasn't going to stop me from commemorating this special moment. I wanted to celebrate not just being nominated but also everyone who had fought for me, had been there for me, had stood by my side and helped me endure the tsunami of criticism and adversity, and everyone who believed in me and put their heart and soul into this album. My party planner went all out. We had a mini red carpet and everything in my home reflected this award show, down to my own huge Grammy awards that said "Chiquis" on them. I loved it. It was the next best thing to attending the live event.

As we poured into the room, everything was absolutely perfect. Bursting with excitement, I stood behind a gold podium waiting for our category to come on the big screen and took a moment to glance down in silence to prepare for whatever came next. When I heard "Mejor álbum de banda" and the list of nominees, my heart started racing and I closed my eyes and thought, *This is ours, this is ours, get ready, get your speech ready.* Then I heard it: "Playlist." My guests exploded in cheers, screaming and clapping, and I felt my heart skip a beat. I quickly composed myself from the initial shock and calmed my wonderful circle down so that I could give my thank-you speech. I was so awestruck that I forgot to look at my notes, but I didn't need them. I just spoke from my heart. I started by thanking God first for giving me the courage I needed to persevere, and then went on to thank my team, my fans, everyone, because we all won that day. I've never felt such a rush before. We were the list's underdogs and we'd made it to the top.

Unfortunately, it didn't take long for the toxic voices to come out in full force, saying that I had "bought" the win. Juan called to congratulate me, but my tía Rosie said some very hurtful things regarding my win, and it not only affected my relationship with her, but it also cost her her relationship with Johnny and Jenicka.

It was such a surreal few days. Despite feeling hurt by this new wave of bullshit, I was still on cloud nine.

Meanwhile, Lorenzo had sent me two more emails that day, one of encouragement before the announcement, and another congratulating me and my team. I missed him so much, but I remained quiet. I didn't know what to say, and I needed to protect my heart. The pain was there, latent, but the last thing I wanted was to give it a starring role in this particularly unique and wonderful moment in my life.

One meaningful surprise came from my tío Lupe. While a lot of my family didn't reach out to congratulate me or post anything on their social media, the person I least expected called me right away and then posted a congratulatory YouTube video. While chatting with Lupe, he said, "I know what it feels like to not get a call from anyone." He didn't refer to our family directly, but I could read between the lines. We hadn't been close for a long time, but that moment meant so much to me. I was so grateful.

That day, after a five-hour text war among relatives, I decided to exit the family group chat. I was finally beginning to create some much-needed boundaries, yet I felt so alone. I asked God for forgiveness because I didn't want to be ungrateful—my siblings were with me, my grandma and a handful of relatives supported me, as well as my friends. People who didn't even know me seemed genuinely happy for me. Despite the sadness, I knew I was truly blessed to be surrounded by so many people who were genuinely rooting for me. That gives me life. It inspires me to do better, to be better.

I'm very competitive with myself, and these moments don't just feed my sense of accomplishment, they light a fire that pushes me to set a higher bar in every aspect of my life. I strive for every album to be better than the last, for every red carpet look to outdo the previous one. It's all about leveling up with myself. I'm here as proof that when you have faith and you work hard, dreams really do come true. It's about perseverance. It's about not giving up. It's about believing in yourself when no one else believes in you. Don't let anything or anyone stop you from manifesting your vision.

If you've been told that you can't,
that you shouldn't,
then I'm here to tell you
that you can and you should!
¡Sí, se puede!

18

TABLE FOR ONE, PLEASE!

The last few days before Thanksgiving, I had on my Chiquis suit and was so entrenched in work mode that I didn't realize I was neglecting Janney, my essence. I was neglecting the side of me that was immersed in a pool of pain, trying to navigate through a divorce, tension with my family, and an indescribable emptiness in the pit of my stomach. My neck hurt, my muscles hurt, everything within me was screaming: You need to put yourself first! I was on the brink of falling apart, and I crossed that edge during my last day recording *Tengo talento*.

Something snapped. As soon as I finished filming the show that day in late November, I felt like I was hanging on by a thread. I didn't realize how hard I had been pushing through the past couple of months until I stepped off the stage and Don Cheto gave me a hug and said, "I know you're not okay, I feel it. But you're going to be fine, you've been through worse." His words pierced through to my soul. I will never forget that moment, that hug, one I hadn't received in a long while. I walked off the set in tears and suddenly realized, *Okay, you need time for yourself. You need to heal.* The producers asked if I would do some promos, but I could barely gather the strength to make it to my dressing room. When I walked in, I headed straight to the bathroom, collapsed to my knees, and let the pent-up tears flow out of me. I didn't realize I had been holding all of that in for so long until then.

When I got home that night, and took off my Chiquis suit, I felt so bare and vulnerable. Up until that day, I had no choice but to be strong, to chingona up and smile through my sorrow because I had obligations, responsibilities, and work. I had just released my single, "Me Vale," and it definitely reflected part of what I was feeling, but I suddenly realized I desperately needed time to process the intensity of everything that had gone down in the past couple of months. I had been putting a Band-Aid on my open wounds and now it was time to heal and recharge my batteries. I asked my friends Vanessa and Helen to come over and, after a two-week alcohol cleanse, I got really drunk while we listened to music, and later cried myself to sleep.

The following day was Thanksgiving. I had planned to spend it with my grandma, but with all the issues with my family, I chose to stay home instead. I needed time to be alone. I didn't want to shower, dress up, and front that everything was fine because it wasn't. So instead, I stayed in bed and wore my pj's all day. Vanessa brought me food, and I just let myself be. I realized I was reaching rock bottom when a few suicidal thoughts crossed my mind. This was no joke. I had to take care of myself.

I visited my grandma on Friday and spent the following two days with her, and then I canceled all of my commitments. I needed to take December off and really figure out what was going on with me—something I wish my mom had been able to do back in 2012.

Momma was feeling off the year she passed. She was on a self-destructive path, blinded by what others said instead of listening to her gut. From what I heard later from Vanessa and Rosie, she spent days on end obsessively watching the infamous blurry video and filling in the gaps with her unstable mind. When you look at the same image incessantly, you can start seeing things that aren't really there, like when you look up at the clouds and discern shapes of objects or animals. The power of the mind is so great that if you really want to see something, you can.

I think my mom was going through something, and it was driving her to a very dark place. From what I heard, she had gone to the doctor to figure out why she felt so off, and they said she had the hormones of an eighty-six-year-old woman. I think she started taking supplements of some kind, according to what people who were close to her during those last months told me. I was also told that she was afraid to be alone, which wasn't like her at all. Maybe she sensed something was coming. I'll never know, but after putting all of the pieces together, I do believe she was acting out of character.

Now I believe this instability may run in the family. I was talking to my grandma recently about this, trying to understand if there could be a chemical imbalance that we've inherited from our ancestors. My grandpa has some crazy-ass ideas about what happened in our family back in the day, what my grandma's family did to some of his relatives, I'm talking some horror movie shit. I've heard stories about my grandpa's dad making his wife march, naked, down the street like a soldier. Sounds like my great-grandpa was probably mentally unstable.

When I hear these family stories, I don't find them funny or colorful; I find them worrisome because I see a pattern of instability running through our bloodline that no one seems to be aware of or take seriously. Now, after chatting with my grandma about all of this, I've come to think that maybe my mom was going through something far beyond the influence of toxic voices and a hormonal imbalance that began to overpower her logical state of mind.

Unfortunately, I'll never know for sure. What I do know is that I went to a very dark place while we were estranged that fall. And once it was confirmed that her plane had crashed and she wasn't coming home, it got even darker for me. I locked myself in my grandma's bathroom and I thought, *I don't know if I want to continue living.* As I stared into oblivion, suddenly I heard Momma's voice say, "You cannot give up. You need to be strong for your siblings." And I immediately snapped out of it. *Oh my goodness, what am I thinking.* I took a deep breath and, before opening the bathroom door, I recalled something else she always said, "You can't take the easy way out." I'm so glad I didn't because now I am here, alive and able to share this story and hopefully help other women pull through these all-consuming thoughts.

I honestly didn't think depression was real until I experienced it in 2012. Before living it in the flesh, I naively believed we had the choice to not be depressed. But sometimes life is stronger than your will to choose. Sometimes it's not that easy to leave the darkness behind—some people never make it out at all. I'm glad I went through what I did in 2012 because it helped me quickly recognize the profound sadness that was hitting me in 2020. My body ached, and as much as I wanted to move and work out, it was hard to even get myself out of bed. That's when I realized, *Oh my god, I'm depressed.*

Depression is a demon, that's how I see it, an evil demon that wants to rob me of my light, of my future. But I wouldn't let it. I fought it off once before in 2012, and I was determined to do it again in 2020. I prayed, I lit candles, I read spiritually positive books, I went to therapy and, slowly, I began to climb out of that damn hole. I made an intentional effort to get back on my feet.

What I realized was that it was finally time for me to be alone with myself. My codependency—that need to feel needed—had me jumping from my mom, to Angel, to Lorenzo, without ever giving myself the necessary space between relationships to be with myself. And when my relationships went south, my friends helped fill that void. I almost fell into this pattern again in October with Mr. Tempo. I thought he was everything I had asked God for in a man, but when the kiss leaked, I had the sense to slam on the brakes. It was time to listen. It was time to pay attention to the red flags rather than ignore them. I had to start applying the lessons learned. I initially interpreted that moment with him as the universe sending a sign that it was listening to me, but what it was really saying is that it was time for me to be alone.

That space with ourselves is crucial. It can teach us what we like and dislike, and it can make us aware of what we'll tolerate, compromise, and where we draw the line. It allows us to sort through our crap so that we have a better chance of not dragging our old baggage into the new chapters of our lives.

I now know that by not giving myself time and space after my relationship with Angel, I definitely dragged some of my past issues into my budding romance with Lorenzo, even though they were night and day. And that was not right, or fair to him. I also know it's common. When we're in pain and feeling down on ourselves, it's so easy to fall into someone else's arms because they offer the comfort we so desperately seek. We also can't think straight because we are what I call "dick-stracted." I had been dick-stracted this entire fucking time, and I was done. I needed to stop and take stock.

The first change to my pattern came in early 2020, when after one of those emotional roller-coaster rides with Lorenzo, I stopped and asked myself, *Do I have peace?* And the answer quickly manifested itself: *No.* I immediately started praying. *God, please show me the way. If I'm not meant to be with this man, please give me signs. Give me the courage to walk away.* For a while there, I was afraid to be alone. But the signs I had prayed for, my spiritual awakening in this regard, came only a few months later, in June, when Lorenzo was in rehab and I was alone at home.

That space without distractions, that quiet time without love or pain, allowed me to level up in my spirituality and honestly check in with myself. That's when I woke up from my love-blind slumber and thought, *Wait, what the hell happened here? Something is wrong.* My fear of abandonment had turned me into a clingy wife who accepted all kinds of nonsense—I barely recognized myself. We had fallen into a toxic cycle that I was only able to identify during that time apart. It allowed me to gain my strength back. I even dressed up and took myself out to dinner one night, alone. Being able to sit there, at a table for one, and simply be was incredibly empowering. I once again began to feel enlightened and clear on what I needed to be happy. During those last couple of months of our marriage, I wanted to give it one final shot, not because I needed him but because I loved him.

I soon realized I would be okay no matter what happened because I had finally fallen in love with myself. That strong self-love is what allowed me to seek the help I needed later in the fall. And I've been building myself up ever since.

If you feel someone is taking away your peace, try to quiet the voices, your surroundings, and the dick-stractions, and have an honest check-in with yourself. We don't do this often enough. Does the person you are with make you happy? Do they make you feel joy? Do they give you peace? Do you worry and question them? In that space, you may realize that the answers you've been looking for have been living within you all along, you just didn't have the clarity to see them. Taking time for ourselves allows us to learn the lessons from our past before jumping into the future. I'm still processing this myself because it's something I've barely learned in the past year, but I'm getting there.

We all need to work on ourselves, regardless of our age. Coaching, therapy, counseling, whatever works for you, do it. I've done a lot of therapy. It started when the whole thing with my dad went down, then continued when my mom pushed me out of her life in 2012, and I've sought out help when I've needed it ever since. It's my way of doing everything I can to get better. It's what I did at the end of 2020 to get out of my dark hole and really digest the lessons to be learned from all of that suffering. I had a life coach and a counselor who helped me understand the masculine and feminine energies and how they communicate. I was determined to put in the time and work so that I do my best not to bring the same baggage to any future relationship.

Taking care of our mental health is crucial. Don't be afraid to seek help if you need it. Asking for help is not a weakness, it's a strength. It shows you're brave enough to admit you need support to get back up and running again. It means you are finally giving yourself the love you deserve.

In this journey inward, I've discovered that I seek partners who will be my family, the united front I currently lack, and that pushes me to be on a constant search for that one guy who will fulfill several roles and complete me. Now I know that first I need to be okay with myself and learn how to receive rather than give all the time until I can complete myself. I can't put all that pressure on my future partner. He doesn't need to complete me; he needs to love me and elevate me just like I hope to love and elevate him.

I'm done with allowing other people to say I'm egocentric or self-centered because they make me feel like I can't and shouldn't think about or love myself. But if I don't take care of myself, who will? Self-care isn't equivalent to being selfish; it's about fixing whatever is no longer serving you. It's okay to put yourself first. It's okay to say no. And if people get upset, they will just have to get over themselves. This doesn't mean that we're selfish. We're just reprioritizing our lives, and other people who've been on the receiving end of all our giving may not like it, but they're just going to have to deal with it.

We have the power of choice in every aspect of our life. There's always a choice. I've been taking care of my family since I was a kid. First my mom, then my siblings and romantic partners. Now I choose me. I've earned this space; I deserve it. I'm learning how to stand on my own two feet and love myself through and through. Now that I'm starting to prioritize myself, I feel I am building the tools to choose a better partner in the future. Someone who chooses me and knows how to love me. There are days when I feel sad and a little lonely, but I know it will all be worth it in the long run. Life is a journey full of seasons. I've just been through one of my worst winters. I turned inward, reassessed my situation, and now that I can feel spring at my fingertips, I'm ready to bloom again.

Practice doesn't make perfect, it makes better. And that's all I strive for . . . to be a better me, each and every single day.

19

BUILT TO THRIVE: I EITHER WIN OR I LEARN

When I left my grandma after Thanksgiving, I drove back home, crawled into bed, and spent the next day in my feelings, crying it all out. I was profoundly sad, still in the thick of my pain, trying to figure out how to break free from this dark spiral and get back to me. Suddenly, I felt an urgency to see Lorenzo. I needed to have a conversation with him face to face. Without telling anyone, I booked a red-eye flight to El Paso and took an Uber to the airport instead of driving there to avoid the media. I traveled with the clothes on my back. My plane landed at nine in the morning, and I rented a car and drove straight to Lorenzo's mom's house. After parking outside, I grabbed my phone and emailed Lorenzo.

"I'd like to speak to you," I wrote.

"I'd like to speak to you as well," he replied.

"Well, would you like to speak to me in person."

"Yes."

"Okay, I'm outside."

I then called him and broke down. My vulnerability was running high. Maybe this gave him the impression that I was there to beg him to come back to me. But I wasn't there to beg. I was there to talk. If I had cheated, if I had been at fault, I would've been the first one to beg for his forgiveness and ask him to come home. But that wasn't the case. After I decided to take December off to heal, I realized I needed to close cycles and detox myself from toxic patterns, and this relationship was one of them. I wanted one last heart-to-heart conversation. This is something I needed to do for myself, and I didn't want anyone to sway my resolve. I didn't owe anyone an explanation either. That's why I didn't share my plan with anyone, and I mean *no one*. In fact, the following day, I texted Johnny to let him know I was okay, but I didn't disclose my location—that's how far I went to keep this trip private.

When Lorenzo came out of his mom's house, we drove to a nearby park to talk. It was horrible. He was obsessed with my rendezvous with Mr. Tempo. But that was after we separated. It wasn't the cause of our impending divorce, but a consequence of it. I'll say it again and a million times over: No, I did not cheat. My mistake was falling into someone else's arms so soon after we separated. I take full responsibility for that. And when I realized my misstep after the whole media debacle, I took action and stopped talking to Mr. Tempo. It was clear I needed to spend time with myself before finding a new companion. I couldn't get lost in another relationship without doing the work on myself first. But I was never unfaithful while with Lorenzo. I apologized because I never meant to harm him. But I was also brutally honest with him.

"I needed to be loved. I wanted to be with someone. I wanted a companion," I said, then added, "I'm sure you've been with women—"

"No, I haven't," he said, cutting me short.

"Okay, I'm not asking you. I'm just saying it's human nature and

I'm okay with it. I'm not here to demand any type of explanation on that front. After September 16, I have no right to demand anything. And you don't either."

For some reason, he was convinced that Mr. Tempo had paid for my birthday trip to Ensenada (I have no clue where he got this idea from), so I brought proof to right this wrong in his mind. I showed him how my friends and I all pitched in to pay for the rental. I also showed him Mr. Tempo's first DM with the October 7 date stamp—which was not even close to June. I did all of this in person because the last thing I wanted was for him to say that it had been photoshopped. I needed to clear the air from the incessant and poisonous rumors swirling around our separation. His ego was hurt, and he was lashing out. It seemed he was angrier about what people thought about him than anything else.

"So you're not here because you love me?" he asked.

"Of course I'm here because I love you. I don't want to hurt you. I don't want you to ever think that I cheated on you." I didn't want him to live with that pain.

"Oh, okay, so you're only doing this for yourself."

Nothing I said got through to him. Nothing I said was enough.

"I come in peace," I said. "I'm not here to fight. I have no energy left to fight. I'm going through things with my family. This is something I need to do for myself and for you because we need closure." I had nothing to hide. I told him to ask me whatever he wanted. I was very honest, which he didn't like. But I vowed to myself that whatever happened, I would remain transparent.

He kept yelling at me, "I'm angry, you hurt my manhood, you humiliated me."

While he continued to point out everything I did to harm him, I just sat there and cried. I didn't want to fight. I was so tired. I came to him vulnerable. I told him I was going through a lot, that I was sad, heartbroken by our situation and by the deception I'd suffered from so many people in my family.

"You see me on the floor," I said, "and instead of picking me up, you're kicking me while I'm down."

This conversation was going nowhere. I was ready to call it a day and go back home, but he didn't want me to leave. He was upset, at times furious, and yearning for his freedom, but he was also asking me to stay longer. I felt there was still stuff we had to hash out, so I missed my flight. But when we picked up the conversation the next day, it was just as awkward and upsetting.

"What did you think was going to happen when you left?" I said at one point. "You told me you'd never abandon me, and I felt abandoned."

"But you said you wanted to separate," he replied.

"I did it for you because you were expressing your need to be free. You felt confined; you said that you weren't independent. That my world had become your world. That you left your life behind in Texas. I felt like you were saying 'I wanna be here but I don't.' So I gave you the option to leave and you took it without even thinking twice."

He expressed that at the time he thought we'd work things out. If he truly believed that, then why the hell did he drive all the way to Arizona the day he left our house? Why didn't he stay nearby? Was it that he was eager to be with someone else?

"This isn't a game. It's not a hotel that you can check in and out of whenever you want. It's a marriage. You shouldn't have left. Especially not to another state."

We had to interrupt this conversation because he had a video shoot scheduled that day.

"Since you're here, can you help me with my video? You're so good at all this stuff."

"Wait, but I thought I didn't support your career?" I replied, annoyed. He kept publicly claiming that I never supported his career and now there he was asking me for help. WTF!

"No, look, I want to clear that up. They took my words out of context."

"Yeah, you let them use you. And, in turn, they hung me out to dry. That show really hurt me and hurt us. And you deliberately went there because you know they don't like me." I was talking about the same show that had revealed our wedding invitation to the world. When he gave them an interview after our separation, I felt it was a deliberate move on his part. I was so hurt and disappointed. I didn't expect such a low blow from him. But he said he now realized he'd messed up and vowed to clear it up. I was so physically and mentally drained that I couldn't argue anymore, so I just went with the flow and helped him with his wardrobe for the video. I needed to focus on something else for a bit. I needed to feel normal. We drove to the set and I gave him pointers on how to move. Then I stepped in and took over, using my phone for lighting, directing the camera guy, and even suggesting that his daughter run into the closing frame at the end of the video. I was in Chiquis mode, in my element, and for a brief moment I felt okay. And he was incredibly grateful.

When we drove back to his mom's that night he said, "I'm not letting you leave. We need to speak to a counselor. This is where you belong. You belong next to me." He wanted us to stop talking about the past and enjoy the moment; he wanted to take me out to eat, and I let him. I canceled two more flights.

On Saturday, he took me to get a massage because he knew I was in physical pain—my arms, fingers, neck, and back all hurt from the tension. Afterward we grabbed a bite to eat, and then he said he wanted to get a pedicure. I did too, so we went to a random place that neither of us had been to before. I was off social media at the time and trying to keep this visit under wraps. He was still connected though, so as we sat and got what I felt was the longest pedicure of my life, he posted a picture of his feet. Nowhere did it say where he was or that we were together. However, the minute we walked out of the salon, we were met by *Suelta la sopa* reporters who had been lying in wait, ready to pounce. I was so taken aback and upset that I turned around and went back inside. Lorenzo followed me to the back of the salon.

"How do they know we're here, Lorenzo?" My voice was scarily calm and assertive.

"I don't know. I just posted a picture of my feet. I'm assuming they went to every nail shop around my mom's house until they finally found us," he said innocently.

"Well, now you can't blame anyone on my side because I didn't tell anyone where I am," I said, referring to the time the paparazzi found us in San Diego and he said it was my people's fault. "I haven't texted or talked to any of my friends. Look at my phone."

I sat down and watched as he suddenly tightened his fist. Then I looked up at him standing beside me and had a clear view of his clenched jaw. I knew these cues all too well. He felt under attack. I wasn't accusing him of anything, I just wanted to know how those damn reporters found us at that unassuming nail shop we'd never gone to before. Then he started yelling. This was the third day with him, the third day of entering this endless loop of discussions that were getting us nowhere. We eventually speed-walked past the reporters, climbed into the car, and left. I remained quiet during the ride to his place. My mind was made up. I needed to get back home. This wasn't the closure I had hoped for, but at least I tried.

That night I received a text from my grandma: "I know where you are and I'm worried about you. Please come home. That man isn't good for you. You're going to suffer a lot, mija." That's exactly what I needed in that moment. I clung to my grandma's message and bought my ticket home the next morning. Then I told Lorenzo I had to go, that my grandma needed me back home, especially since December is a tough month for all of us. He went from insisting that I belonged by his side—being all sweet and loving and doing the things that I missed so much—to this aggressive, accusatory, cold guy who didn't even offer me a ride to the airport. I requested an Uber, he walked me to the door, and that was it.

On my way back home, as I reflected on those last three days, I understood that although I still loved this man, and missed him, I no longer trusted him. Introspection didn't come easily for him. Instead of sitting down and accepting what each of us could've done better, he simply pointed the finger at me. Did he forget how his addictions had affected our relationship? No. When I brought that up, he blamed me. He said that the white lies; the disappearing acts; the not texting or calling me back; all those times I was worried sick, thinking something had happened, were all my fault because he was scared of losing me. While with me, he claimed that he felt disrespected and that's what made him fall into a depression and drink. But I checked him then and there, "Dude, you've been drinking and doing coke for ten-plus years. How is that my fault?" The only way he would stop and listen to me was if I started cussing and yelling. "I don't like the person you bring out of me," I said to him. I didn't like how he pushed me to step out of my essence. Then I told him, "We're toxic for each other." I wanted to be a positive source in his life, but clearly that wasn't possible if he felt I was to blame for everything. That was it. I guess that was all the closure I was going to get.

As depleted and defeated as I felt, that trip did help me. It reminded me of why this relationship had come to an end in the first place. Maybe that's what I needed to move on. To realize I hadn't made a mistake, that I was on the right track, that this was definitely not the man for me. He only confirmed this further when, later that day, he FaceTimed me after going to church, while with some friends, completely drunk. "Dude, really, what is the point of this call?" This was the root of our issues. *What was he thinking?*

By the time I arrived in LA, the media was in a frenzy. They said I had gone to beg for his forgiveness. They started a rumor that I was pregnant. And they kept talking about how I had been crying while I was there. Wait a minute . . . the only photos they caught of us were the one when we were leaving the nail salon and a group pic at his video shoot. I was not crying in either of those shots. So how did they know about my tears? I hadn't spoken to anyone on my side. How did they have those details? Strangely enough, every time the media caught me by surprise over the past few years, I was with Lorenzo. I've done crazier things with crazier people and managed to keep it private. He liked the attention. I didn't. I preferred the relationship I had with Angel, where no outsiders were involved in any of our ups or downs. Could Lorenzo have been the one leaking stuff all along? I'll never know for sure, but I wasn't the only one who suspected this. The thought was disturbing to say the least. If this was a guy I was just meeting now, I'd say to myself, "Bitch, run!" And, although it took me a few years, I finally did.

I went from LAX straight to my grandma's house for comfort. As I sat in her kitchen while she cooked up some food for me, we chatted and she asked if the rumors were true, if I was pregnant.

"No, Grandma, of course I'm not."

"This is getting ugly. I'm angry at what's happening," she said and then repeated what she'd texted me while I was away. "Deep in my heart, I feel you're going to suffer a lot with him."

Tears streamed down my face. When someone like my grandma,

who's had my back and has been there for me since I was a little girl, says something like that, it's worth paying attention. And she was right. During those first few months after our separation, it felt like he was using the end of our marriage for publicity, to his benefit—painting the picture of the good guy, the hurt husband—when what was going on behind closed doors told a different story. Yet I so wished the relationship would've worked out. I envisioned something different for myself at thirty-five. I wanted a constant companion, not this tumultuous tug-of-war. I think, in part, it's why I couldn't stop crying during those three days with Lorenzo, and even when I got back. I was entering the acceptance stage. There was no turning back. My tears were now in mourning for a relationship that had reached the end of the line.

As if all of this wasn't enough, December 9, 2020, was suddenly here. Eight years since my momma passed. Every anniversary is different, so I didn't quite know what to expect this time around, or how I'd react. The past few years, I had been focused on the pain caused by her absence and everything we went through together, but this year was different. I felt her presence, guiding me along the way. I wasn't focused on how we left things because I knew she was right there with me. I started thinking about her in a new light, in a more mature way. The pain gave way to gratitude. It was like she was helping me by unlocking doors and opening my eyes so that I didn't make the same mistakes she made. Throughout the years I've had to live without her, I believe she's helped carry me through my ups and downs. Now I felt she was saying to me, "Look, daughter, because of what I put you through, here's this platform. I'm going to open these doors for you. I'm helping you heal, and I'm helping you see things because starting next year, you're on your own."

My circumstances had brought me to my knees, but that day I

suddenly understood her more than ever before, and that gave me peace. I could hear her voice telling me that somehow it was all going to be okay, that darkness is always followed by light. I will always be her daughter, but now I'm also Chiquis. I've proven that I can do this on my own, and that has earned me respect now. I feel like she's pushing me to finally spread my wings, to let go of the past, and to soar into the future knowing that I got this. I will be okay.

I wish I could say everything started looking up from then on, but the rest of December sucked. One doesn't magically heal overnight, it takes time. I felt the weight of that entire year in my heart. So when I decided to interrupt my social media hiatus and upload one more post to end the year, I wanted to be as forthright and honest as possible. I felt we needed to take a moment to acknowledge and reflect on the unprecedented year that was finally coming to an end. My management team advised against this, but when they saw my resolve, they jumped in to help. We had talking points. My manager did his best to guide me through it and asked me to not be too vulnerable on camera. We filmed the clip seven times, and I was about to post one of those takes when I thought, *I can't do this. It doesn't feel right. Fuck this, I'm just going to be Janney*. I set aside the talking points, sat in front of the camera one last time, and spoke from my heart. First, I acknowledged what a rough year it had been for all of us and then countered that by listing some of the great things that had happened, like the music I managed to release and the amazing Grammy win in November. Then I went on to say:

> At the end of the day, I'm human. I'm letting Chiquis rest
> right now, and now I'm focused on Janney, I'm focused on
> my heart, on my mind, on my spirituality, on healing a lot

of things that have happened. The pressure of being Chiquis sometimes makes me forget to allow myself to be human, to feel wounded, to [take] time to heal. To give you the best of me I have to be well in my mind, my soul, my heart. This has been a year of loss. In one way or another, we've all lost something. So believe me, I understand you. Believe me, I'm with you.

Leave the heaviness behind and move forward with your head held high. In order to do that, you need to face yourself. You need to be intentional and adamant about wanting to be a better person. About wanting to change. I know why I'm here, I know my purpose, but sometimes with so much chaos around us, we tend to forget that, we tend to lose our way. Who am I? Where do I want to go? What is my purpose in life? What footprint do I want to leave on this earth? That's what I recommend you do. Write it all down. Who and what do you want to leave behind? What's good for you, what isn't? What will serve your higher good so you can lift your purpose on this earth?

With that post, I realized I wasn't alone. I received so many messages from followers and fellow artists that my heart swelled with all the love. That sense of community is priceless. It filled me with light and inspired me to do all in my power to let go of the past and start the new year with less pain and more peace in my heart.

Then, on New Year's Eve, I received a message from Lorenzo. He wanted to ring in the new year with me and do a year of sobriety together. Before midnight, I got on my knees and prayed, "God, let me see what I need to see because I'm so confused." I knew I shouldn't respond but I was fighting between my mind, which knew best, and my heart, which couldn't help but hope that this might be the grand gesture, the turning point I had been waiting for all along.

However, when the clock struck twelve, he was nowhere to be found. Then my phone rang at one in the morning. It was Lorenzo. He was in Las Vegas, drunk. Thank you, God, for sending me that sign—another nail in our relationship's coffin. *How is it that I'm starting my New Year like this?* Frustrated, angry, exhausted, and in tears, I finally fell asleep at 2:30 a.m.

The next day he texted me asking for forgiveness. He wanted to talk, to start the new year sober with me, like a blank slate, where we no longer spoke of the past. "But the past is the reason I feel the way I feel," I explained. We couldn't magically erase it with the snap of our fingers without ever really dealing with it. "I've been doing this for four years—a series of unanswered calls and texts followed by a drunk reply and a plea for forgiveness the following day—I can't do it anymore." I had asked for a sign and I got it. God was showing me his true colors, once again, in full display, and now it was up to me to stand by my decision and no longer give in to him.

This time I didn't change my number. I wanted the messages to come through so I could exercise my willpower and make not responding a conscious choice. A couple of days later, he showed up at my house and texted me, "Janney, can I invite you to breakfast?" He was taking a page out of my playbook, but it was too little too late. I ignored him. "Janney, I'm here just to see you," he wrote and then posted a photo of one of our favorite restaurants, which is down the street from my house. But I stood my ground. I didn't cave. For the first time, I didn't let him back in after messing up. "No, I'm not going to see you. You are not good for my heart. Leave me alone. I'm trying to heal."

I was so proud of myself for finally breaking that toxic pattern in our relationship. But I was so rattled that, in the end, I blocked him. I needed peace of mind. When he realized this, he reverted back to emails and sent me our very first picture together.

"What do you want from me? You were living your best life only a few weeks ago, and now that I'm finally feeling better, you want to come back? No, no me vas a tumbar—you're not taking me down."

"I'm sorry I wasn't there for you," he replied.

More apologies. I couldn't handle them anymore. It was classic addiction behavior—the binges, the apologies—and I was done with the manipulation. It was obvious he wasn't willing to genuinely break that cycle and deal with his issues, and no one could do it for him. And I wasn't going down with him.

Meanwhile, after a month off, I had to start thinking about work again, I had to continue living my life. I gave myself those weeks to go deep, and now it was time to dust myself off and keep going. I set out to organize and clean my house, revamp the interior, and make the space my own. That's when an image of Tulum, Mexico, popped up on my phone. It spoke directly to my chill and relaxed essence, and I decided I wanted a New Year redo. I needed to start 2021 right, before I revved up my work and life. So I texted my friend Rose and said, "Hey, let's go to Tulum." I wanted to stay at a hotel, I wanted to be spoiled, I wanted my bed to be made. I wanted to be with people that I loved and who loved me back. I visualized this trip as a reset button, a way to reconnect with the energy I required in my life. A handful of friends who were single and also in need of a getaway joined us, and off we went.

With the passing days, the sadness that I had been carrying in my heart for months on end began to dissipate. I felt happier and spiritually aligned. I'd never been to a place like that, where every corner had a spiritual and healing element to it. The more time I spent there, the less I wanted to leave. I felt right at home. I wrote down my thoughts in my journal, I read books that fed my soul, and I reconnected with my essence—of course the girls and I had some fun too. I was sleeping in, and not even worrying about what I was eating because I was feeling so good that I was inspired to make the right choices for my body.

While I was out there, I kept thanking God. For the first time in my life, I felt truly free. Johnny was twenty, and he could take care of himself. My mom didn't need me. I didn't have a partner pressuring me to come back home. Even my dog, Pancho, was in good hands. It meant I could just be. It also meant that when our return was delayed, I didn't stress out. I decided to make the most of it and enjoy the extra days in this oasis. So when the paparazzi found me on the beach and took pictures of me, I didn't even notice because I was honestly living my best life. I came to find out about them through Omi when she called to tell me they'd been leaked to the media. I asked her to send them to me. She hesitated, then said, "They're not good." But I told her to send them to me anyway.

When I got them, I started laughing. I showed the girls and they began to crack up too. Were they flattering? No. But I didn't care. I know who I am. I know I'm not the thinnest girl in the world, I know there's room for improvement, and I know I might not meet the bikini beauty standards, but I don't give one fuck. When I see those shots, what I remember is that I was walking on that beach like I was freaking Tyra Banks, with long legs and everything toned and in place, and I held on to that feeling. I was determined not to let anyone take that moment from me.

On my last day in Tulum, I had a healing massage, and even though there was a party for hotel guests, I decided to stay in. So did my friends. I didn't want to do anything to contaminate my body. By then, I was ready to leave. I missed home; I missed my structured life.

Reality hit in full force that first Monday after I returned. There was so much to get done and only myself to do it. But I didn't let that stop me. I acknowledged my feelings and reconnected with the blissful energy of Tulum, knowing one day I'd return. So, refreshed and revived, I pushed myself and got back into the flow of things.

For now, this is what I have to do. I must take care of my responsibilities in the real world so I can accomplish my goals and build my future dreams. I'm doing things at my pace, I'm not rushing myself, I'm taking my time. If I don't get it done today, I'll get it done tomorrow. I've realized that paradise can be sunshine and a beach, but it can also be a state of mind. Paradise is within me.

Don't wish for things to be easy. Pray for them to be WORTH it!

20

UNSTOPPABLE

I'm here, still standing, still singing, still learning, still thriving. I'm done second-guessing myself. I've learned that if you don't love yourself first, you will never be able to truly love and receive the love you deserve from others. Self-love means feeding yourself the right food, feeding your mind the right literature, and surrounding yourself with the right friends and partners. I haven't grown jaded because of my divorce and all that it entailed. I've grown stronger, smarter, and I now have a clearer vision of what I want from the man in my life. I'm also pushing myself to acknowledge any red flags that pop up along my path, because ignoring them hasn't served me well at all.

During the past few years, I've suffered the end of relationships with romantic partners and close friends. Each of these losses pained me greatly, but they've made me grow as a person. This particular pain helped me open my eyes to what I could do better as a partner and as a friend, and also to what I won't tolerate or don't deserve. There are people who are meant to be with us for the long haul and others who are only there for certain seasons of our lives to teach us specific lessons, and that's okay too.

For a long time, I felt that I had to suffer for good things to happen in my life. No hay mal que por bien no venga, right? Well, yes and no. Every cloud does have a silver lining, I believe that, but I've also realized that good things don't come only from cloudy days; sunny days also provide wonderful gifts. I don't always have to go through shit in order to experience the positive outcome that's around the corner. I don't want to needlessly suffer any more. I want to live, learn, and evolve.

I've also come to terms with the fact that I don't owe anyone an explanation about who I'm banging or dating, whether that's one, five, or ten guys. After enduring such a painfully public relationship, I now want to go back to keeping that part of my life to myself. Being in reality shows during my formative years as an adult really skewed my perception regarding what to share and what to keep private. I'm known for being open and honest in the public eye about what I'm going through, but now I know that being a public figure doesn't mean I am obliged to share everything. Some things are best enjoyed in the privacy of my own heart. At the end of the day, it's my body, my vagina, and my life.

My momma was the first one to teach me how to be unstoppable. If I was stuck, she'd tell me, "Figure it out." If I fell, she'd say, "Dust yourself off and keep going." No obstacle was too large or too difficult to overcome in her eyes. And after she passed away, when I was about ready to give up, what kept me unstoppable were Johnny and Jenicka. I couldn't let them down, I couldn't abandon them; they'd already lost both their parents. Even though I wasn't sure how to continue living, I picked myself up and did it for them. They are my pride and joy.

Many people in my family criticize me because of how I've raised Johnny and Jenicka. They think I've been too liberal with them, that I should've taken away their cars and phones when they were exploring their sexual identities. I heard it all: It was my fault because I have gay friends; it was my fault because I had my own gay experience and was open about it; it was my fault because I wasn't strict enough. They will never know what it's like to raise other people's children.

When I had to step out of my sister role and into the role of mom, I vowed to be patient, loving, and accepting. I guided them and was determined to embrace their individuality. I aimed to respect their process, while striking a balance between my mom's way of doing things and my own. She was very traditional and frowned on experimentation and nontraditional sexual preferences, but I wanted to be there to support them along the way. The last thing I wanted to do was drive them into a depression. I know firsthand how devastated and lost that can make you feel. Now that doesn't mean they didn't respect me as a mom. To this day, when I get down and serious, they're like, "Oh shit, she's mad," and they respect what I have to say. I love them so much and want to help them navigate every stage of their lives. I'm so proud that I helped raise these great-hearted kids.

I've seen Jenicka, the shy and self-conscious girl, blossom into this strong and confident woman who embraces her body and is wise beyond words. She taught herself how to do her own makeup and developed that passion into a career. At her age, I wasn't even on my own two feet yet. Now she's making her own money and building her own empire. I wish for her to keep at it so that she can become an even bigger influencer and succeed at everything she sets her sights on. Far from my competition, she's my sister, she's my baby, and she's ultimately my inspiration. I wish only happiness for her, and love too. May whomever she chooses to be with give her the love she deserves. When I last texted her "I'm so proud of you," she texted back, "I am who I am because of you." My heart flipped from how good that made me feel.

I think Johnny's the smartest of the five of us. At the moment, he's still searching for his purpose, that thing that will make him passionate and happy at work. We sit down and have conversations about this as I try to guide him when needed, but I know he's going to do great things. Like Jenicka, he's such an awesome kid, and I know that I don't really have to worry about him (though I always will!). If he's out with friends and I ask him to come home, he does. Our communication is open, honest, and on point. I allow him to be himself and to experiment, but I also step in and draw the line when needed, and he respects that. He listens to me and I trust him. To all the fake pages on social media that talk so much crap about him and how he's never going to let me be happy, you have absolutely no clue what you're talking about. Johnny's not jealous, he's protective. We've been through hell and back together, and all he wants is for me to be happy. He's my son, he's my brother, and he's my little partner in crime. I will always have his back and he will always have mine.

When people look at me with pity in their eyes and say, "Wow, your mom didn't leave you anything?" I say, "Yeah, she did." She left me my two younger siblings; they're my inheritance. When my family gets upset because I don't promote my mom's stuff the way they want me to, I remind myself I took care of the most important job: I raised her kids. I'm taking care of their minds and hearts. If they ever need anything, I'm here. They know that they can count on me. I'm taking care of the most important part of my momma's legacy and her most valuable possession: her children.

What makes me unstoppable now? God. He inspires me to give my best, to do better, and to continue moving forward so that I can fulfill my mission and purpose in life: to help people. I refuse to be a victim of my past. I feel confident, I feel accomplished, I love who I am, and I want to help you love who you are. Singing isn't just my passion, it's a vehicle to reach my long-term goal of motivating and empowering others. I want to bring light to people's lives through my music and eventually also through motivational speaking. I've often experienced a vision of me singing in a huge arena filled with thousands of people and then falling to my knees in tears. After taking a few deep breaths, I pick myself up and start singing a worship song.

I wasn't supposed to make it. I was sexually abused by my dad as a child, I had a fallout with my mom and she died without us having a chance to reconcile, I've been through rough-and-tumble relationships, I've lost friends along the way, and I have been estranged from my own family. I should've been a fucked-up crack whore living in a garage for the rest of my life. But I'm not. Despite the adversities I've had to face, I'm still standing, I'm still growing, and I know I can do more. Finding balance in life is a constant struggle, but if I can do it, I know you can too, because we're all unstoppable.

I've decided that no matter what
has or hasn't happened in the past,
I will be the hero of my future.

EPILOGUE

*L*ife is in constant and unexpected motion. It shocks us, surprises us, makes us shed tears and burst out laughing, and it also calls on us to pause and contemplate our journey and, when necessary, redefine our paths. A few weeks ago, I decided that the time had come to sell my beloved yellow house. The overriding reason that pushed me to make this decision is that I no longer feel safe there anymore. So many people know where I live because of *The Riveras* and the series *Mariposa del Barrio* that I often see Tik-Tokers standing outside my gates filming videos for their profiles, not to mention that the paparazzi drive by on the prowl. Each time I have to travel, I'm knotted with worry thinking about Johnny in there alone. His safety is my priority, and so is my peace.

It's with a heavy heart that I came to this decision because I fell in love with my yellow house the moment I stepped foot on the path leading to its front door four years ago. That place made me a first-time homeowner. It was the scene of my love and my heartbreak, it's where I celebrated my friends and family, and where I received my first-ever Latin Grammy. After we separated and Lorenzo moved out for good, I renovated the entire place, changing the furniture and replacing the floors. I was on a mission to get rid of the bad energy of that failed relationship and bring in the good vibes. I have great memories of all the fun times and parties I hosted in that house, but a lot of shit went down there too. That's why when my financial adviser first ran the idea of selling past me, I thought, *Maybe this is for the best.* I'm ready for a change that will attract a more stable chapter in my life, a fresh wave of energy that will open new doors for my future. I'm ready to upgrade my home and my life.

Something has already come knocking on one of those new doors: love. It happened when I least expected it, at a surprise birthday party I was hosting for my longtime friend Becky G on March 1, 2021. When I came downstairs to greet my guests, I saw Emilio and my heart skipped a beat. We'd met about a year earlier, at my photo shoot for the video of my hit song "Jolene." Becky G asked if we could use her photographer, and my team and I said yes. It was May 2020 and Lorenzo had just moved out of the house after one of our last major fights. When Emilio and I were first introduced, I said, "Oh, you have pretty eyeballs," because he does. The shoot was all small talk and super professional. I never saw or spoke to him again until that night in March the following year. Earlier that day, I had decided to take the plunge and start exploring some dating apps, but that evening changed everything. *Oh shit, it's the guy with the nice eyeballs*, I thought, when our smiles met and we fell into comfortable conversation—we were hooked.

Soon after, we began dating, and everything was moving along just fine, until I noticed he and Lorenzo were following each other on social media.

"Wait a minute, how do you know Lorenzo?" I asked Emilio during one of our early dates.

"I just know him from a party we both went to seven years ago."

It turns out he'd gone to a party with Becky G, and Lorenzo also happened to be there. They all hung out that night and later followed one another on social media. They have mutual friends, but they never saw each other again. They never exchanged numbers, never hung out, never talked, or texted, or DM'd, and never wrote anything on each other's pages. Until recently, when out of the blue, after seven years, Lorenzo commented on one of Emilio's posts. Then soon after, he came out saying that the guy I was rumored to be dating was his friend, his "compa." Ay dios mío. When will it stop? When will he stop?

The reason I'm not divorced yet is not because I don't want to be, it's because Lorenzo isn't complying. Contrary to what I've heard him say to the media, last time my attorney checked, there was absolutely nothing from him, no signed papers, no new clauses, nada. I've been waiting for months now, and you best believe I won't be putting my life on hold because of this new hurdle in my path. All I know is that I dodged a diamond bullet. But as infuriated as Lorenzo has made me sometimes, I honestly don't wish him harm. Our relationship simply didn't work out, and that's okay. It happens. I think that being together taught us both valuable lessons and now it's time to move on. I really do wish him only the best.

Meanwhile, I'm dealing with other relationships that are on thin ice once more in my life. I no longer talk to my tío Juan and my tía Rosie—we don't even follow one another on social media. Jacqie is once again caught in the middle, unsure of how to handle it all. But I'm being as patient and understanding as I can with her because I don't want to lose her. I've even distanced myself from my abuelita; we still talk, but not like before. I miss driving to her house and eating her home-cooked meals. I hope we can find our way back to each other soon.

Why is this happening now? Because of the accounting I'm helping Johnny do on our mom's estate. Because after being told time and again that by the time he turns twenty-five he wouldn't have anything to his name, we just want to know if that's true. There's nothing wrong with what we're doing. My momma worked tirelessly for us. We know that. The world knows that. She said it herself in countless interviews. Johnny simply wants to see the numbers of an estate that partly belongs to him. We're not bad children for asking questions. Knowing what's there and what he can or can't count on in the future will allow him to better plan his next steps in life.

At the end of the day, as much as I wish we could come together as a family, I also have learned that sometimes it's just better to love certain people from afar.

Now, for the first time in my life, I can confidently say that I'm no longer afraid to stand up for myself and what I believe in. I'm not afraid of the idea of getting married again. And I'm even not afraid of having children anymore. I'm eager to see what God, fate, and the future have in store for me. In the meantime, I will continue to work tirelessly for what I want. Starting with my new show with Telemundo Universo: *Chiquis y lo mejor de ti.* This is not a reality show. I'm finally being called to the set to use my experiences to help others overcome their own battles, and I couldn't be happier. God gave me this life and this voice for this purpose, to help other people navigate their own shitstorms and come out better on the other side. This is the highlight of my new chapter, my high note. It's all coming together, and I can't wait to see where I go next.

ACKNOWLEDGMENTS

Thank you to my siblings, Johnny, Jenicka, Mikey, and Jacqie, for your love and support through this roller coaster called life. We have laughed together, we have cried together, and we have grown together—I couldn't have gotten through it all without you. I love you more than you will ever know.

To my amazing team, my work family, thank you for being my rock, for supporting my evolving vision, and ultimately for believing in me. Here's to many more years of evolution, opportunity, and success. ¡Arriba Team Thrive!

To Johanna Castillo, my brilliant literary agent, we've been working together for a long time and I'm still amazed by your tenacity and go-getting spirit. Thank you for always having my back and helping me bring my book ideas to fruition.

To Cecilia Molinari, thank you for being my friend (and practically my therapist!) and someone I could talk to with an open heart, knowing you would interpret my words, tears, pain, and laughter beautifully on the pages of this book. What a journey!

To Michelle Herrera Mulligan, senior editor at Atria, your thoughtful edits, guidance, and support helped elevate this book even further, cementing the intimacy and honesty we set out to con-

Acknowledgments

vey. Thank you and the entire team at Atria for giving me the opportunity to once again speak my mind and share my heart.

To my Boss Bees, my followers, my steadfast supporters, thank you for being my rock, for cheering me up when I'm feeling down, for always reminding me why I chose to be on this path. I wouldn't be where I am today without all of you. This book is for you. Ya saben, son los mejores del mundo mundial.

And last but never least, thank you to God, for being my guide, my moral compass, my light in the depth of darkness, my beacon of hope. Con Dios todo, sin él nada.